T0323801

Thinking to Some Purpose

'I am convinced of the urgent need for a democratic people to think clearly without the distortions due to unconscious bias and unrecognized ignorance. Our failures in thinking are in part due to faults which we could to some extent overcome were we to see clearly how these faults arise. It is the aim of this book to make a small effort in this direction.'

– Susan Stebbing, from the Preface

Despite huge advances in education, knowledge and communication, it can often seem we are neither well trained nor well practised in the art of clear thinking. Our powers of reasoning and argument are less confident than they should be, we frequently ignore evidence and we are all too often swayed by rhetoric rather than reason. But what can *you* do to think and argue better?

First published in 1939 but unavailable for many years, Susan Stebbing's Thinking to Some Purpose is a classic first-aid manual of how to think clearly, and remains astonishingly fresh and insightful. Written against a background of the rise of dictatorships and the collapse of democracy in Europe, it is packed with useful tips and insights. Stebbing offers shrewd advice on how to think critically and clearly, how to spot illogical statements and slipshod thinking, and how to rely on reason rather than emotion. At a time when we are again faced with serious threats to democracy and freedom of thought, Stebbing's advice remains as urgent and important as ever.

This Routledge edition of Thinking to Some Purpose includes a new Foreword by Nigel Warburton and a helpful Introduction by Peter West, who places Susan Stebbing's classic book in historical and philosophical context.

Susan Stebbing (1885–1943) was a leading figure in British philosophy between the First and Second World Wars. The first woman in the UK to be appointed to a full professorship in philosophy, in 1933, she taught at Bedford College (now Royal Holloway University). She was best known for her work on logic before turning more generally to the study of thinking and reasoning. At a time when analytic philosophy was largely confined to technical questions, her work stood out for engaging with contemporary issues and addressing a wider public audience. *Philosophy and the Physicists* (1937) and *Thinking to Some Purpose* (1939) were critiques of the language used in popular science communication and in everyday genres such as political speeches, advertisements and newspaper editorials.

Susan
Stebbing

Thinking to Some Purpose

With a new Foreword by Nigel Warburton and
a new Introduction by Peter West

 Routledge
Taylor & Francis Group

LONDON AND NEW YORK

Cover image: © Sergi Calaff Bayes / Getty Images
Back cover image: Susan Stebbing, by Howard Coster, half-plate
film negative, 1939, © National Portrait Gallery, London, CC-BY-NC-ND 3.0

First published by Routledge in 2022
by Routledge
4 Park Square, Milton Park, Abingdon, Oxon OX14 4RN

and by Routledge
605 Third Avenue, New York, NY 10158

Routledge is an imprint of the Taylor & Francis Group, an informa business

Foreword © 2022 Nigel Warburton
Introduction © 2022 Peter West

First published in 1939 by Penguin Books Ltd.

British Library Cataloguing-in-Publication Data
A catalogue record for this book is available from the British Library

Library of Congress Cataloging-in-Publication Data
Names: Stebbing, L. Susan (Lizzie Susan), 1885–1943.
Title: Thinking to some purpose / Susan Stebbing ; with a new
foreword by Nigel Warburton and a new introduction by Peter West.
Description: New York, NY : Routledge, 2022. | First published
in 1939. | Includes bibliographical references and index.
Identifiers: LCCN 2021059971 (print) | LCCN 2021059972
(ebook) | ISBN 9781032280660 (hardback) | ISBN
9781032155951 (paperback) | ISBN 9781003295181 (ebook)
Subjects: LCSH: Thought and thinking.
Classification: LCC BC108 .S83 2022 (print) | LCC BC108
(ebook) | DDC 153.4/2—dc23/eng/20211217
LC record available at https://lccn.loc.gov/2021059971
LC ebook record available at https://lccn.loc.gov/2021059972

ISBN: 978-1-032-28066-0 (hbk)
ISBN: 978-1-032-15595-1 (pbk)
ISBN: 978-1-003-29518-1 (ebk)

DOI: 10.4324/b22927

Typeset in Joanna
by codeMantra

And if we have a right to know any Truth whatsoever, we have a right to think freely, or (according to my Definition) to use our Understandings, in endeavouring to find out the Meaning of any Proposition whatsoever, in considering the nature of the Evidence for or against it, and in judging of it according to the seeming Force or weakness of the evidence: because there is no other way to discover the Truth.

Anthony Collins, *A Discourse of Free-Thinking, 1713*

CONTENTS

FOREWORD

Can we learn to think better? I hope so. Children quickly pick up reasoning skills and catch out adults using inconsistent arguments or making a special case for themselves without warrant. They instantly see through 'Do as I say, not as I do' and other self-serving rationalisations. Motivated adults can build on this foundation and refine and extend these skills, though it would be naive to think that studying critical thinking immunises us from logical error and skewed thinking. Sometimes it just provides a more sophisticated vocabulary with which to rationalise our prejudices. And if you begin arguing from false premises, no matter how good your logic, you might still end up with false beliefs. Daniel Kahneman and Amos Tversky have provided impressive experimental evidence about a range of cognitive biases to which human beings are prone,[1] biases which make it very likely that we'll be led astray in our thinking much of our time.

Susan Stebbing was an astute observer of wishful thinking and evidence avoidance. She was well aware how easily even highly intelligent people could be swayed by propaganda or by faulty reasoning that leads to desired conclusions. She was self-aware enough to see that she too could be misled, and knew that she needed the check of having her own beliefs challenged and criticised from time to time. Although parts of her *Thinking to Some Purpose* are straightforward expositions of logical moves and fallacies, much of it deals with the dangerous patterns of thought that can lead anyone to false or unsupported beliefs, and with psychological motivations for blinkered, slipshod or crooked thinking. She anticipated some of the erroneous patterns that Kahneman and Tversky provided experimental evidence for.

There is an urgency about Stebbing's book that most of today's primers in critical thinking lack, an urgency that came from growing threats to freedom, democracy and the rule of law in the 1930s. Though its language, syntax and choice of examples give it an archaic flavour at times, this is still very much worth reading today, and not simply as a historical relic. Stebbing is a sharp, clear thinker who moves easily from the abstract to the particular and back again, and she combines the ideal virtues of the philosopher: the strength of character needed to challenge received opinion, and the humility to recognise that she too could be wrong.

The germ of the book was a talk Stebbing gave in 1936 to the annual conference of the British Institute of Adult Education. Adult education in Britain following the First World War was, from the government's point of view, a self-conscious attempt to equip the general population for the duties of citizenship through publicly and philanthropically funded lifelong learning available to all. It wasn't about training for a job, but training to be a responsible citizen. Stebbing's book is written in that spirit. The mass circulation Pelican series was ideal for this. It is a book that would have appealed to motivated autodidacts too. Its slim paperback format meant that it was readily portable for service-men and women wherever they were posted. In wartime, the publishers encouraged readers to maximise its readership – the 1942 reprint included this note:

'For the Forces
   When you have read this book, please leave it at your nearest Post Office, so that the men and women in the Services may enjoy it too.' (p. 186)

The patterns of lazy thinking that Stebbing anatomises here haven't gone away. If anything, the Internet has amplified them. Algorithms used by social media have a tendency to serve up selective evidence and examples that support our beliefs rather than challenge us to reflect on them. Many of us are in media bubbles that never present the case against the views we hold. Meanwhile, through smartphones and other demands on our at-tention we are continually distracted from deeper critical think-ing of a kind that takes time and patience.

Nigel Warburton, *November 2021*

NOTE

1   Kahneman, Daniel. 2011. *Thinking, Fast and Slow*. London: Allen Lane.

Introduction

In the Preface to *Thinking to Some Purpose*, Susan Stebbing writes:

> I am convinced of the urgent need for a democratic people to think clearly without the distortions due to unconscious bias and unrecognized ignorance. Our failures in thinking are in part due to faults which we could to some extent overcome were we to see clearly how these faults arise. It is the aim of this book to make a small effort in this direction.

This is Stebbing's mission statement: we must learn to recognise and make ourselves conscious of the faults in our ways of thinking if we are to continue living in a free and democratic society. Stebbing treats this as a universal truth, albeit one which was of particular importance at the time of writing. In 1939, when the text was published, the twin threats of fascism and communism were on the rise in Europe (Stebbing refers to social and political developments in Germany and Russia throughout the text).This is no hyperbole; Stebbing really believed there was an 'urgent need' to develop the skills to 'think clearly'.

Thinking to Some Purpose is thus a piece of applied philosophy, an attempt to use the tools of critical thinking to step in and make a difference to the lives of ordinary people. The text, which is written in a manner accessible to a non-specialist readership and full of colourful examples from politics and culture that would have been familiar to her audience, is both an artefact of its time and of immediate relevance today. While Stebbing saw herself as offering a solution (instructing readers to think clearly) to a particular problem (threats to democracy in Europe), there is nonetheless much that we can learn from her lessons on combatting our own prejudices, bringing truth back into politics, and separating how we *feel* from how we *reason*.

In this Introduction to the text, I want to introduce Stebbing to readers who may be new to her work, situate *Thinking to Some Purpose* in its historical context, provide some insight into what Stebbing thinks thinking clearly involves, and critically examine the text as an attempt to bring philosophy into the public sphere. Throughout the text, Stebbing articulates herself clearly, assumes no prior knowledge on behalf of the reader, and shows that a little bit of philosophical know-how can make a great deal of difference. For these reasons, my own view (and one I hope you will agree with) is that *Thinking to Some Purpose* should be a go-to text for anyone asking '*Why is philosophy important?*'

L. SUSAN STEBBING (1885–1943)

Stebbing was born in North London in 1885 and educated at Girton College Cambridge and King's College London between

1904 and 1912. She died in 1943 aged just 57 from cancer. 'Lizzie' was her given name, but she disliked it and was always known as 'Susan'.

In 1933, Stebbing was the first woman in the UK to be appointed to a full professorship in philosophy – at Bedford College, where she spent much of her career (there is a Susan Stebbing Professorship and a Susan Stebbing Studentship at Kings College London, which Bedford College merged with in the 1980s). Throughout her career, she inhabited a world almost completely dominated by men and published as 'L. S. Stebbing' because, according to a friend, she disliked philosophical debates getting distorted by questions of gender or status.[1] While her appointment at Bedford made national news at the time, Stebbing is now a relatively unknown figure in philosophy's history, and has accrued nothing like the almost mythic aura that surrounds philosophical 'greats' like Bertrand Russell or G. E. Moore (both of whom were her contemporaries). She is also less well known than other women philosophers who came to the fore in the post-war period, such as Elizabeth Anscombe, Philippa Foot, Iris Murdoch and Mary Midgley.

There is no doubt that, despite her best efforts, both Stebbing's reputation and career were adversely affected by her status as a woman in an academic landscape that was dominated by men from Cambridge and Oxford. For instance, in 1939 Stebbing applied for a chair in philosophy in Cambridge soon to be vacated by G. E. Moore. In a letter to a friend from the time, she explains that Gilbert Ryle (another prominent Cambridge philosopher) informed her that 'everyone thinks you are the right person to succeed Moore, except that you are a woman'.[2] Ultimately, the post went to Ludwig Wittgenstein, suggesting that (as Siobhan Chapman puts it in her philosophical biography of

Stebbing) 'any opposition to Stebbing on the grounds that she was a woman was probably immaterial' (2003, 127). Nonetheless, it is clear that Stebbing was fighting an uphill battle in attempting to surmount the social prejudices of her intellectual environment.

Today, Stebbing's omission from many contemporary histories of twentieth-century philosophy is made especially glaring by her impressive academic credentials. Between 1924 and 1939 she published at least one article each year in leading philosophy journals.[3] She also served as president of the UK's two leading philosophical associations, the Mind Association and the Aristotelian Society (1931–32 and 1933–34, respectively), and helped found the journal *Analysis* in 1933. She was well regarded by most English-speaking academic philosophers at the time and also engaged with 'continental' philosophers, most notably Henri Bergson in her MA thesis (later published as *Pragmatism and French Voluntarism* in 1914).

However, Stebbing was always interested in doing things and actually solving problems, not just thinking about them. As she explains in *Thinking to Some Purpose*, 'there is a danger of indulging in an academic detachment from life' (p. 15). Thus, in the 1930s and 40s, she spent a considerable amount of time and energy securing the safety of refugees from Germany and Nazi-occupied countries at her own personal cost. In line with her more applied interests, Stebbing established a reputation as a public philosopher (although she was wary of doing so for the sake of fame or public approval). In 1930, she published *A Modern Introduction to Logic*, regarded by many as the first textbook in formal logic. In 1937, she published *Philosophy and the Physicists*, a critical examination of popular scientific writing. Two years after *Thinking to Some Purpose* was published, in 1941, Stebbing released

Ideals and Illusions – another attempt to use the tools of critical thinking to promote healthy public discourse.

FREE-THINKING AND HUMANISM

By suggesting that her readers (the general public) must learn to think clearly, and helping to provide the means, Stebbing was adding herself to a long line of philosophers known as 'free-thinkers'. 'Free-thinking' dates back to the European Enlightenment (towards the end of the seventeenth century) and originally involved rejecting religious authority and academic dogma in the light of new developments in science. Essentially, Enlightenment free-thinkers pushed for a democratisation of knowledge and believed we should follow our own reason over the Bible or ancient philosophical texts.

The frontispiece to *Thinking to Some Purpose* features a quotation from the eighteenth-century philosopher Anthony Collins, whose treatise *A Discourse of Free-thinking* (published in 1713) was a call to arms for free-thinkers everywhere and was criticised by more conservative thinkers at the time, including the satirist Jonathan Swift.[4] The quotation includes Collins' definition of free-thinking as:

> [Using] our Understandings, in endeavouring to find out the Meaning of any Proposition whatsoever, in considering the nature of the Evidence for or against it, and in judging of it according to the seeming Force or weakness of the evidence, because there is no other way to discover the truth.

Stebbing evidently thought Collins was right. Like the free-thinkers of the Enlightenment, she believed we should eschew authority (whether that be the church, politicians or the media) and instead rely on our own rational abilities. She even encourages the reader not to take her word on various claims without scrutinising them:

> It remains possible that my beliefs on these matters are erroneous (although naturally I cannot myself believe that they are), and that my reasons for holding them are insufficient. Whether this be so or not the reader has to decide for himself. (p. 29)

Stebbing's main aim is not to call out any particular individual or organisation (although she criticises various politicians, newspapers and advertisers in the text) or to simply impart knowledge to a passive audience. Instead, her message is this: it is each person's duty to learn to think clearly and play their role in fostering healthy public discourse. It isn't easy to examine our own beliefs and biases, but it is what each of us must do if we are to remain free.

Stebbing's commitment to free-thinking also manifested itself in a more formal manner. There is a strong historical and organisational connection between the free-thinking of the Enlightenment era (which continued into the nineteenth and twentieth centuries) and humanism, an ethical movement which emphasises independent thinking and a secular approach to various aspects of public life, such as education. Stebbing was president of Humanists UK (then known as the Ethical Union) between 1941 and 1942 and was involved with the organisation before and after her presidency. She no doubt would have been influenced by the meetings she presided over and her engagement with other humanists, and there are clear thematic connections between humanism and Thinking to Some Purpose.[5] In particular, her view that independent critical thought is crucial to democracy and her wariness of the dark arts of persuasion and propaganda, often employed by politicians or journalists, align with humanism's opposition to dogma and tradition.

THINKING CLEARLY

While it would be impossible to summarise the whole text in this introduction, it is nonetheless worth looking at some of the advice Stebbing offers her readers. This will help paint a picture of what she thinks healthy public discourse looks like. Again, she places considerable emphasis on the role of the individual:

> I ... seek to convince the reader that it is of great practical importance that we ordinary men and women should think clearly, that there are many obstacles to thinking clearly, and that some of these obstacles can be overcome provided that we wish to overcome them and are willing to make the effort. (p. 29)

Part of Stebbing's aim is to show that reason, rationality and logic do not belong only in the halls of Westminster or the ivory towers of Cambridge and Oxford. In fact, Stebbing believes that 'all people resemble one another in one important respect, namely, in having some capacity to follow an argument' (p. 21). She is strongly opposed to the idea that logical reasoning is something that only belongs in abstract discussions. She points to the example of a young girl, Emily, who, after being told by a nurse that 'nobody eats soup with a fork', replied that 'I do, and I am somebody'. Stebbing takes this as proof that people untrained in logic, even children, can still reason successfully (in this case, by identifying a false generalisation). As she puts it, 'it is human to reject a contradiction' (p. 21). In other words, an example like this shows that we all have the potential to do what trained logicians do; namely, not only *disagree* with certain claims but work out what is wrong with the reasoning that lies behind them. She also opposes the idea, propagated by British politicians like Stanley Baldwin (a three-time Conservative prime minister), that logic stands in contrast to common sense (p. 9). If anything is common to us all, Stebbing argues, it is our innate ability to follow an argument.

Although Stebbing believes that the ability to reason is innate, we must make the effort to learn how to employ that natural ability. This is where her own instruction comes in. Throughout the text, Stebbing provides the reader with a series of lessons in how to detect faults in our reasoning and rectify them. I will run through a few examples.

First, Stebbing argues that we must identify and then question our most cherished beliefs. In line with David Hume's mantra that 'A wise man proportions his belief to the evidence',[6] Stebbing writes: 'The strength with which we hold a belief ought to bear some proportion to the amount of evidence upon which it is based' (p. 27). She then explains that inevitably, when it comes to our most deeply seated commitments, this will not always be the case. In fact, many of our most cherished beliefs are held 'unquestioningly' (p. 34). For instance, she suggests that capitalists believe that the interests of their class are more important than the interests of their country. Or that patriots unquestioningly believe that 'our country is superior to other countries' (p. 34) (both examples are clearly intended to be provocative). In such cases, Stebbing advises, we should ask ourselves: how did I come to think that? And would I accept that claim now? Of course, simply asking such questions may not result in a change of mind-set. But we can nonetheless work out which beliefs are supported by evidence and which are formed by emotional responses. To use a different example, I might strongly *feel* that I want to eat meat, while also acknowledging that this belief cannot withstand critical scrutiny. If I become aware of such a discrepancy between how I feel and what I rationally judge to be the case, I can at least make myself *aware* which beliefs are supported by reasonable evidence and work towards either justifying or changing them.

Another of Stebbing's lessons focuses on what she calls 'potted thinking', which involves oversimplifying ideas by using crude characterisations or slogans. While slogans are not always a bad thing, Stebbing thinks they have a tendency to oversimplify more nuanced or sophisticated views and to hide the intricacies of an idea behind a catchy phrase. As an example of potted thinking, she points to how some people think Freudian psychoanalysis can be encapsulated in the slogan 'Everything is sex.' This falsely gives the impression that Freud's theory reduces everything to sex, that his approach is easy to understand, and (worst of all) makes Freud's views sound utterly ridiculous – so ridiculous, in fact, that one begins to wonder why on earth anyone ever paid any attention to them in the first place. In talking of 'potted thinking', Stebbing is drawing a comparison with potted *meat*: a vacuum-packed product that one might have found in a ration pack, such as Spam. She explains:

> Potted meat is sometimes a convenient form of food; it may be tasty, it contains some nourishment. But its nutritive value is not equivalent to that of the fresh meat from which it was potted. Also it must have originally been made from fresh meat, and must not be allowed to grow stale. Similarly, a potted belief is convenient: it can be stated briefly, sometimes also in a snappy manner likely to attract attention. (p. 66)

Her point is that potted thinking takes something that once had high 'nutritive value' and packages it in a way that is easier to sell but harder to find any genuine nourishment in. The worst type of potted thinking, according to Stebbing, is when we grow into the habit of 'using words repeated parrot-fashion' – in other words, when we start talking in slogans that have no thought or consideration behind them.

One area in which Stebbing's views seem particularly prescient is in her discussion of how language gets manipulated to invoke strong emotional (and often irrational) responses from an audience. Stebbing draws two distinctions: between 'bad' and 'good' language and between 'scientific' and 'emotive' language. She explains that bad language 'fails to achieve the purpose for which it is used' while good language does achieve its purpose (p. 54). Although most of us fail to recognise it as such, Stebbing argues, much of the language employed in public and political discussions is 'bad language'. That's because we assume most language is 'scientific' – i.e., intended simply to indicate or describe things 'objectively' (p. 54) when in fact that isn't the way language is often used. Instead, such language tends to be 'emotive' – it has the 'deliberate intention of evoking emotional attributes in [its] hearers'. Many of the words commonly used in political discourse, Stebbing claims, have 'tied suggestions'; they 'have a significance in addition to their objective meaning' (p. 55). For instance, Stebbing picks up on the fact that newspaper reports use the term 'dole' to describe unemployment tax – which has negative connotations. Similarly, in the context of discourse surrounding the Spanish Civil War, she explains that a careful analysis reveals:

[W]ords used by *The Times* [newspaper] to refer to the Spanish Government became increasingly derogatory, whilst the words used to refer to the opponents of the Spanish Government became increasingly favourable. (p. 60)

To use a contemporary example, one might think of how the term 'woke' has gone from being a descriptive moniker to a loaded term, designed to invoke a particular kind of reaction in a reader or audience. Stebbing claims that an awareness of whether language is used well or not can help us to identify which sort of claims we should be convinced by and which require greater scrutiny.

PHILOSOPHY IN THE PUBLIC SPHERE

Stebbing was not alone in advocating for an increased role for philosophy in the public sphere. Bertrand Russell, in his essay 'Philosophy for Laymen' (published in 1946),[7] argues that if everyone were equipped with philosophical training then, on a societal level, there would be considerably fewer disputes and, on a personal level, we would all lead more peaceful and fulfilling lives. As Russell puts it:

[Philosophy] supplies an antidote to the anxieties and anguish of the present, and makes possible the nearest approach to serenity that is available to a sensitive mind in our tortured and uncertain world.

Some of Russell's advice (published after *Thinking to Some Purpose*) strikes a similar tune to Stebbing's own views. He advocates avoiding 'emotional bias' in political discourse, examining the sources of our opinions, and questioning even those beliefs 'we find it most painful to doubt'.

However, drawing on the ancient, Aristotelian notion of leading a good life by accruing wisdom, Russell promotes philosophy as something of intrinsic personal value. In that sense, Russell's approach to public philosophy is more idealistic, and perhaps less practically applicable, than Stebbing's. Stebbing presents the tools of philosophical thinking (e.g., detecting fallacies, avoiding inconsistences, proportioning our beliefs to the evidence) as a means to an end. Thinking clearly is something that will allow us to continue to hold those who speak in public contexts (like politicians) to account and, in turn, live in a genuinely democratic society. As Stebbing explains, politicians are only able to win us over by using emotive language *because we allow them to*: 'We are sometimes too lazy, usually too busy, and often too ignorant to think out what is involved in the statements we so readily accept' (p. 65). But if we avoid reacting emotionally to politicians' claims, and learn to examine them logically, then they will have to start *proving* things to us on the basis of evidence.

Like Stebbing and Russell, many philosophers today are trying to find the best way to bring philosophy into the public sphere. In a blog post from 2020 that was widely circulated online,[8] the Oxford philosopher Timothy Williamson argued that while the democratisation of knowledge in general should be encouraged, it should nonetheless be up to professional, academic philosophers to find ways to communicate their research and ideas to a public audience. For Williamson, philosophy is not something we can all do equally well; like any other science, it is something one must be trained to do since it involves adopting highly sophisticated research methods and familiarising oneself with a considerable amount of both historical and contemporary literature. Good public philosophy, Williamson argues, is just like good popular science. It occurs when a specialist in the field finds a way to communicate their findings to non-specialists in an engaging and informative manner.

However, I think Stebbing's approach in *Thinking to Some Purpose* provides us with a different model of public philosophy (to both Williamson and Russell). For Stebbing, philosophical knowledge (of what such-and-such thinker said about such-and-such topic) is of little intrinsic use. For Stebbing, all thinking is *thinking to some purpose*. In other words, thinking or reasoning is only worthwhile when it is directed at a particular problem or question – and it has got to be readily available to those who wish to use it. This means that if it is really going to make a difference, philosophy must involve more than simply the transfer of knowledge between individuals. Thus, public philosophy must be a two-way street. Stebbing explains:

> An educator has two main objects: to impart information and to create those mental habits that will enable his students, or pupils, to seek knowledge and to acquire the ability to form their own independent judgment based upon rational grounds. (p. 93)

Again, Stebbing places the emphasis on the individual: the learner. For philosophy to play a positive role in public discourse, it will not be enough for 'educators' (academic philosophers) to try and disseminate as much knowledge as possible. Rather, the role of philosophers should be to instruct an audience on *how* to think in certain ways. That way, regardless of the subject area, ordinary people should be able to avoid the errors in reasoning that, Stebbing believes, threaten both our individual freedom and the democratic society we inhabit.

***

Thinking to Some Purpose is an accessible and engaging text suitable for a range of audiences, from advanced readers to undergraduates, and even (with the right instruction) at school level. It was written as an in-the-moment response to threats to individual liberty that Stebbing saw growing in the world around her. Yet, even today, the text serves as a reminder that we are *always* reasoning; not just when we step into a philosophy seminar but when we listen to the radio, open a newspaper or decide where to purchase a coffee in the morning. As Stebbing remarks, it is 'persons who think, not purely rational spirits' (p. 18). Thinking is the foundation upon which our society is built. Stebbing's message is that as long as we wish to continue to live in and benefit from that society, we ought to ensure we are thinking clearly.

Peter West, *November 2021*

NOTES

1   https://plato.stanford.edu/entries/stebbing/.

2   Siobhan Chapman. *Susan Stebbing and the Language of Common Sense.* London: Palgrave Macmillan (2003), 126–27.

3   Frederique Janssen-Lauret. 'Susan Stebbing's Metaphysics and the Status of Common Sense Truths' in *Women in the History of Analytic Philosophy.* Peijnenburg, J. & Verhaegh, S. (eds.). Springer Nature.

4   Jonathan Swift. *Mr Collins' Discourse on Free-thinking.* London: John Morphew (1713).

5   Thanks to Andrew Copson from Humanists UK for talking me through Stebbing's involvement with the organisation and for access to records that reveal Stebbing was present at many Humanist meetings.

6   David Hume. *An Enquiry Concerning Human Understanding.* (1777), 11.4, 110.

7   Bertrand Russell. 'Philosophy for Laymen,' *Universities Quarterly* 1 (Nov 1946), 38–49.

8   https://dailynous.com/2020/06/08/popular-philosophy-populist-philosophy-guest-post-timothy-williamson/#:~:text=and%20Populist%20Philosophy-,Timothy%20Williamson,also%20to%20the%20general%20public.

PREFACE TO THE 1939 EDITION

In the autumn of 1936 at the annual conference of the British Institute of Adult Education I gave a lecture entitled 'Thinking'. This lecture was published and I am indebted to the Institute for permission to use some passages from it. This book originated, however, in a proposal made to me by the B.B.C. that I should expand the topic of that lecture and draw up a synopsis for twelve Talks. For good reasons I did not give the Talks, but I submitted the synopsis. Although the manuscript was not returned to me, this book is based upon my original scheme and nine of the chapters have the same titles as the proposed Talks. Pressure of work as well as other difficulties prevented me from completing this book until the summer of this year.

I am convinced of the urgent need for a democratic people to think clearly without the distortions due to unconscious bias and unrecognized ignorance. Our failures in thinking are in part due to faults which we could to some extent overcome were we to see clearly how these faults arise. It is the aim of this book to make a small effort in this direction.

I am much indebted to Mr A. F. Dawn both for helping me to find examples of dishonest thinking and for his generous aid in the correction of the proofs.

L. Susan Stebbing, London, November 1938

1

PROLOGUE

ARE THE ENGLISH ILLOGICAL?

There is a belief prevalent among foreigners that we English are illogical. This belief is not confined to foreigners. Our own statesmen, especially since the Great War, have been proud to proclaim that 'we shall muddle through', being apparently just as anxious that we should *muddle* as they are confident that we shall somehow come through. Of this professed pride in our inability to be logical I shall select, at the outset, two examples made to very different assemblies. The first is taken from a speech made by Lord Selborne at the annual festival of the Community of the Resurrection, in 1924. The *Church Times* (June 20th) reports:

DOI: 10.4324/b22927-1

> Lord Selborne... referring to the missionary work in South Africa, made some apt remarks about 'the glorious incapacity for clear thought which is one of the distinguishing marks of our race. It is the cause of our greatest difficulties and has been the secret of some of our greatest successes. If you say sufficiently often and loudly and clearly that the moment the black man comes in contact with the white man his education has begun, your scoffer at mission work may at last understand.'

One wonders whether the Church Times reporter judged the remarks to be 'apt' because this 'glorious incapacity' was the cause of our greatest difficulties or because it is a glorious incapacity, or because it was the secret of some of our greatest successes. An open secret at least. Or is it, perhaps, not true that the muddling was a cause of these successes? Is it not odd that an incapacity for clear thought should be deemed glorious? Further, it is difficult to believe that saying something 'often and loudly and clearly' should end in producing understanding, since, presumably, 'clearly' was used by Lord Selborne to refer to the tone of voice.

The second example is taken from a speech by Mr (as he then was) Austen Chamberlain, speaking in the House of Commons, on March 24th, 1925. He criticized the proposals of the Geneva Protocol, and, replying to Mr Arthur Henderson, said:

> I am really not sure what the right hon. gentleman himself thinks of it [the Protocol]. At one moment he declares that we undertake no new obligation, and at another moment that it is merely the logical conclusion of the covenant. I profoundly distrust logic when applied to politics, and all English history justifies me. [Ministerial cheers.] Why is it that, as contrasted with other nations, ours has been a peaceful and not a violent

development? Why is it that, great as have been the changes that have taken place in this country, we have had none of those sudden revolutions and reactions for the last three hundred years that have so frequently affected more logically-minded nations than ourselves? It is because instinct and experience alike teach us that human nature is not logical, that it is unwise to treat political institutions as instruments of logic, and that it is in wisely refraining from pressing conclusions to their logical end the path of peaceful development and true reform is really found.

(*The Times*, March 25th, 1925.)

We shall shortly have to consider this unfounded fear of 'pressing conclusions to their logical end'. It must be admitted that Austen Chamberlain showed himself to be thinking very unclearly with regard to what a logical conclusion is.

'Democracy is government by discussion, by talk.' Such was the considered opinion of the Lord Rector of the University of Edinburgh in 1925, as stated in his inaugural address to the students. If this dictum be true, must we suppose that a democratic nation will be expected to flourish if it be governed by discussion revealing a glorious incapacity for clear thought? Will the policy the nation adopts be wise if 'the talk' eschews consideration of what is logically relevant to the conclusion to be established? Apparently the Lord Rector was of this opinion, since he was none other than Mr (as he then was) Stanley Baldwin. Lord Baldwin is commonly regarded as a typical Englishman, impatient of logic, a little stupid it may be, but indubitably honest, not wasting time upon fine-spun arguments, but guided by common sense and experience. So, too, I fancy he likes to regard himself. Or is it only that he likes others thus to regard him?[1] The address he gave as Lord Rector is extraordinarily interesting. It is entitled 'Truth and Politics'.[2] In what he then said he showed himself to be sensitively aware of the difficulties of a political leader who has to persuade an electorate to support a policy but dare not assume that the electors are capable of being rationally convinced.

'The advocate and the politician', said Baldwin,

> are more interested in persuasion than in proof. They have a client or a policy to defend. The political audience is not dishonest in itself, nor does it desire to approve dishonesty or misrepresentation in others, but it is an audience only imperfectly prepared to follow a close argument, and the speaker wishes to make a favourable impression, to secure support for a policy (p. 96).

I am writing this book partly because I am in considerable agreement with this statement. I am hopeful that the British electorate neither desires to think dishonestly nor to approve dishonesty in political speeches. I agree, again, with Lord Baldwin that most electors are 'only imperfectly prepared to follow a close argument'. That being so, the politician who seeks to win an election must resort to persuasion. He 'must' because, first, he seeks to get something done – to put a policy into effect; secondly, in order to achieve this policy, his party must be returned to power; thirdly, the victory of the party at the polls depends upon the votes of electors who are beset by hopes and fears and who have never been trained to think clearly. Consequently, rhetorical persuasion will in fact be substituted for rational argument and for reasonable consideration of the difficulties that confront any democratic government. This grim practical necessity is, however, no matter for congratulation. If the maintenance of democratic institutions is worth while, then the citizens of a democratic country must record their votes only after due deliberation. But 'due deliberation' involves instruction with regard to the facts, ability to assess the evidence provided by such instruction and, further, the ability to discount, as far as may be, the effects of prejudice and to evade the distortion produced by unwarrantable fears and by unrealizable hopes. In other words, the citizens must be able to think relevantly, that is, to think to some purpose. Thus to think is difficult. Accordingly, it is not surprising, however saddening it may be, that many of our statesmen do not trust the citizens to think, but rely instead upon the arts of persuasion.

To think logically is to think relevantly to the purpose that initiated the thinking; all effective thinking is directed to an end. To neglect relevant considerations would entail failure to achieve that end. There is prevalent a strange misconception with regard to the nature of logic – a misconception that seems to be deeply rooted in the beliefs of Lord Baldwin and the late Sir Austen Chamberlain, to mention only two of our prominent statesmen. On many occasions Lord Baldwin had warned his hearers against the dangers of logic. In his rectorial address, speaking to university students, he said wisely:

> Ability to read is not synonymous with ability to reflect on what is read. Better to doubt methodically than to think capriciously. Education that has merely taught people to follow a syllogism without enabling them to detect a fallacy has left them in constant peril. And as with the fallacy so with its near relation, the half truth. For though it has been accepted through the ages that half a loaf is better than no bread, half a truth is not only not better than no truth, it is worse than many lies, and the slave of lies and half truths is ignorance (pp. 90–91).

On another occasion, speaking at Philip Stott College, on 'Political Education', he insisted that the purpose of such education

> is always twofold; it is, in the first place, to clear the mind of cant, and in the second place, not to rest content with having learnt enough to follow the syllogism, knowing perfectly well that to follow the syllogism alone is a short cut to the bottomless pit, unless you are able to detect the fallacies that lie by the wayside (p. 153).

Surely it is odd to suppose that we can have 'learnt enough to follow the syllogism' without having learnt also 'to detect the fallacies that lie by the wayside'. Certainly professional logicians often think illogically and act unreasonably; they too are human beings subject to all the obstacles that beset men who have to think in order that they may achieve their aims. But a knowledge of what these hindrances are and of the difference between thinking logically and thinking illogically may at least serve to put us on our guard. Some of these hindrances will be discussed in the following chapters. Here I wish to emphasize two considerations: first, that a knowledge of the conditions of a logically sound argument does help us to think clearly *provided that we wish so to think*; secondly, that not all sound arguments are syllogistic. What Lord Baldwin is thinking of when he speaks of 'the syllogism alone' as 'a short cut to the bottomless pit', I do not profess to know. Perhaps both phrases are mere rhetorical devices. Yet he is very sincere in his detestation of logic. This detestation is so relevant to the purpose of this book that I propose to quote at some length from Baldwin's last public speech as Prime Minister, just before he was elevated to the peerage. The occasion was a dinner given by the combined Empire Societies at Grosvenor House, on Empire Day, 1937. The audience was mainly composed of statesmen from the Dominions, the Colonies and India; the speech was to propose the toast of 'The British Commonwealth'. The passage quoted below was reported in *The Times* with the sub-heading

CONSTITUTION AND LOGIC WARNING AGAINST A STRAIT WAISTCOAT[3]

Baldwin was not, of course, responsible for this sub-heading but, in my opinion, the *Times* reporter had accurately assessed the emphasis laid upon these contentions by the speaker:

Now I would like, as but an indifferent historical student, to make an observation about our Constitution... One of the most interesting features about it historically is that the Constitution was not evolved by logicians. The British Constitution has grown to what it is through the work of men like you and me – just ordinary people who have adapted the government of the country in order to meet the environment of the age in which they lived, and they have always preserved sufficient flexibility to enable that adaptation to be accomplished.

Now that is extremely important, because it seems to me that one of the reasons why our people are alive and flourishing, and have avoided many of the troubles that have fallen to less happy nations, is *because we have never been guided by logic in anything we have done.*[4]

If you will only do what I have done – study the history of the growth of the Constitution from the time of the Civil War until the Hanoverians came to the Throne – you will see what a country can do *without the aid of logic, but with the aid of common sense*. Therefore, my next point is: Do not let us put any part of our Constitution in a strait waistcoat, because strangulation is the ultimate fate.

And I would say one more thing – don't let us be too keen on definition. I should like to remind you, if I can remind an audience so educated as this, that it was that attempt to define that split the Christian Church into fragments soon after it came into existence, and it has never recovered from that, and therefore *I deduce – and I hope that it is a logical thing –* that if we try to define the Constitution too much we may split the Empire into fragments, and it will never come together again. Politically, if ever a saying was true, it is this: 'The letter killeth, and the spirit giveth life'.

A consideration of these statements will, I think, reveal that Baldwin mistrusts logic because he misconceives its nature. We may dismiss rather hastily the statement that the British Constitution was not evolved by logicians. Probably no one has ever supposed that it was. No doubt Baldwin intended merely to make the point that the British Constitution 'has grown'; in other words, it is of the flexible, not of the rigid, type of Constitutions. There is no single enactment wherein its precise form is laid down. It is true (that is to say, I agree with the statement) that a flexible Constitution suits the English temperament. This may be in part the reason why parliamentary institutions originated in this country, for such institutions could hardly have been thought out in principle, *de novo*, and then embodied in a single written form. The important question to ask is whether there is anything specifically illogical in such a development? It is hard to see why anyone should regard growth and development as illogical. It is to be hoped that if a Constitution were to be developed by logicians, then they would take note of the relevant facts. Among these relevant facts would be the characteristics of the people who have to work by, and live within, the conditions laid down by the Constitution. Baldwin's warning not 'to be too keen on definition' suggests wherein lies his mistake. He supposes that a logician must demand a definition, and that the definition must necessarily set forth precisely determinable characteristics. But whosoever demands such a definition of that which lacks precisely determinable characteristics is being illogical. The mistake consists in demanding that a sharp line should be drawn concerning characteristics which are not in fact sharply distinguishable. Later in this book I shall consider this illegitimate demand.[5] To fail to realize that such a demand is illegitimate involves a logical error. Many people besides Baldwin erroneously suppose that it is impossible to think logically about anything that is not clear-cut. If that were so, then very few of the matters that concern us as practical men could be thought about in a rational manner. We do not live in a world that has the neatness of a card-index. It is not logical to ignore so relevant a fact; it is logical to recognize it. Baldwin apparently supposes the contrary. He seems to attribute to common sense what may well be attributed to logic, even though he does not disdain to hope that his deduction (on occasions) is logical.

I suspect that he confuses logical thinking with attempting to derive knowledge about what happens in the world by purely *a priori* speculation. Such an attempt is, however, thoroughly illogical; it is anti-scientific. Yet this confusion is strikingly illustrated both by the claim of a French statesman that the French are logical and by the pride of an English statesman in his distrust of logic. An examination of their statements may, perhaps, help to remove these prevalent misconceptions of the nature of logical thinking.

The reader may remember that the Protocol of 1924 led to a certain amount of tension between the English and the French. At the Assembly of the League of Nations in September 1925 an attempt was made to arrive at a clearer understanding of the situation. M. Painlevé and Mr Austen Chamberlain suggested that their misunderstandings were in part due to differences of mental outlook. M. Painlevé said:

> The Protocol's universality, the severe and unbending logic of its obligations, were framed to please the Latin mentality, which delights in starting from abstract principles and passing from generalities to details. The Anglo-Saxon mentality, on the other hand, prefers to proceed from individual concrete cases to generalizations.[6]

Mr Austen Chamberlain replied as follows:

> We are prone to eschew the general, we are fearful of these logical conclusions pushed to the extreme, because, in fact, human nature being what it is, logic plays but a small part in our everyday life. We are actuated by tradition, by affection, by prejudice, by moments of emotion and sentiment. In the face of any great problem we are seldom really guided by the stern logic of the philosopher or the historian who, removed from all the turmoil of daily life, works in the studious calm of his surroundings.[7]

I do not doubt that these spokesmen correctly represented the different mental habits of their respective nations. But, if so, it is difficult to see why the Frenchman claimed to be logical, or why he considered the English to be illogical. For, it must be remembered, the Protocol was concerned with political affairs in this world, not with a Utopia. Consequently it hardly seems logical to start from abstract principles instead of proceeding 'from individual concrete cases to generalizations'. On the other hand, the Englishman prides himself upon the small part played by logic in our everyday life, because he is 'fearful of these logical conclusions *pushed to the extreme*'. But is it logical to push a 'conclusion' to an extreme, i.e. to a point beyond which it applies? Certainly there are dangers in being actuated by tradition, affection, prejudice, emotion and sentiment without regard to the consequences of being thus actuated. It is not, however, illogical to base conclusions upon the fact that people are sometimes so actuated and that, in consequence, a change that would otherwise be beneficial cannot in fact be brought about. There is something comic in the suggestion that the philosopher or historian is being sternly logical when he 'studies a problem' by ignoring all its conditions. Yet Austen Chamberlain does not seem to have spoken sarcastically. He was but repeating what he had said in the House of Commons, when discussing the Protocol the previous year. To claim to be illogical is to claim to be drawing conclusions that are not warranted by the relevant facts; it is to be in the position of a man who declares that black is white and that what is sour is also sweet. Austen Chamberlain seems to me to have supposed that a logical thinker is unable to notice the difference between black and grey or between grey and white. He was 'fearful of these logical conclusions pushed to the extreme'. It is not logical to push a conclusion to an 'extreme', i.e. farther than the facts warrant; on the contrary, a conclusion is logical only if it does follow from the premisses upon which it is based. Thus, for example, we are not being 'sternly logical' if we devise a scheme to control the actions of human beings and forget, in making that scheme, that men are actuated by emotions and prejudices; further, if the scheme be devised to apply to changing conditions, we are not being logical if we proceed upon the false assumptions that these conditions do not change.

I am afraid that Mr Austen Chamberlain and M. Painlevé have but provided us with another example of the very common confusion between thinking logically and thinking abstractly about matters of fact. This is a strange confusion indeed. M. Painlevé, in common, I believe, with many of his countrymen, seemed to suppose that to think logically is to think within the limits of a system. Indeed, I believe that the most fundamental difference between the French mental outlook − or 'the Latin mentality', as Painlevé preferred to call it − and that of the English is that the French tend to seek systems at the expense of the facts to be systematized, whilst the English tend to avoid anything approaching to a system. In this untidy world the advantage hardly seems to lie with the French attitude. An Englishman, I suggest, is prone to believe that men have diverse interests, diverse aims, and diverse problems to solve; he recognizes that these diverse aims and diverse interests cannot always be harmoniously solved, nor can these diverse problems admit of neat solutions. Consequently, English statesmen are tempted to adopt piecemeal solutions, leaving unsolved problems to be dealt with later. If M. Painlevé may be taken to represent the attitude of French statesmen, we may be justified in supposing that their temptation is to adopt solutions that seem to be logical only because they have unduly simplified the details of the problems.

Truly the English cannot be said to be logical. Is there any nation of which this could be truly said? Such a nation, could it be found, might confer upon this unhappy world the incalculable benefit of pointing out the consequences that must logically follow from the schemes we so unreflectively adopt and the policies we so blunderingly pursue.

NOTES

1 See the revealing remark made by Baldwin in 1931, which is quoted on p. 98.
2 Reprinted in *On England*, by Earl Baldwin (Penguin Books). The page numbers inserted in this text refer to this edition. Much may be learnt from reading this valuable collection of addresses by a statesman who has thought carefully about the difficulties of democratic government.
3 *The Times*, May 25th, 1937.
4 Italics throughout this speech are mine.
5 See p. 192.
6 *Official Report of the Proceedings of the Assembly. September 7th, 1925.*
7 *Official Report of the Proceedings of the Assembly. September 10th, 1925.*

2

THINKING AND DOING

'But what can we *do*?' This is the question that is likely to be asked by those who are at all sensitive to the avoidable suffering that is being endured to-day throughout the world. Some will be impatient at the suggestion that, if we seek to bring about some widespread and permanent improvement in the conditions responsible for this suffering, we must pause to think. They would be even more impatient if they were told that, in a time of such stress, it is nevertheless worth while for us to overhaul our mental habits, to attempt to find reasons for our beliefs, and to subject our assumptions to rigorous criticisms. Yet, apart from idle thinking more aptly described as day-dreaming, thinking is always purposive. To think effectively is to think to some purpose. To pursue an aim without considering what its realization

DOI: 10.4324/b22927-2

would involve is stupid: the result may be fortunate but it cannot be wise. Swift, unpremeditated action is sometimes necessary. A person who is called upon thus to act is more likely to act fortunately the more he has previously meditated upon actions of a similar kind. If we wish to play an effective part as members of a community, we must avoid two opposed dangers. On the one hand there is the danger of rushing into action without thinking about what we are doing, or – which in practice comes to the same thing – by taking it for granted that it is 'all right' to do as others do, although we don't in the least know why they act thus. On the other hand, there is the danger of indulging in an academic detachment from life. This is the peculiar temptation of those who are prone to see both sides of a question and are content to enjoy an argument for its own sake. The present writer is at times beset by this temptation. But thinking is primarily for the sake of action. No one can avoid the responsibility of acting in accordance with his mode of thinking. No one can act wisely who has never felt the need to pause to think about how he is going to act and why he decides to act as he does.

We do not think with a part of ourself. Our thinking involves our whole personality. *How* I think is conditioned by the kind of person I am, whosoever 'I' may stand for. The word 'person' is used here in the same sense as it is used in such expressions as 'He is a person to be avoided', or 'He is a person worth knowing'.

Consider the following example. Four men were travelling in the same compartment of a train that had a head-on collision with another train. None of them was injured, though all were badly jolted. It was a bad accident. Some coaches were derailed, some were telescoped, and one was on fire. The four men went along the line to see whether they could give any help to the injured people. One of them was so overcome by the scene of suffering that he backed away, unable to do anything. The second man, anxious to help and able to control his emotions, tried one ineffective thing after another; he tugged at doors that were jammed without realizing the fact, whilst ignoring an iron rod – obviously usable as a crowbar. The third man was a surgeon. He had special knowledge relevant to the situation; he was able at once to attend to those who were freed from the wreckage. The fourth man kept beside him and did what the surgeon told him to do. The reader may wonder what is the point of this example in a discussion about thinking. Everyone knows, it may be urged, that people of different temperaments react differently to the same general situation; everyone knows that certain jobs can be performed only by specialists. That is the point. A specialist is a person who has special knowledge, that is, knowledge about certain states of affairs. He is in possession of certain information of which the layman is ignorant, and he has been trained to discern relevant connexions. He is the right person to tackle a given job. The job may be the comparatively humble one of obeying the specialist's instructions. How we react to a given situation reveals what we are. Our reaction is the outcome of ourself.

The example just considered is an example of a practical situation in which there was an immediate call for action, a need to do something definite. Consider now how different are the judgments of different persons with regard to the conditions prevailing in Russia. Many people who have not themselves visited Russia but have read some of the numerous books professing to tell us what is the state of affairs in the U.S.S.R. find it difficult to ascertain what has been done and what is the aim of 'the great Russian experiment'. André Gide, Eugene Lyons, Sir Walter Citrine, Mr and Mrs Sidney Webb, each interpret in his or her own way the structure of Soviet Communism. I am not speaking of differences in explicit judgments of value, but differences in the records of what is being done, or has been done. These various interpretations spring from the differences in mental habits, prejudices, hopes and fears of the different interpreters. I am not suggesting that these interpreters are in any way trying to make out a case, or being intellectually dishonest, nor that they are incompetent observers. On the contrary, I assume that each of them aims at giving us an impartial account of the facts. This is easy to say, but what are the facts, an impartial account of which is to be given? The selection of what is to be reported, as well as the significance attributed to various items in the report, is the outcome of the personal attitude of the reporter.

Consider, finally, possible differences in the point of view of, say, an Italian, an Englishman, a Frenchman, an American, with regard to the Italo-Abyssinian war. I have noticed that some Englishmen are much surprised to hear that some intelligent and not markedly Fascist Italians hold that a reasonable justification can be made out for the Italian invasion of Abyssinia. To some people it is no less of a surprise to learn that the French view British action with regard to the Italo-Abyssinian crisis very differently from the way in which most of us view it. Again, many Englishmen might be surprised to discover that a large number of Americans consider that British policy with regard to Abyssinia was definitely self-interested, that the discussions in the House of Commons were not frank, and that the prevailing attitude adopted by the newspapers was hypocritical.

I am not suggesting that every Italian takes up the same point of view differing from that of every Englishman, nor, likewise, with regard to Frenchmen, Americans, and members of other nations. I am pointing out that certain beliefs are prevalent among the members of one nation, other beliefs are prevalent among the members of some other nation, and that these beliefs are held so strongly and so unreflectingly that they are not questioned by those who hold them. In consequence, we each approach a problem concerning a nation other than our own from a point of view that is specifically our own. This is surely a commonplace. But platitudes are not necessarily unimportant merely because they are boringly familiar. The importance of this platitude in the present context is that certain persons (i.e. definite individuals, such as I, or you) have certain characteristics in common, differentiating them from some other set of persons. Each different set of persons, bound together by some common interest or by ties of sentiment and common traditions, will tend to think differently from some other set even when both are regarding what is so loosely termed 'the same facts'. It is, we need to remember, persons who think, not purely rational spirits. When I think, I think about a subject-matter, i.e. about some topic or other. There is no thinking in a vacuum. Always there is a topic thought about, but there is no such thing as a quite simple topic. In nearly all the affairs of life with regard to which we are called upon to act it is more or less difficult to ascertain what is in fact the case. As Algernon remarked, in Oscar Wilde's play *The Importance of Being Earnest*, 'The truth is rarely pure and never simple. Modern life would be very tedious if it were either, and modem literature a complete impossibility'. Whatever may be the case with regard to literature, contemporary or nineteenth-century, it is at least true that our difficulties in thinking effectively for our various purposes are enormously increased by the complexity of the topics with which we have to deal and our consequent inability to discern what is and what is not the case. There is not merely the difficulty of ascertaining 'the facts', though that is often difficult enough. There is the additional, and even more serious, difficulty of discriminating with regard to one fact or another its significance for our purpose. This difficulty is, I think, evident in the various interpretations of Soviet Communism to which reference was made above. Yet to make such a discrimination of what is significant is essential to thinking clearly and acting effectively.

Thinking involves asking questions and trying to find answers to these questions. By 'asking questions' I do not mean framing interrogative sentences. This is not necessary, and is never sufficient. Rhetorical questions are questions only in form; they are a stylistic trick. A genuine question logically demands an answer. To be thinking something out is to be in a questioning frame of mind. A necessary and sufficient condition of asking a question is being puzzled about something, i.e. about a topic. What we are puzzled about may be how to open a door that has got stuck; or it may be how to earn a larger income, or how best to learn Arabic. We may be puzzled with regard to which candidate we ought to vote for in a parliamentary election. A Member of Parliament may be puzzled as to which way he should vote on some motion that he considers to be important No doubt some of these Members are saved from this puzzle because they have already made up their minds to vote as 'the Whips tell 'em to'. These examples of puzzles, or problems about which we might have to think, are of very different kinds. But they have this in common, that we should not be puzzled unless we already know something about the problem that sets us on thinking and are aware that there is more to be known about it. Both complete absence of knowledge and complete knowledge about a topic are logically incompatible with the questioning frame of mind. Certainly a writer or lecturer who 'knows his subject' is not all the time having to ask himself questions, for he already knows the answers. But even in the exposition of a familiar topic, to judge by my own experience, the expositor may suddenly find himself confronted with a fresh question. Sometimes he may see what the answer is almost as soon as he asks himself the question; sometimes he may have to reconsider what he has been asserting because the fresh question throws a new light upon his topic. Whenever the topic of our thinking is at all complicated, which is usually the case, the business of thinking effectively is apt to be slow. In the process of thinking out a problem questions may, and indeed ought to, arise which are literally unthinkable until the thinker had begun to consider the problem. When the matter is of grave practical importance, for example, the problem of how to bring about the removal of some social injustice, the need to ask and answer these questions which arise in the course of our thinking may present itself as an intolerable hindrance to getting on with the job. It may even be resented as a merely pedantic delay. Sometimes it may be pedantic; more often it is not. The difficulty here is to strike the right medium between undue academic detachment and adopting a policy that has not been sufficiently considered in all its relevant aspects. When is the academic detachment rightly described as 'undue'? When is the consideration 'sufficient'? How are we to know what are 'all the relevant aspects'? There is no fool-proof method of obtaining answers to these three questions. That is not news. But it is important, at this point, to remind the reader of these difficulties, because our decision with regard to what is relevant and with regard to the moment when we must act on such considerations as have been possible are alike determined by our personal outlook. Each person formulates his questions from a given point of view, determined by the context of his own experience. Sometimes a violent shock may profoundly alter the point of view, but it is still from a point of view that the questions are asked and from which the satisfactoriness of possible answers to these questions will be judged. The context of the experience of each one of us includes the influence of those with whom we come into contact. Members of the same society, whether it be a nation or a church or a trade union or a public school or a profession, to some extent have the same outlook. For them certain questions are already settled, certain other questions are never asked. No one, I suggest, can be wholly uninfluenced by the prevailing attitudes of those with whom he is in any form of close association. Many of our beliefs are due to our unquestioning, i.e. unthinking, acceptance of the beliefs commonly held by the members of our group. Those belonging to other groups will, in the same unthinking way, accept other beliefs concerning some topics. An individual who does not accept some belief unquestioningly held by the members of his group may react violently against that belief; his thinking will be partly determined by the violence of that reaction.

Fortunately, all people resemble one another in one important respect, namely, in having some capacity to follow an argument.[1] Even if we cannot admit that men are primarily rational animals, still it remains true that it is human to reject a contradiction. No one knowingly accepts both of two contradictory statements. No doubt we all hold fast to some beliefs that are contradictory; in other words, our beliefs are not always consistent, and may be in flat contradiction one with another. This is possible only so long as we fail to confront these beliefs or to recognize them as contradictory when confronted. If we can be brought to see the contradiction, then one of the conflicting beliefs will be surrendered. Now, it is usually the case that the mere confrontation of two beliefs is not sufficient to make evident the contradiction. If, however, we examine what each implies, the contradiction may be made manifest. It is in bringing out concealed contradictions that one person can sometimes help another to think more clearly, and thus more effectively for his purpose. Mrs Ladd Franklin tells the story of a little girl, aged four, whose nurse objected to her table manners. 'Emily,' said the nurse, 'nobody eats soup with a fork.' 'But', replied Emily, 'I do, and I am somebody.'[2] This retort left the nurse with only three alternatives: silence, resort to immorally exercised authority, or an explicit qualification of the original 'Nobody'. We are not told how the nurse responded to the situation created by Emily's recognition that an indisputable fact contradicted her nurse's statement. The demand that a generalization should be applied to particular instances often shows the need for an explicit qualification of the generalization by restricting its scope. If such a qualification be necessary, then the original assertion must be abandoned. We are prone to make statements of the form 'Everybody does so and so', 'Nobody behaves in such and such a way', although a little reflection would suffice to convince us that the statement is untenable in this unrestricted form. In Chapter 10 I shall consider the dangers that arise from our tendency to exaggerate and thereby to neglect the important differences between statements about *all* so and so's and statements about *some* so and so's. This neglect involves us in muddled thinking.

In so far as a person is thinking clearly he is intelligent. A distinguishing characteristic of intelligence is the ability to discern relevant connexions – to put together what ought to be conjoined and to keep distinct what ought to be separated.[3] Anyone who holds that *Nothing good can come out of Nazareth* and also that *Jesus Christ came out of Nazareth* must rationally hold that *Jesus Christ was not something good.* It is logically necessary that the first two italicized statements cannot both be true whilst the third is false. The three statements together constitute a syllogism. The first two have been conveniently called 'the premisses' and the third 'the conclusion' of the syllogism. This example of a syllogism is a special instance of a logical principle which may be formulated as follows: *Whatever is affirmed (or denied) of every member of a class must be likewise affirmed (or denied) of any specified member, or any specified set of members, of that class.* This fundamental principle is acceptable also to those who have never heard of logic. It was by reasoning in accordance with this principle – despite her ignorance of it – that the child Emily confounded her nurse. Like Emily we are all capable of drawing the conclusion that follows in accordance with this principle; we can see other people's mistakes in such simple instances. A little reflection shows us that if what we are maintaining is false, then anything implied by what we are maintaining is also false. I must, however, admit that I know a learned man who professed himself unable to give unhesitating assent to this contention. When two statements are so related that, given that the first statement is true, then the second statement must also be true, we say that the first statement *entails* the second statement. Sometimes the word 'implies' is used as a synonym for entails. The relation of *entailing* (or *implication*) is the relation upon which deductive inference depends. Provided that we know that one statement entails another, and also that the former is true, then we can validly infer that the latter is true. In this way we can sometimes obtain new knowledge. Thus we can make use of knowledge we already possess in order to discover something we did not know, but need to know in order to answer our questions.

When we are puzzled we ask questions. A question is intelligent only if an answer to it would resolve the puzzlement that led to the question or would be at least a step towards its solution. To give a satisfactory answer more than intelligence is needed. A little boy, playing with his circular railway, found that the train would not run. Thereupon he proceeded to grease the mechanism. He had answered his question intelligently, drawing upon his past experience for a relevant connexion. But the answer was not satisfactory. The train did not move; it was worked by electricity and the battery had run down. The child did not show lack of intelligence; he lacked the experience needed to provide him with the appropriate knowledge. This lack of knowledge prevented his answer from being effective; it did not serve the purpose of his thinking. To find satisfactory answers we must take account of the facts. We fail if we take an electric toy railway to be a clockwork one. Most of the topics in which we are interested concern the behaviour of people and things in the world. Accordingly, we need to know how they behave; we need knowledge of their characteristics.

An illustration may make this point clear. Aristotle was puzzled by the problem: 'How can we justify the use of other men as slaves?' Few of his contemporaries were puzzled by this problem; it was natural that he should take it for granted that it was right to have slaves. His difficulty was that he could not see how it could be right. Finally, he came to the conclusion that there was a difference in the nature of men by virtue of which some are natural tools, others are the natural users of these tools. He supposed that natural tools (i.e. living men) resembled the masters in their bodily characteristics, but lacked rational souls. He supposed them to be rather like what we should nowadays call 'robots'. Clearly, Aristotle's answer was intelligent up to a point. It insists that there is a fundamental distinction between slaves and masters, i.e. between tools and users of tools. This

fundamental distinction is wholly relevant to the question concerning the justification for one man's using another as a slave.
Unfortunately, the answer is not satisfactory, for it is not true
that some men lack rational souls whereas other men have rational souls. It is not inconceivable that the world might have
contained such convenient robots, but it happens to be the case
that our world does not. It may be remarked that not a few people have taken a view very like Aristotle's. For example, Harriet
Martineau's philanthropic efforts were based upon the assumption that God had created 'the rich man in his castle, the poor
man at his gate', that each must be content with the station thus
assigned to him by God, whilst the rich man should help the
poor man so long as he kept his lowly estate. If an intelligent
woman living in the nineteenth century could hold such a view,
we need not be surprised to find that a Greek philosopher of
the fourth century B.C. held a similar view. Indeed, the Greek
philosopher had the advantage over Harriet Martineau in that
he saw clearly what sort of distinction there must be between
masters and slaves in order to justify the treatment of the one by
the other. Further, Aristotle noticed that some natural masters are
slaves, some natural slaves are masters. This fact was inconvenient; it showed that there was something wrong with Aristotle's
answer. The problem of justification breaks out anew. Since the
original question was a question about the justification of behaviour, the untrue answer is found to be unsatisfactory as soon
as this answer is used to guide subsequent behaviour. It is a sure
indication that something is wrong with an answer if the answer itself leads us to ask another question of exactly the same
form. Possibly Aristotle did not want to go on puzzling about
this problem. He seems to have taken it for granted that there
must be an answer to any question about the way men behave

which would be in accordance with his moral principles and yet not involve a radical alteration of his mode of life.

To make these comforting assumptions is surely dangerous although very common. Reluctance to be shocked as well as laziness may prevent us from questioning the assumptions upon which are based the answers we give to questions directly concerning our daily lives. It is perhaps hardly necessary to stress the point that thinking is a tiring process; it is much easier to accept beliefs passively than to think them out, rigorously questioning their grounds by asking what are the consequences that follow from them.

NOTES

1   I hope this is not an unduly optimistic statement.
2   See my *Modern Introduction to Logic*, p. 95.
3   Here 'ought' means 'must, if rational.' This is the logical *ought*. I shall, throughout this book, use 'ought' only in this sense.

3

A MIND IN BLINKERS

One of the gravest difficulties encountered at the outset of the attempt to think effectively consists in the difficulty of recognizing what we know as distinguished from what we do not know but merely take for granted. Further, it is not always easy to distinguish between what we may reasonably believe and what we ought to hold as doubtful and in need of confirmation. It is reasonable to accept a statement as true, i.e. to hold a belief, provided that there is some evidence in support of it and that it does not contradict what we already know to be the case. Perhaps few people would deny that we are all apt to hold beliefs which are not in this sense reasonable. The strength with which we hold a belief ought to bear some proportion to the amount of evidence upon which it is based. Often, however, we

DOI: 10.4324/b22927-3

hold a belief much more strongly than the evidence known to us warrants; again, we sometimes refuse to entertain an opinion for which there is considerable evidence. Thus, for instance, some people believe that all pacifists are cowardly. These people may have known men whose adoption of pacifist principles during the Great War and their subsequent behaviour did support, more or less strongly, the belief that these men were lacking in courage rather than steadfast to a principle. But it would not follow that this was true of all who proclaimed themselves to be pacifists. There is much evidence to the contrary. Hence to accept as true the statement *All pacifists are cowards* is unreasonable, in the sense indicated above. To take another example. Some people dismiss as being obviously absurd the contention that telepathic communication between persons is possible, i.e. that there are some kinds of extra-sensory perception. There is, however, some evidence that such communication does take place. Others, again, will say that psychoanalysis is all rubbish, that there is nothing in the theories of Freud, Jung, Adler, and their numerous supporters. Some have rushed to the opposite extreme and have supposed that every slip of the pen is evidence of a psychopathological state.

These examples of beliefs which are held either in direct opposition to the evidence or more strongly than the evidence warrants should be regarded by the reader merely as examples. It must be understood that I am not, in this book, concerned to persuade the reader to accept the beliefs which I give as examples of sound thinking, or to reject those which I give as examples of unsound thinking. A conclusion may be true, even though it has been accepted as the result of an unsound argument. My concern is to discuss some of the causes which lead all of us at times to accept unsound arguments and to hold unreasonable beliefs; further, to consider some ways in which we may find good reasons for our conclusions. For this purpose I must take definite examples. Sometimes I shall take examples I have derived from listening to discussions, sometimes from my reading of newspapers and books, sometimes from my recollection of mistakes I have myself made. Often the examples will be drawn from controversial topics. I do not seek to persuade the reader to take sides in the controversy in question. If the reader is sure that he has adequate evidence for some position, an argument for which I have criticised, he should pay attention only to the grounds on which I allege that the conclusion of the argument is not justified. Many unsound arguments have been used to support conclusions that are in fact true. When, however, the argument is unsound, we have not justified our acceptance of the conclusion. Our belief is to that extent unreasonable, although not false.

On the other hand, I do seek to convince the reader that it is of great practical importance that we ordinary men and women should think clearly, that there are many obstacles to thinking clearly, and that some of these obstacles can be overcome provided that we wish to overcome them and are willing to make an effort to do so. Accordingly, both in Chapter 1 and in the last chapter of this book I make many assertions which I not only believe to be true but also of whose truth I wish to persuade the reader. It remains possible that my beliefs on these matters are erroneous (although naturally I cannot myself believe that they are), and that my reasons for holding them are insufficient. Whether this be so or not the reader has to decide for himself. This is an argumentative book about arguing. I should like to say only what is true about the process of arguing. I am not anxious to defend the examples used to illustrate our ways of arguing.

At this point we need to remember that it is *persons* who think, and, therefore, persons who argue. I think, not *something* thinks in me. My intellect does not function apart from the rest of my personality. This is a statement about all thinking beings. A person who is trying to think or is seeking to acquire knowledge should not be compared to an empty bucket waiting to be filled. Nor should he be compared to a pure devouring flame or to a light that illumines a path. On the contrary, from infancy upwards we are forming habits, reacting to situations, experiencing emotions of various kinds; we are being constantly affected by the beliefs and modes of behaviour of those belonging to the various groups with which we have contact. All these play a part in determining our point of view. In the last chapter I called attention to the fact that people belonging to different groups differ in their points of view and that this difference leads them respectively to select different facts for consideration and to interpret differently what they have selected. I, the writer of this book, believe that it is very important in discussing thinking to keep constantly in mind the part played by the thinker, who is a person having definite habits and emotional tendencies. For this reason, the word 'I', in this book, will generally be used to stand for L. S. Stebbing (i.e. the writer), whilst 'you' will be used to stand for the reader. (Thus 'you', though plural in form, is singular in meaning.) This mode of speaking (to use a convenient idiom) is not well adapted for writing. It is more elegant and usually clearer to use a non-personal 'I' and a non-personal 'you', still more a non-personal 'we'. By 'non-personal' is meant 'not referring to a *given* individual but to any one of some set of individuals, the selection of the set being determined by the context'. In this book I (the writer) am making many assertions that call for criticism; some of these assertions will be about you (the reader); hence it is desirable that we should not slip into the mistake of supposing that our discussion is about quite other persons. When we do concern ourselves with others, we must be clear what we are doing. Occasionally the use of a non-personal *we* will be permitted, as has been the case in preceding pages where 'we' has been used to stand for 'people in general' or even for 'English people'. I hope that the context will suffice to make this deviation in usage clear. In talking face to face no difficulty would arise, since I should use a bodily gesture pointing to my-self when I wanted to make clear that 'I' is not being used for *any* I. When a discussion is in book form, then I, the writer, and *you*, the reader, must do the best *we* can. It is indeed only by courtesy that a book written by a single person can be said to contain a discussion, since it takes two to discuss. A book, however, is written to be read; the reader contributes his part, although the writer may not benefit from the contribution.

To return after these preliminaries to the importance of the person's point of view. The expression 'point of view' is meta-phorical, and a very good metaphor it is. Mountains seen across a bay look very different from those same mountains as they are being climbed. In the National Gallery there is a picture painted by Holbein which has in the foreground a curious ob-long-shaped, yellowish patch. Looked at from one position, however, this patch is seen to be the representation of a skull. The painter has taken advantage of his knowledge of the prin-ciples of perspective to paint an object that looks like a skull only from one position. As there are many other positions it is natural to say that the patch is 'curious', since, in order to make it fit in with the rest of the picture, the spectator must be in a unique position. The unmetaphorical usage of a 'point of view' emphasizes the fact that we see things differently in so far as we are different one from another. I must see from my point of view; you must see from your point of view. Fortunately, people's points of view often overlap. Otherwise, there could be no communication one with another. Sometimes one person can bring about a considerable alteration in another's point of view with regard to some topic. That is why argument is sometimes useful and preaching is occasionally effective. But such an alteration is possible only in so far as one person can make another adopt his own standpoint. No doubt you have sometimes begun to discuss some topic with someone else and have come to feel, after a short time, that the discussion is useless, since the other person's point of view is so different from your own that there is no ground common to them. I, at least, have had that experience.

Let us consider some of the obstacles to thinking effectively that arise from our being the sort of persons we are. Our fears and hopes, our ignorance (often not easily, if at all, avoidable), our loyalties, these lead us to entertain prejudices which are an effective bar to thinking a problem out. By 'entertaining a prejudice' is usually meant 'accepting without evidence a belief for which it is reasonable to seek evidence'. We shall see later that it is reasonable to accept statements upon the evidence of expert testimony. We shall then have to consider what are the grounds for trusting the expert. At present our concern is with beliefs for which we have no evidence that can withstand critical questioning. We do not know how we have come to have these beliefs; we are often impatient at the mere suggestion that they may be untenable. It is a good habit to ask, with regard to our cherished beliefs, 'Now, how did I come to think that?' An honest answer would sometimes be both surprising and enlightening; it could not fail to be useful.

Notice, first of all, that we do have habits of thought. Just as our bodies may bear the stamp of our daily occupation, so too may our minds. Sailors are well known to have a characteristic sort of walk. Some people believe that sailors have characteristic mental attitudes, for example, straightforwardness and gullibility to an unusual degree. I have heard both these characteristics attributed to sailors, with what truth I do not know. Possibly you have come across the phrase, 'the alert face of the lawyer'. No doubt lawyers get into the habit of looking alert. We speak also of 'the legal cast of mind'. It is hardly necessary to multiply examples. If it be true (as I think it is) that we think with the whole force of our personality, then it follows that our habits of thought will not be unaffected by the way in which we spend our working hours. I suggest that each of us form the habit of asking ourself a definite sort of question.

Notice, secondly, that I am recommending the habit of asking a question about (i.e. thinking about) a cherished belief. By saying that the belief is 'cherished', we show that it is one we want to retain; it is a belief pleasant to hold. We have to be on our guard against supposing that a belief that is cherished could not be false because it would be so dreadful if it were. I do not believe that anyone is wholly without cherished beliefs. Indeed, I would go farther and say that I, for my part, am quite sure that every normal person passionately believes some things and with equal passion disbelieves other things. Enthusiasm is not necessarily an enemy of thinking clearly, whilst it is indispensable for achieving great and difficult ends. The danger arises from the feeling that the passionateness of a belief provides any guarantee of its truth. Our safeguard lies in an ability to ask the question: 'How did I come to believe this?' It is the answer to this question that may be surprising. Then another question may have to be asked: 'Well, no matter how I came by it, is it tenable?' It is the answer to this question that may be enlightening. If I find that the belief is tenable, since I can find evidence in support of it, then my belief is now not only cherished but also reasonable. If I find that it is not tenable, then I have saved myself from believing a falsehood. In either case the result of my inquiry is useful in clearing up my mind. You will notice that I am taking it for granted that to be clear-headed is worth while for its own sake. Without this assumption I should not have wanted to write this book. It is, however, enough if you will admit that muddled thinking ends in bungled doing, so that to think clearly is useful for the sake of achieving even our most practical aims. Unless you admit at least as much as this, there will be no point, so far as you are concerned, in what I have to say. Our points of view would be too different for discussion to be possible.

Cherished beliefs are derived from many different sources; they are, moreover, about such diverse matters that it is hardly possible to do more than select a very few examples in the hope that they are fairly typical. Some of our cherished beliefs are, as the saying is, 'imbibed with our mother's milk', i.e. they are common to our culture. Some are the unquestioned assumptions of our particular class and age; some are thrust upon us by authority, by those whom we take to be our superiors in knowledge and whose opinions we have not learnt to question. That capitalists set the interests of their own class above those of their country; that our own country is superior to other countries; that white men are more intelligent than Negroes; that war can never be abolished; that no country should tolerate the growth of its industrial rivals – all these are beliefs that someone or other holds unquestioningly. That to start a journey on a Friday is unlucky is a superstition still prevalent among sailors. You will notice that by dubbing this belief a 'superstition' I have shown that I do not share it. Indeed, I was once surprised to learn that a ship, on which I was sailing from New York, would not leave until 12.1 a.m. (i.e. one minute *past* midnight) to avoid leaving on the Friday night. You will, I expect, often notice examples of superstitions, that is, of foolish beliefs that *other* people hold. It is scarcely wise for you and me to assert that we are quite free from superstition. Perhaps you have seen someone who, having spilt salt, throws a pinch of salt over his left shoulder. If he does it with a laugh, you can judge that he has labelled the belief – it is unlucky to spill salt – as superstitious. But he has not quite rid himself of a superstitious feeling. Do you feel like that about any popular superstition, for example, being the thirteenth person at a dinner-party? There are strange survivals of primitive superstitions which crop up at times in the behaviour of the most rational people. This is to be expected. The roots of our behaviour are very deep in the traditions of the past. We are not purely rational beings. We may succeed in avoiding many errors if we can bear that in mind. It is only too easy to dismiss other people's beliefs, including their religious beliefs, by condemning them as superstitious whilst failing to notice the superstitious elements in our own attitudes.

In the sense in which I defined a 'prejudice', a superstitious belief is a prejudice. Sometimes, however, a prejudice is defined as a belief, or opinion, that the thinker holds because it is to his advantage that it should be true, and in consequence he believes it. This account of prejudice emphasizes the tendency to be partial where we should be impartial. In entertaining a prejudice we have prejudged the question at issue, and thus, whether there is any evidence for it or not, our acceptance is not based upon evidence. In the main this is true of what we call superstitions. Most, I suspect all, superstitions have an origin that makes them seem not absurd. The superstition about spilling salt is due to the significance attached to salt by primitive peoples. The superstition about the unluck attached to the number '13' is perhaps connected with Judas Iscariot. In what I said above there was contained the suggestion that to say 'This is a superstition' implies 'That is a foolish belief which other people hold'. We cannot, however, draw a sharp line between a prejudice in the narrower sense, which excludes superstitions, and in the wider sense, which includes superstitions as beliefs accepted without adequate evidence. My main purpose, however, in dealing with these two together is that I wish to emphasize the fact that both have an emotional foundation of which the thinker is not aware. Ignorance of the connexion between the belief and the emotional interest inducing the belief is an essential element in being prejudiced. A person who owns capital may very firmly believe that the private ownership of capital is vital to the industrial prosperity of a country. This belief may be casually dependent upon his desire to retain what he has. Subsequently he may construct an argument designed to justify his desire. In such a case he does not believe because the belief follows from the premisses of his argument. He first believes and then finds reasons for his belief. This process has been called 'rationalization' – a somewhat unfortunate name. It must not be taken to mean that the belief thus 'rationalized' is in fact reasonable. Someone else may believe equally firmly that the abolition of private ownership of capital is vital to the industrial prosperity of a country. He, too, may rationalize his belief. Both are the victims of prejudice. On this topic their minds are closed.

At this point you may object: 'But surely one of these two beliefs is correct?' Let this be granted. That would not in the least alter the fact that anyone who holds the belief first and rationalizes it afterwards is prejudiced. If you have ever read a series of letters appearing in the newspapers on the topic of fox-hunting, or on vivisection, and if you do not yourself feel strongly for, or against, fox-hunting, or vivisection, you can hardly have failed to notice many prejudices masquerading as arguments on both sides of the controversy. If you do feel strongly on one side, you will at least notice the prejudices on the other side. Or, consider Colonel Blimp. In him Low has constructed a perfect caricature of a prejudiced mind, a mind in blinkers. Some of Colonel Blimp's beliefs are, no doubt, true. But he is not prepared to question their truth. Colonel Blimp, being a caricature, does not rationalize: he shouts and splutters. He, it would seem, believes in speaking loudly, in the manner recommended by Lord Selborne. Colonel Blimp is a laughable, because a grotesquely exaggerated, type of a closed mind. He is portrayed as having emotions so strong that he is not even aware that any reasonable person could dissent from his beliefs. Consequently, he would not want to offer even bad reasons for his explosive statements. No 'decent' person, he would feel, could disagree.

I do not think that it can be reasonably disputed that there is something of a 'Colonel Blimp' in all of us (though it may be on the other side of the political fence). We are all of us prejudiced about something or other. Whilst we can see the mote in our neighbour's eye it is often difficult to discover the beam in our own. It is, however, possible to get into a way of remembering that, whenever our emotions are aroused, we are prone to prejudge the point at issue. We can then try to make clear to ourselves what our prejudices are. It is then possible to make an attempt resolutely to discount them. This, though easy to say, is hard to do. Certain recommendations can be made. Yet in making them I am sadly aware how difficult it is to observe them. First, we must remember that a strong emotion, such as hatred, love, or loyalty, tends to close our minds. Hence, when we are thus strongly moved we must deliberately pause in order to consider whether we have so prejudged the matter that we have made no attempt to weigh the evidence. One way of finding out whether we have fallen into this mistake is to compare our sentiments (as we so correctly call them) with those of other people who disagree with us on this matter and yet seem to us to be as reasonable as we are. Secondly, we must take note of the fact that an emotional bias in favour of a view tends to make us select instances favourable to it and simply fail to notice anything that tells against it. Consequently, it is desirable to make a deliberate search for contrary evidence. Thirdly, we must not allow a prejudice to lead us to overstatement. 'To believe nothing good of the enemy' is a sign of prejudice. The following quotation from an article in the *Daily Mail* provides, I think, an example:

> What should the British attitude be? This can best be decided by noting what the Soviet would have this country do and taking the opposite course.

The influence of prejudice in our beliefs is very extensive. We shall frequently have to consider its distorting effects in our arguments. In a sense the next chapter partly continues the topic of this chapter. Moreover, several erroneous forms of argument with which we shall later be concerned could be fittingly considered here. It is, however, more convenient to limit the discussion of prejudice in the above manner. So far I have been mainly concerned to emphasize the danger of not questioning our beliefs, of being unwilling to drag our assumptions into the light, and of forgetting that my argument, in so far as it is mine, may suffer from the defects of my personality.

I must obviate a misunderstanding that I have often met at this point. I do not in the least wish to suggest that it is undesirable for us to be set on thinking by emotional considerations. On the contrary, nothing else will suffice to make us think to some purpose. Nor do I wish to suggest that the presence of a strong emotion is incompatible with thinking clearly. Certainly the more strongly we feel the more difficult it is to take account of what is alone relevant. But the difficulty may be overcome, provided that we also desire to reach sound conclusions. 'It is not emotion', said André Malraux, 'that destroys a work of art, but the desire to demonstrate something.' I would say, somewhat similarly, that it is not emotion that annihilates the capacity to think clearly, but the urge to establish a conclusion in harmony with the emotion and regardless of the evidence. This urge is incompatible with the impartial weighing of evidence which is an essential condition of ascertaining all the relevant facts and deducing conclusions from these facts alone. A comment made by an adult student, who had been asked to state his opinion of his tutor, will serve to illustrate this point. The student's criticism was:

> The tutor always insisted that he was unbiased. I cannot see how education of this description will assist us in the emancipation of the working class.[1]

This student's emotional attitude to the subject he was studying must, I think, have been inimical to his thinking clearly about it. He does not seem to believe that an unbiased presentment of the topic could lead to the fulfilment of his purpose in studying. If that were so, he could not be in the temper of mind necessary for the sifting of evidence. Perhaps he was making the assumption that no one who was not biased in favour of the class war could possibly present correctly the facts that (so he felt sure) show it to be inevitable. If so, he was taking it for granted that historical facts are in accordance with the Marxist philosophy of history. But if the Marxist philosophy of history is true, then an unbiased thinker, given the relevant knowledge, will discover this truth. If it is not true, then a bias in favour of its truth is a hindrance to thinking effectively, unless this bias be consciously recognized and allowed for by the thinker. People of other political parties make equally dogmatic assertions with regard to the historical facts, without in the least recognizing that they are making assumptions. The old adage, 'Nothing like leather', has a very wide application.

NOTE

1   *Learn and Live*, p. 109.

4

YOU AND I
I AND YOU

In the last chapter we noticed some of the obstacles to thinking clearly that come from having a mind in blinkers. It will be remembered that the blinkers are our prejudices, including those assumptions that are so fundamental to our point of view that we do not even know that we are taking anything for granted. We have noticed how difficult it is to drag our assumptions into the light. There are still other ways in which having a mind made up may prevent us from thinking effectively.

Whenever I write, or talk, about the difficulty of thinking clearly, with a view to suggesting possible ways of avoiding some of the difficulties that beset us, I am apt to feel uncomfortable. I

DOI: 10.4324/b22927-4

remember some of the bad blunders I have myself made, and I realize that my readers, or hearers, may well reply: 'Those who live in glass houses should not throw stones.' But I cheer myself with the reflection that we can properly understand the causes of distorted thinking only when we have followed it in our own minds and have come to detect it in ourselves as well as in the speeches and writings of other people. None of us can entirely free our thinking from the influence of deep-seated prejudices and strong desires to establish some case at any cost. I ought to avoid making elementary mistakes in logic, since I have been thinking about the conditions of sound reasoning and have been trying to teach logic for years. But eager haste to establish a conclusion may lead me to make elementary blunders. You must not suppose that I, though a woman, am peculiar about this. You also, I believe, will at times fall into fallacies, that is, violate some principle of sound reasoning. When *you* argue with me I can more easily see any fallacies into which you may fall; when I argue with you, then I do not so easily detect a fallacy in the argument. In carrying on an oral discussion we have less time to reflect than when we write and re-read what we have written. It is not very difficult to reconsider what we have written in the detached and critical way in which we examine other people's arguments. Even so, however, we may fail to detect some fundamental assumption that has not been tested and that might not survive the test. Naturally I cannot provide an example of my own failure in this respect; to have recognized the error would be to have avoided it. It is, however, worth while to notice that when anyone begins an argument with such a remark as 'It is indisputably true that ...', 'Everyone knows that ...', or 'No reasonable man can doubt that ...', then the people addressed may be sure that the speaker has taken for granted what he is about to assert, and that any argument he may produce in favour of the assertion is for export only. The assertion may be true, but there is generally a danger that 'reasonable men' means no more than those who agree with the speaker and share his outlook. 'I' just means the speaker, or writer; 'you' just means the hearer, or reader. You and I change places as we argue. Now, when I make an assertion that is intended to apply to everyone, then it must logically apply to me also. One of our commonest mistakes is due to our forgetting this fact − a fact so obvious when stated that it may seem unnecessary to mention it, yet so difficult to bear in mind when we are arguing.

Some definite examples may help to bring out the importance of these considerations. When I want to find examples of mistakes in arguments I look at the correspondence columns of the newspapers, for people who take the trouble to write these letters often feel too strongly about the topic under discussion to be able to scrutinize their reasoning with sufficient care.

My first two examples are taken from the correspondence to *The Times* on the topic of 'the dwindling family'. This topic aroused a good deal of interest in the autumn of 1936. One correspondent sought to put the case for a big family. He wished to insist that there were good reasons why people should desire to have a large number of children. He assumed that we ought to try to establish conditions which would make for the development of fine characters, i.e. unselfish and disciplined men and women. 'There are two conditions,' he said, 'about which there is no reasonable doubt.' These conditions are: (1) that a child who has four or five brothers and sisters will develop good qualities from living with them in the same house; (2) that the home should be poor. He argued that children living in a large family where there is very little money will have to fend for themselves, and they will thus be forced to think of other people and be considerate. Accordingly, he concluded, 'they learn by ten years of age that there is more joy in service than in sweets; more interest in the welfare of others than in their own.'[1]

Whatever may be our views with regard to the desirability of arresting the decline in the birth-rate, it seems to me easy to recognize that this argument reveals a mind in blinkers. The writer is quite unaware that there may be another side to the question. You will probably have guessed that he is a man who has not himself been brought up in a poor family. He has not been able, it seems, to think himself into the position of a member of a large family all of whom are so much taken up with getting enough food and coal, and enough money to pay the rent, and are, moreover, so crowded together that they may not have enough energy left to be considerate one to another. It simply has not occurred to the writer to think that there might be better ways of learning to be unselfish, ways involving much less suffering and waste of human effort. Suppose that, having been reminded that his circumstances are very different, he should nevertheless persist in maintaining that if you wish to produce fine men and women, it is an advantage for your family to be large and also poor. Then we may ask him to state explicitly the general principle underlying his argument. This seems to be that poverty combined with a large family is the most effective builder of fine and disciplined characters.[2] Then we proceed to ask him to apply the general principle to the special case of his own family. Does he seriously believe – we should ask him – that it would have been a moral advantage to his own family had he been poor? If he assents, then he ought in consistency to wish that he had given up his income, worked hard for a low wage, and lived in a poor, overcrowded neighbourhood. If, on the contrary, he is unwilling to apply the principle to the case of his own family, then he has fallen into a serious logical confusion. The mistake consists in making a special plea in one's own favour. It is called by logicians 'the fallacy of special pleading'.

A safeguard against this mistake is to change *you* into *I*. We often forget to do this. Accordingly, I feel that you can't see what is straight in front of your nose; *you* feel that I can't see what is on the other side of my blinkers. We often make bad blunders because we forget that what is true of one of us is true also of the other in the same circumstances. A rule that seems quite sound when I apply it to you may seem to me to be very unsatisfactory when you ask me to apply it to myself. Such an application would be unsatisfactory provided that there were 'extenuating circumstances' in my case. Usually there are not. The only difference is that I am I, whilst you are you. Both you and I make this sort of mistake, not usually because we want to be unfair in making exceptions for our own benefit; we make the mistake because our blinkers – our general outlook, dependent upon our prejudices and unquestioned assumptions – prevent us from seeing that what is sauce for the goose is sauce for the gander.

Two days after the publication of this letter, an extract from another correspondent[3] on the 'Dwindling Family' was published in *The Times*. It was as follows:

> I would like to be permitted to endorse the remarks made by the Rev. Dr Lyttelton in *The Times* of October 7th on the interesting discussion of the 'Dwindling Family'. A well-known obstetrician has stated that in his experience he had always found that the larger the family the greater was the happiness among the children – poverty did not seem to matter in such cases.

This correspondent stresses the connexion between the size of the family and the happiness of the children – the greater the one the greater the other. (Perhaps we need not take too seriously this precise quantitative variation.) He evidently accepts the second of the two conditions laid down by Dr Lyttelton, namely, that the family should be poor, since he 'endorses' the remarks made. The quotation from the 'well-known obstetrician' suggests, however, that both he and the obstetrician were thinking rather of the contrast between large and small families, in respect of happiness, than of the contrast between a wealthy and a poor family of the same size. One wonders, indeed, what would be the opportunities of a well-known obstetrician to view at close quarters the behaviour of poor families. It is one thing to maintain that belonging to a large family promotes 'the growth of strong, disciplined, unselfish characters'; it is quite another to maintain that poverty is a condition of developing such characters. Both these contentions were made by Dr Lyttelton. I hazard the suggestion that these gentlemen were primarily impressed by the happiness that may come from the companionship of brothers and sisters; that they remembered that such companionship often involves a 'give and take' that has beneficial effects (in some cases) upon the children; that they had realized that poverty necessitates sacrifices for those one loves; that those who are poor often have fine and strong characters and have learnt to sacrifice 'sweets' for 'the joy in service'. Thereupon, they draw the wholly unwarranted conclusion that poverty is the most effective means of building up such characters. It seems clear to me that either this is an example of exceptionally muddled thinking or it provides an example of very flagrant special pleading.

The fallacy of special pleading is extremely common. I imagine that few, if any, of us escape it altogether. It is so difficult to be detached from one's own circumstances and regard other people's troubles and pleasures as we do our own. You may hear a person who lives on a large inherited income complaining that the 'dole' given to the unemployed 'pauperizes' them by giving them the means of subsistence without working for it. Or, again, wealthy people sometimes argue that, if higher wages are paid to bricklayers and miners, for instance, they will only spend their extra money on amusements, such as the cinema and football pools; yet these same people may defend their own expenditure on amusements and luxuries on the ground that they are giving employment. On the other hand, a man who has very little money may complain of the luxurious way in which rich people live; yet he may be only too ready to spend money in the same sort of way if he is lucky enough to win a fortune from a football pool.

Certainly there are sound arguments with regard to the con-nexion between poverty and the development of character, and there are sound arguments with regard to the most desirable ways of spending money; there are, no doubt, good reasons why people's incomes should be unequal. But these arguments, if sound, will hold both in your case and in mine. An exception in my own case, just because my own interests are peculiarly important to me, can never be correctly maintained. Accord-ingly, I ought (and this, you will remember, is a *logical* ought) to test my argument by seeing whether it holds in your case too. Unless I do this I shall be thinking unclearly, perhaps even dishonestly.

The contrast I – You holds, not only between individuals, but also between nations. Whatever may be your opinion with re-gard to what is called 'the German Colonial Problem' you may not find any difficulty in seeing that its discussion has involved a good deal of special pleading. To the German demand that their colonies should be returned to them, since colonies are an economic necessity under present world conditions, many Englishmen have replied that colonies are a liability rather than an asset, so that Germany would be better off without them. Naturally, the Germans will reply: 'Why, then, do you refuse to get rid of this liability by returning the colonies to us?' Such a reply seems to be logically justified. If, however, the Germans were told that the British wish to keep their colonies and to prevent the return of the German colonies, not on the ground of economic utility, but on the ground of their strategic value, then the reply would be free from fallacy. I do not say that the reply is satisfactory, nor do I think that these are the only considerations raised by this current problem. It is not my concern here to discuss political affairs, save as examples of the way in which we do actually argue. In my opinion the accusations and counter-accusations made by one nation against another at the present day provide very striking evidence of our difficulty in entering into the other person's point of view. Mussolini's indignation against Great Britain for her reluctance to recognize the King of Italy as Emperor of Abyssinia is not wholly without ground. Italy belongs, at present, to the unsatisfied Powers who desire a change in the *status quo*. Great Britain belongs to the satisfied Powers who do not desire such a change. Accordingly, it is to the advantage of Great Britain to defend the *status quo*. This being so, it is not unnatural that Italians should feel that the British are dishonest in condemning Italians for bombing Abyssinian villages whilst the British Government were themselves permitting bombs to be used to quell disturbances on the northwest frontier of India. Certainly there are differences between the two cases. Italy was an aggressor, whereas the British were in possession in India. But these cases are not, I think, so relevantly different as they seem to be in the opinion of most British people.

A striking example of this failure to see the point from the other man's position is provided by an argument designed by Archdeacon Paley (in the eighteenth century) for the purpose of preaching resignation to the poor:

> The wisest advice that can be given is never to allow our attention to dwell upon comparisons between our own conditions and that of others, but keep it fixed upon the duties and concerns of the condition itself ... We are most of us apt to murmur when we see exorbitant fortunes placed in the hands of single persons; larger, we are sure, than they can want, or, as we think, than they can use ... But whenever the complaint comes into our minds, we ought to recollect that the thing happens in consequence of those very rules and laws which secure to ourselves our property, be it large or small ... To abolish riches would not be to abolish poverty but, on the contrary, to leave it without protection and resource ... It is not for the poor man to repine at the effects of laws and rules, by which he is benefited every hour of his existence; which secure to him his earnings, his habitation, his bread, his life; without which he, no more than the rich man, could eat his bread in quietness, or go to bed in safety. ... Besides, what after all is the mischief? The owner of a great estate does not eat or drink more than the owner of a small one ... Either, therefore, large fortunes are not a public evil, or, if they be in any degree evil, it is to be borne with, for the sake of those fixed and general rules concerning property, in the preservation and steadiness of which all are interested. Frugality itself is a pleasure ... the very care and forecast that are necessary to keep expenses and earnings upon a level form, when not

embarrassed by too great difficulties, an agreeable engagement of the thoughts. There is no pleasure in taking out of a large unmeasured fund ... But no man can rest who has not worked. Rest is the cessation of labour. It cannot, therefore, be enjoyed, or tasted, except by those who have known fatigue. The rich see, and not without envy, the refreshment and pleasure which rest affords to the poor, and chuse to wonder that they cannot find the same enjoyment in being free from the necessity of working at all.

(Reasons for Contentment addressed to the Labouring Part of the British Public (1793), pp. 4, 11.)

I cannot believe that this argument was likely to appeal to the poor as providing them with good reasons for contentment. They may have found it difficult to believe that the rich, who showed no eagerness to become poor, were in fact envious of the conditions imposed by poverty.

It would be an error to assume that arguments involving special pleading are always evidence of hypocrisy. Those engaged in arguing may be completely unaware of the irrational grounds of their arguments. They may not in the least realize that their personal desires and repugnances have led them to put forward a plea which, had their desires and repugnances been different, they would have seen through at once. When a line of action chimes in with our desires, we may wholeheartedly and honestly support it with wrongheaded arguments. Many examples can, I think, be found in the debates, in the House of Commons and elsewhere, concerning the policy of non-intervention in the Spanish Civil War. The explicit ground for the adoption of this policy was (so it was asserted) the desire to localize the war in Spain. Different politicians had diverse sympathies; these sympathies led them to favour, or to oppose, this policy of non-intervention in accordance with the fluctuations of the war. For example, in March 1938 General Franco's forces seemed to be winning. In the House of Commons the Labour Party urged the need 'to consider the grave menace to British interests arising out of the armed intervention in Spain by certain Powers.' Captain H. Balfour is reported in *The Times* (March 17th) as having said that the Opposition 'were using non-intervention for just so long as it suited their political affinities, to throw it over as soon as it suited them, irrespective of whether it was helpful to the cause of peace.' The charge of bias has also been brought against the Non-Intervention Committee. Sir Peter Chalmers-Mitchell in a speech at the Queen's Hall (April 24th, 1938), stated that he had followed closely the dates of the Non-Intervention Committee meetings and the successes and failures of Franco, and that he had found that whenever Franco was gaining, the Non-Intervention Committee did not meet; whenever he was losing, the Non-Intervention Committee got together. Granted that these observations were correctly made, then there is some evidence that the Government were using non-intervention only when it suited their purposes.[4]

We need not inquire whether either of these accusations was justifiable. Our concern is with the way in which the divergence between *my* interests and *yours* may lead me to use an argument the force of which I should be unable to recognize were our positions reversed. To be sensitive to the danger of this temptation need not, however, prevent me from admitting that there are not two sides to *every* question. In some disputes the right is on one side alone.

NOTES

1 Dr Lyttelton, in *The Times*, October 7th, 1936.
2 I do not *think* that his two 'conditions' admit of any other interpretation.
3 Mr Charles Horwitz (*The Times*, October 9th, 1936, p. 10).
4 See pp. 175 for a further discussion bearing on this point.

5

BAD LANGUAGE AND TWISTED THINKING

We use language in order to communicate one with another, to express our personal reactions to situations, to stimulate a response in someone else, and for the sake of thinking something out. Language may be described as a means of conveying something that the user of the language wants to convey. In this wide sense the word 'language' is so used as to cover any means used to convey emotions and thoughts, from gesture language at the one extreme of simplicity to mathematical language at the other extreme. It is with language regarded as an instrument that we are here concerned. An instrument is efficient to the extent to which the using of it enables the purpose, for which

DOI: 10.4324/b22927-5

the instrument is designed, to be achieved. An inefficient instrument is bad; an efficient instrument is good. An instrument is for use. A carpenter's tool, for example, is, strictly speaking, an instrument only when someone is using it. I am myself very inefficient in using a hammer. I might say: 'This is a good hammer, but I am not using it well.' Such a judgment implies that the object called 'this hammer' is well devised for its purpose of hitting nails on the head, but that the person using it is not very successful in hitting the nail. There is some similarity between using a tool and using language; indeed, language is often metaphorically called a 'tool'. Bad language (in the sense in which the phrase is being used here) is language that fails to achieve the purpose for which it is used; good language is language that achieves the purpose for which it is used. A word is a tool only in so far as it is used in a context by someone who has some purpose in view. Whether, therefore, we are using language well or badly depends upon the purpose for which we use it.

When we use a word (or combination of words) either in speaking or in writing, our most obvious purpose is to indicate some thing, or some relation, or some property. What the word is used to indicate is sometimes called its 'meaning'. For example, suppose that you and I are standing on the shore of Sligo Bay and suddenly we see a large white bird flying overhead. I say to you: 'That's a swan'. I thereby indicate to you that the object we are looking at is a member of the class of birds called swans. The word 'swan' as I used it has a plain, straightforward meaning. This meaning is non-personal, or, as it will be more convenient to say, 'objective'. Since the primary purpose of the usage of language in any scientific inquiry necessitates that the words used should be non-personal or objective, we may call such a use of language scientific. Sometimes we use words with the deliberate intention of evoking emotional attitudes in our hearers; we want them to respond in a certain way to what is said. Language thus used may be said to be emotive.[1] A word used in this emotive manner can be said to be emotionally toned. If we speak for the sake of arousing emotional attitudes, then the use of emotionally toned words is good for the purpose. When, however, our purpose is to give a straightforward account of what we believe to be the case, emotionally toned language is bad language. In poetry and in oratory the use of emotionally toned language may be essential for the purpose the speaker wishes to achieve. It is, then, good language, for it is fitted to its purpose. If, however, we want to think something out, then we are hindered in our purpose by using emotionally toned language. Such language may be an insuperable obstacle to thinking effectively. This is a point of such importance that it is worth while to spend some trouble over it.

As we noticed in a previous chapter, there are two parties to any discussion. We can refer to them respectively as the speaker and the hearer. What is said about the speaker and the hearer can, for the most part, be applied to the pair – writer and reader. Now it is not always the case that I, the speaker, have the same purpose in our discussion as *you*, the hearer, have. You may ask me simply to give you information. In replying I may, by using emotionally toned language, give you information with a twist to it. This twist is imparted by the use of words carrying with them more or less strong suggestions of emotional attitudes. These suggestions are what psychologists call 'tied suggestions'; we cannot hear the words without having the emotional attitude. Much in the way in which ice *looks* cold as well as feeling cold to the touch, so certain words have a significance in addition to their objective meaning. This additional significance may be called emotional meaning. I may deliberately impart this twist to the information I give you because I want to arouse your emotions. In that case I am replying to your question dishonestly. My language is, then, good (i.e. effective) from my point of view, since it achieves the end for which I use it. From your point of view it is bad language, since its use arouses an emotional response in answer to a request for information. It may be, however, that I have so fallen into the habit of using emotionally toned words in connexion with certain topics that I am not aware that the information is twisted. In such a case I mislead not only you but also myself. It is regrettable enough if I mislead you, but it is even worse if I mislead myself, since I shall be unable to think straight. Unfortunately we are often in this state. Controversial discussions concerning morals, politics, art and religion abound in the use of emotionally toned words.

Let us consider a few examples.

In one of his weekly articles on the theatre, published in the *Observer*, Mr St John Ervine wrote:

> *The Sea-Gull* can scarcely be called a trivial play, though it may be overrated by young Eaton-Square Bolshies who fall into a coma every time a Russian name is mentioned in their presence.

'Bolshies' is a term of contemptuous abuse – a little old-fashioned nowadays, but still current in Mr Ervine's vocabulary. In the article from which the above statement was taken he was defending the English stage against the charge of triviality brought by certain American critics. He cites in his defence the production that summer of *The Sea-Gull*. This is, at least apparently, his purpose. But Mr Ervine is a man with a mind made up; he feels strongly and speaks passionately. The recollection that the play was written by a Russian seems to have diverted his aim; he cannot refrain from a thrust against those whose political views he detests. Consequently he uses an abusive term and is led into an absurd exaggeration. The reader is left wondering whether Mr Ervine's statement is intended to assert that young men of certain political views are, in virtue of holding these views, rendered incapable of distinguishing a good Russian play from a bad one. Perhaps, however, we should not try to draw out the implications of what, after all, is nothing but a shout – a sort of equivalent to waving a flag. I may be doing Mr Ervine an injustice but I have the impression that he is a man with a mission, so that his articles are primarily intended to induce his readers to agree with him rather than to convince them that what he says is sound. His exaggerated modes of expression and his frequent use of emotional language may serve to impress some of his readers; on the other hand, some readers may be tempted to ignore his serious criticism because they have come to discount his exaggerations. I am myself unsure exactly what Mr Ervine wanted to achieve. In summing up his statement as a *shout* I have deliberately used a word that, in the context, is emotionally toned, for in so doing I have expressed, I believe correctly, the impression made upon me by what Mr Ervine said.

Possibly my readers will be familiar with Ruskin's expression of opinion about Whistler's *Nocturnes*:

> I have heard and seen much of Cockney impudence before now, but never expected to hear a coxcomb ask two hundred guineas for flinging a pot of paint in the public's face.

Such violent language may be regarded as inexcusable in a man who was capable of being a serious art critic. I hardly think, however, that it can be regarded as misleading; its violence defeats itself.

Sometimes strongly toned language is deliberately used for the purpose of exciting a strong emotional response:

> Over the whole of this Abyssinian dispute rises the stink of oil and stronger than the stink of oil is the stink of the Jews.
>
> Sir Oswald Mosley (*New Statesman and Nation* – 'This. England', 1935.)

If I am not misunderstanding Sir Oswald Mosley's purpose, he has used language fitted to achieve it. In the sense in which we are now considering the distinction between good and bad language, his language is good. His purpose was, I believe, to stir people to action by arousing or fomenting hatred; he sought to be offensive, and his language is too blatantly offensive to impart a twist to the understanding of what he said. It is important for the purpose of this chapter that I should try to make this point clear. I personally disapprove of Sir Oswald Mosley's intention; I very much dislike his impolite and deliberately offensive language. But I am not concerned here to state agreement or disagreement with anyone's views on art or on politics; I am concerned only with the ways in which our usage of language hinders us from thinking effectively. The habit of using strongly toned language does make for twisted thinking. It is difficult to distinguish clearly between intentionally using forcible language because we feel strongly and want other people to know that we do and unintentionally mispresenting the facts by using words to the emotional significance of which we are deaf.

If we bear in mind the important difference expressed by I – You, then we may expect to find that it is easier to recognize the distorting influence of emotionally toned words upon other people's thinking than upon our own. To abuse our opponents and to praise our supporters is a temptation to which we are all liable to succumb. The temptation lies in the attempt to present abuse as honest criticism and praise as impartial appreciation. This very common frailty was pointedly made the topic of a joke in *Punch*, just before the General Election of November 1935. Advice was given to election candidates to remember certain useful phrases:

Your Side	The Other Lot
Comprehensive programme of reform.	Unscrupulous electioneering manifesto.
Trenchant criticism.	Vulgar campaign of personal abuse.
Shrewd thrust.	Unmannerly interruption.

These six phrases might each of them be used to state a fact in a wholly neutral manner. There is such a thing, for instance, as trenchant criticism; there are also vulgar campaigns of personal abuse. *Punch* hits the nail on the head by confining one set of phrases to *your side* whilst allocating the second set to *the other lot*. Apart from the context we could not easily tell whether or not the use of these phrases proceeded from twisted thinking. The danger in using emotionally toned language lies in its tendency to dispel our critical powers. Mr A. P. Herbert has put this point well:

Those who say 'Deeds – not Words' should note how, in politics, one cunningly chosen word may have more power than a thousand irreproachable deeds. Give your political dog a cleverly bad name and it may do him more harm than many sound arguments.[2]

This is true. Many politicians are possessed of this cunning. They cast, as it were, a spell upon their hearers, appealing to their emotions in such a way as to destroy their judgment. Mr Herbert calls such 'cunningly chosen words' *witch-words*. But not all 'witch-words' are cunningly chosen; they may be used honestly although stupidly. Certain words have been used so frequently with a strong emotional significance that we are likely to use them in this way without realizing that our thinking is dominated by the emotional meaning that has been associated with these words. Similarly, we react to them emotionally when used by other people. Examples of such words are: *Bolshevik, Fascist, Communist, Capitalist; sex, sexual; Liquor* used for 'Wine' or 'Beer'; *dole* used for unemployment pay. It is easy to find examples. Whether these words are emotionally toned depends upon the context in which they are used. Some combinations of words reveal the speaker's attitude in any context, for example, 'a staunch Conservative' will be used by a member of that political party, 'a hide-bound Tory' by an opponent. The terminology used to refer to the two sides engaged in the Spanish Civil War is often indicative of the speaker's attitude. Prof. Julian Huxley, in a letter written to the *New Statesman* (August 8th, 1936), gave a careful analysis showing how the words used by *The Times* to refer to the Spanish Government became increasingly derogatory, whilst the words used to refer to the opponents of the Spanish Government became increasingly favourable. You will be able to sort out the less from the more favourable terminology in the following lists:

Referring to the Spanish Government: Loyal, Spanish, Spanish Government, Republican, Anti-Fascist, Communist.

Referring to their opponents: Revolt, Insurrection, Fascist, Anti-Government, 'Rebel'.

You will notice, for instance, that by putting 'Rebel' (in inverted commas) there is conveyed the implication that the opponents were a legitimate party engaged in a non-rebellious struggle. Another Conservative paper, the *Observer*, at first, if I remember correctly, described General Franco's side as 'the Anti-Reds' and the other side as 'the Reds'. These descriptions have the emotional significance that readers of the *Observer's* political articles might be expected to welcome; they contain further implications that prejudged the political character of the respective sides. According to the political complexion of a newspaper we find first one, and then the other, side described as 'Nationalists'. Of late *The Times* has used this description for General Franco's side.

The Spanish Civil War has indeed provided opportunities for a large amount of question-begging words. A word is said to beg the question if its meaning conveys the assumption that some point at issue has been already settled. To use such words is to use bad language, since the language implies a conclusion that has not been in any way confirmed. We shall meet these 'question-beggars', as Mr A. P. Herbert calls them, later on in connexion with the mistake of arguing in a circle.[3] Here it is enough to point out that emotionally toned words may conceal from ourselves as well as from our hearers the fact that the question has been begged.

The excitement, amounting to panic, that preceded the General Election of 1931 produced an amount of bad language even exceeding what is, unfortunately, usual in election speeches. I select three examples, taken almost at random from the reports I have at hand.

Lord Grey, appealing to Conservatives 'to play the game', said:

Those who are opposing Sir Herbert Samuel are doing an unpatriotic thing, and if their insistence on tariff reform and opposition to Liberal candidates results, as it might very well result, in a doubtful issue of this election or even in a victory of the spendthrift policy of the Labour Party, they will be in the position of people who, when the nation is in peril, have by their fractious party opposition, stabbed the nation in the back.

(*Manchester Guardian*, October 13th, 1931.)

Mr Baldwin, speaking at Liverpool, said:

The supreme test of democratic statesmanship is courage in a crisis. The courage of some of our countrymen failed them a few weeks ago and brought the nation to the verge of disaster. They ran away, and that is why we find ourselves in an unparalleled position. They quailed. [Cheers.] They forgot that they were Englishmen and only remembered that they were Socialists. The offence of those weeks will remain upon our political history. [Cheers.]

(*Manchester Guardian*, October 20th, 1931.)

Sir Robert Horne, speaking at the Criterion Restaurant, on October 29th of that year, was reported by the *Manchester Guardian* as having said:

The people voted with pride in their breasts for the dignity of their country. They were affronted by the ignominy put upon them by the cowardice and poltroonery of the men who held office in the last Government. Their opponents made a vast mistake when they thought they could seduce the soul of the business people by sordid appeals to them as if they were mercenaries.

I am hopeful enough to believe that, now that seven years have elapsed since these speeches were made, you will detect in these extracts various instances of bad language. In saying that the language is bad, I am suggesting that these politicians were not deliberately misleading their audiences; they were themselves misled by their habit of using language charged with emotional significance – abusing, praising, or appealing to the Englishman's love of fair play.

The next example is more difficult. It is taken from the same speech by Mr Baldwin as the second example above; this part of the speech was reported as follows:

> There must undoubtedly be some difficulty over the question of tariffs. Liberals would approach the problem with a Free Trade bias but with an open mind to examine and decide whether there were measures of dealing with the problem apart from tariffs. Conservatives would start with an open mind but with a favour for tariffs. They would start with an open mind to examine alternative methods, and the Cabinet as a whole would sit down with perfect honesty and sincerity to come to a decision on that matter.

You will notice that Baldwin speaks of a Liberal *bias* for Free Trade and of a Conservative *favour* for tariffs. The word 'bias' carries with it an emotional significance of having *prejudged* the matter in a way that could hardly be regarded as consistent with having an 'open mind'. The word 'favour' does not, I think, have this significance. Consider, however, the following statement, made by the editor of the *Aeroplane*:

> Another example of Foreign Office flabbiness is in the Spanish affair. From the beginning I have argued that our proper game was to be strictly neutral and supply both sides, with a natural bias towards the Nationalist forces.

Mr Grey, the editor, does not seem conscious that there is anything funny in this statement; perhaps the word 'bias' is neutral, so that I was mistaken in suggesting above that it had an emotional significance; perhaps it has been used in such a variety of senses that it has ceased to have any meaning at all. As Alice said: 'It is all very puzzling.'

NOTES

1   Cf. my *Modern Introduction to Logic*, Chapter II.
2   *What a Word?*, p. 229.
3   See Chapter 12.

6

POTTED THINKING

Some forms of ineffective thinking are due to our not unnatural desire to have confident beliefs about complicated matters with regard to which we must take some action or other. We are sometimes too lazy, usually too busy, and often too ignorant to think out what is involved in the statements we so readily accept. Few true statements about a complicated state of affairs can be expressed in a single sentence. Our need to have definite beliefs to hold on to is great; the difficulty in mastering the evidence upon which such beliefs ought to be based is burdensome; consequently, we easily fall into the habit of accepting compressed statements which save us from the trouble of thinking. Thus arises what I shall call 'Potted Thinking'. This metaphor seems to me to be appropriate, because potted thinking is easily accepted,

DOI: 10.4324/b22927-6

is concentrated in form, and has lost the vitamins essential to mental nourishment. You will notice that I have continued the metaphor by using the word 'vitamins'. Do not accept the metaphor too hastily: it must be expanded. Potted meat is sometimes a convenient form of food; it may be tasty, it contains some nourishment. But its nutritive value is not equivalent to that of the fresh meat from which it was potted. Also, it must have originally been made from fresh meat, and must not be allowed to grow stale. Similarly, a potted belief is convenient; it can be stated briefly, sometimes also in a snappy manner likely to attract attention. A potted belief should be the outcome of a belief that is not potted. It should not be held on to when circumstances have changed and new factors have come to light. We should not allow our habits of thought to close our minds, nor rely upon catchwords to save ourselves from the labour of thinking. Vitamins are essential for the natural growth of our bodies; the critical questioning at times of our potted beliefs is necessary for the development of our capacity to think to some purpose.

We are probably all of us familiar with many examples of potted thinking, especially with those forms of it that have become slogans. A slogan may be defined as 'a result of potted thinking expressed in a verbal form that has been adopted by a group of persons' – in short, a catchword, i.e. 'a word caught up and repeated'.[1] Those who are over forty will remember the election cries of 1919, 'Hang the Kaiser', 'Squeeze Germany until the pips squeak'. I imagine that statesmen have since had cause to regret the efficacy of these slogans in determining the votes of the electorate. Baldwin, in 1929, fought an election with the slogan, 'Safety First'. This curious election cry failed and he was decisively beaten. We shall shortly have to consider slogans in relation to the dangerous art of propaganda. The use of slogans is natural and, up to a point, beneficial. That point is passed when the slogan is taken for an argument and relevant complexities in the situation are ignored. Thus, for example, the complicated economic problem of the effects of tariffs upon the welfare of a people has been summed up in the statement: 'Food taxes mean dear food'. This may be true; it is not my purpose to argue for or against the contention. But whether food is dear or not depends partly upon the increase in real wages and in the purchasing power of money. This potted statement is likely to close the minds of unthinking or of ignorant people to any argument in favour of imposing taxes upon food, since no one wants to have dear food. The potted statement, 'The people will not stand food taxes' was taken for granted for many years both by those who wished to impose such taxes and by those who were opposed to them. Lord Beaverbrook challenged this sample of potted thinking when he 'launched a crusade' in favour of 'Empire Free Trade'. He retained the magic words 'Free Trade', but he did not hesitate to proclaim that there must be food taxes, thus questioning whether it is true that 'The people will not stand food taxes'. What the people will stand depends partly upon circumstances.

At one time it was not unusual for people to sum up the results of Freud's work in psychoanalysis under the formula 'Everything is sex'. To say that love, art, politics and religion are nothing but sex seems to most people just plain nonsense. This is, indeed, a peculiarly flagrant example of potted thinking. Freud's works are not easy to read; his views are based upon complicated experimental analysis and are, for the most part, carefully guarded, and are expressed in a highly technical language. Some of us may think (as I do myself) that his choice of language was not always happy. This does not, however, justify the summing up of his doctrines in the manifestly inadequate formula 'Everything is sex'. I imagine that nowadays no one who wanted to support Freud's doctrines would accept such a potted statement, nor should his work be regarded as valueless once this statement has been shown to be absurd.

The opposition between the totalitarian and democratic ideals of the State, which is constantly emphasized to-day, presents great temptations to us to indulge in potted thinking. It is by no means easy to discover what *exactly* are the aims of Fascists, on the one hand, and of Communists on the other. (The emphasis, be it noted, is on the word *exactly*.) It is still less easy to sum up what has been achieved by Germany under Nazi rule or by Italy under the rule of Mussolini. It is equally difficult to assess the achievements and estimate the failures of Soviet Russia. Most of us may well find it difficult to determine what has been the gain and what the loss to the peoples of these States since they have been dominated by dictators. Yet we do need to have beliefs about these matters. What our relations with the totalitarian States are and what they ought to be are questions of practical political importance. In trying to make up our minds on this question we are likely to start with a bias for, or against, the internal policy and the external aims adopted by some one of these States. This is just the sort of problem in which it is extremely difficult to avoid potted thinking that chimes in with our emotional attitude. Most of us cannot get first-hand knowledge of the relevant facts, nor even read such well-informed and comparatively unbiased reports of what is happening as might be available. In any case, the questions are complicated and difficult to grasp. It is easier to set up a simple antithesis: one form of state (whichever you prefer) is thoroughly good, the other is thoroughly bad. We are tempted to behave like the child who asks: 'Was King John a *bad* man?', 'Was Richard I *good*?', and will not tolerate, perhaps could hardly understand, that these questions cannot be answered by a simple 'Yes' or 'No'. It is by no means uncommon to-day to find that anyone who says that Hitler has conferred some benefits on the German people, or that Mussolini has in some ways improved the condition of Italy, is at once accused, by those who detest Fascism, of being himself a pro-Fascist. In the same way an ardent supporter of Fascism may bring an accusation of 'defending those unspeakable Bolsheviks' against anyone who asserts that the conditions of the workers in Russia are better than they were in the time of the Tsars. Such accusations are the outcome of potted thinking. Those who indulge in them have summed up a regime as entirely good (or evil, as the case may be) and are unable to see that some things in it may be good (or evil) without the rest being so. They have made an over-simplified picture in the manner of the child's picture of King John.

Thinking in this potted fashion inevitably leads us to extend an opponent's assertion in a wholly unwarrantable manner. The moderate statement that Mussolini has brought about some much-needed social reforms is extended to mean that Fascism is wholly satisfactory. This extension of an opponent's assertion into one that is by no means implied and from which he may without contradiction dissent may be intentional or unintentional. At the present moment we are not considering deliberate dishonesty in argument, but the insidious dishonesty of allowing oneself to judge a statement about a topic concerning which one's mind has been closed by potted thinking. Our habit of thinking in terms of exclusive abstractions encourages us to undue extension of the point at issue – either democracy or totalitarianism; either good or evil; either black or white. To suppose that the denunciation of Fascism entails acceptance of the view that democratic nations are entirely blameless for the present state of the world is a mistake of similar origin. A recent example is to hand. In the number of the *Spectator* published in Holy Week (April 15th, 1938), Canon Roger Lloyd wrote an article, entitled 'The Cross and the Crisis', the purport of which is to maintain that 'history is at bottom the record of the immemorial effort of Right to overcome Might'. He claims to discern two 'ethical principles of interpretation', namely, evil at first wins the victory, but, secondly, evil 'in its very triumph sets in motion the law of diminishing returns, which in the end engulfs it'. His conclusion is:

> The application of such principles to the existing international situation is clear, and the Cross does provide the basis of a rational hope for democracy to-day. But we must not claim that this ethical interpretation can now be seen in both its phases, or we abandon realism. The fact is, that as things stand on the day these words are written no one can say that the end of the first phase has come. Evil, in the shape of Mussolini and Hitler, is still in process of claiming its initial victory. But those who learn both their ethics and their interpretation of history from the Cross know that sooner or later the law of diminishing returns must inevitably be set in motion by evil's very success.

This article provoked a correspondent the following week to protest against 'Canon Lloyd's facile conception of Democracy and Dictatorship as embodying respectively the forces of good and evil'. The writer urges that 'the issue is not so simple', and asks: 'Are we, then, free of blame for the evil which has been let loose in the world to-day? The nation which gave its consent to the Treaty of Versailles has small right to proclaim itself Christian, or to brand the dictators of Europe as emissaries of Satan.'

To this Canon Lloyd replied that he had never entertained this 'facile conception' and asserts, 'My article does not so much as mention democracy, nor was democracy in my mind when I wrote it'. He adds: 'By the identification of evil with Fascist dictators I am prepared to stand.'

The reader will notice that Canon Lloyd's disclaimer is not strictly accurate since (in the passage quoted from his article) he did speak of providing 'the basis of a rational hope for democracy to-day'. In my opinion, however, he correctly repudiated what was in fact an extension of his statement. His 'identification of evil with the Fascist dictators' does not imply an identification of good with 'Democracy', still less with the democracy established in any given State. The assumption that it does surely arises from an over-simplified antithesis. I do not myself share Canon Lloyd's point of view, but I cannot see that he has been guilty of the 'facile conception' of which he is accused. Elsewhere Canon Lloyd had shown clearly that he was capable of condemning a system as a whole whilst finding much that is good in it. In the course of maintaining that 'Totalitarianism is Anti-Christ', he admits:

> It is the plain fact that the dictatorships of Italy, Russia, Germany and Turkey, were faced by a vast mass of the most loathsome corruption, religious, moral and social. It is also the fact that they have swept them away, restored vitality to their people, given them a new moral self-respect, replaced a corrupt privilege by an ordered social system, and, above all, made of the song, 'Nothing left to strive for, love, or keep alive for,' an irrelevant back number.
>
> The Christian, in fact, who sincerely weighs the published thought and the practical achievements of the Totalitarians, is

alternately stimulated and depressed. If he is hunting for evil, he
can emphatically find it, but he can find good as well.[2]

I have quoted this passage from a carefully reasoned book in
order to show that even such an extreme view as that which
identifies 'evil with Fascist dictators' is not necessarily the outcome of potted thinking nor due to the neglect of relevant facts.
Canon Lloyd certainly detests the Fascist dictators, but he has
not remained content with substituting his personal reactions
for a reasoned argument in support of his views. Whether or not
this argument is successful is not my concern. There is perhaps
a danger that his conclusion might be taken up, parrot fashion,
by those who have made no attempt to investigate the consequences of a Fascist dictatorship, but content themselves with
saying: 'Totalitarianism is Anti-Christ'. Certainly much of what
Canon Lloyd has to say with regard to Fascism and Communism
could only be accepted by those who, like himself, are Christians; only these, too, could accept the ground of his 'rational
hope in the midst of circumstances that tend to despair'. To say
this is only to repeat the point I have already emphasized in previous chapters, namely, that how we think is not independent of
the sort of persons we are.

You will be able to test for yourself the truth of this statement
if you will reflect upon your attitude to the lengthy account I
have given of Canon Lloyd's views on a burning topic of the
day. The introduction of an argument that refers to the Cross
of Christ may have aroused your indignation to such a point
that you could hardly believe that the writer would have anything worth while to say. Or, on the contrary, you may have been
predisposed in its favour as soon as you knew that a Church
dignitary was the writer. Or you may have been prepared to

consider the argument on its merits without any thought about the religious beliefs of its exponent. These three 'you's' stand, of course, for different persons. Nor are they exhaustive of the varieties of persons who argue and are argued with. I am concerned with only two broadly described varieties – those whose minds are relatively open and those whose minds are relatively closed. Even if we believe that we belong to the first class, we must, I think, admit that there are certain topics on which our minds are relatively closed and thus impervious to argument and almost, perhaps quite, insusceptible to any sudden illumination. I have myself strong opinions on some of the topics that I cite as examples; I do not hope to succeed in escaping bias either in my selection or in my exposition of these examples. I should like to be able to do so, but I am aware that on many questions of practical importance I hold views that seem to me so definitely correct that I am unable to believe that those who differ from me thereon have seen clearly what I see (and 'see *clearly*' is the addition I am tempted to add, except that I have so often been mistaken). My personal bias is evident in the examples I shall give in the next paragraph.

Cruder forms of potted thinking than those we have been considering are revealed in the use of such phrases as 'young Eaton-Square Bolshies', 'Trotskyite wreckers', 'lily-livered pacifists', 'bloated capitalists', 'paunchy stockbrokers', and 'milk-sop Christians'. Such emotional language compresses into a phrase a personal reaction and an implicit judgment about a class of persons. To me at least it seems clear that their use results from potted thinking. Possibly I pay too high a compliment when I suggest that any thinking at all precedes their use. It may be that the notions expressed by one of these phrases have been associated together in such a way that the epithet has been tied to the noun it qualifies in a manner which makes it psychologically impossible for the speaker to think, for instance, of a Christian apart from the quality of being a milk-sop. Torn from a context we should not know whether these phrases are used merely to give vent to an explosion of emotion or are used in the course of an attempt to contribute to a serious discussion. In the former case they have merely an exclamatory value. There is no good reason why we should not express our personal distastes, unless the desire to be polite restrains us. In the latter case the language is bad and the thinking is consequently ineffective. It is an extreme form of potted thinking. A reconsideration of the facts (if any) upon which the judgment implicit in the phrase had been based might suffice to convince the thinker that, for instance, a capitalist is not necessarily bloated, nor a Christian necessarily a milk-sop. Those who habitually attach an abusive epithet to a form of government, a policy of action, or a class of people, have at best over-simplified the relevant facts, or are sheerly ignorant of those facts. A person capable of making a reasoned condemnation does not need to shout.

Not all tied epithets are abusive. You will sometimes hear people speaking of 'our magnificent police force' or our 'unbribable police', who are quite unable to believe that some policemen have been convicted of taking bribes. To believe this would upset all their preconceived and firmly rooted ideas about 'our police force'. They can no more entertain the notion that a British policeman has taken a bribe than they could look at ice without seeing it to be cold. I well remember the horror with which a friend of mine heard her brother, an army officer, say – when he came home for his first leave during the Great War – that not every British soldier was brave. It offended her conception of what a British soldier must essentially be. Noble as well as ignoble impulses go to make up this ideal. But to maintain it involves a failure to realize that a British soldier is still a man, just as a French or a German soldier is. It involves further, I think, a failure to realize imaginatively the circumstances in which soldiers on both sides were fighting. This ideal conception of a class of people is the root of much unclear thinking; indeed, it may result in a complete inability to think about the topic at all. A recent letter to the *News Chronicle* affords an extreme instance of such an outcome of potted thinking:

> Twice, in your leading article in last Wednesday's paper, there occur the words 'British cowardice'. One wonders what is the nationality of the man who wrote it, as the combination of these two words, together, is unknown in the English language, or in the tongue of any country in the world. In the present delicate situation in Europe would not the words 'British Diplomacy' be more appropriate?
>   I sign myself,
>   'A Britisher', and Proud of it.

This is so uncommonly silly that it would not be worth while to cite this example, were it not that it reveals very clearly the way in which our admiration (or, in other cases, our contempt) for a certain class makes us unable to contemplate the possibility that we might be mistaken. The signature also reveals the curiously muddled view that a man cannot be proud of belonging to a nation unless every member of it has the quality he admires. Such an attitude is the result of a steadfast refusal to escape from a mental habit that is incompatible with the detachment necessary to think effectively about the affairs of the world.

I do not wish to deny that potted thinking has its uses. On the contrary, we must act, and it is desirable that we should act vigorously at times. I have already spoken of the danger of academic detachment carried to an extreme that makes us unable to decide on which side we shall act because there is much to be urged in favour of both sides. We are not able to refrain from acting, say, in the case where our country goes to war, or in the crisis of a parliamentary election. To abstain from taking part in the war is definitely to act on one side. To refuse to go to the poll is likewise to act, and moreover, so to act that our action can effect nothing useful. All that we can do is to take what opportunities there are for making our minds up; when this is achieved we can act with vigour. If we have found difficulty in deciding how to act, we shall naturally be disposed to view tolerantly those who differ from us; such tolerance is not incompatible with vigorous action. Potted thinking (like potted meat) is not dangerous provided that fresh thinking has preceded it. At this point the metaphor breaks down. We cannot 'unpot' the meat, but we can, from time to time, review the principles in accordance with which we reached the potted conclusion. Further, we can remember to take note of fresh circumstances and admit also that we are capable of having made a mistake. The history of the relations between the European countries during the last twenty years provides sad evidence of the disasters that may result from continuing to act upon beliefs embodied in potted thinking.

NOTES

1   *Shorter Oxford English Dictionary.*
2   *Revolutionary Religion*, p. 37.

7

PROPAGANDA

AN OBSTACLE

The insidious and powerful influence of emotional language that appeals to our hopes or our fears and of potted thinking is nowhere more clearly seen than in a consideration of the art of successful propaganda. The deterioration in meaning of the word 'propaganda' affords sad evidence of the stupidity of human beings. Originally 'propaganda' meant 'a committee of Cardinals of the Roman Catholic Church having the care and oversight of foreign missions'.[1] A derivative of this word is used, I presume, in the same sense in the title of a well-known English missionary society – 'The Society for the Propagation of

DOI: 10.4324/b22927-7

the Gospel'. The avowed intention of a missionary is to convert other people to his faith. To be converted, in this sense, is to change one's point of view and accept certain religious beliefs. Propaganda has sometimes been used in a neutral manner to indicate the spreading of information with a view to enlisting sympathy for some cause.[2] Since the desire to enlist sympathy is often stronger than the desire to obtain sympathy by providing information sufficient to provoke it, propaganda has come to mean any method of inducing people to accept the judgments of the propagandist. Do we not all sometimes feel that if only people knew so and so, then they would act in such and such a way? When we find, however, that the information has not moved them to share our beliefs and act as we want them to act we may be tempted to substitute for information what we know to be at best but half-truths, at worst lies. A firm belief in the righteousness of their own cause has seemed to many otherwise honest people to justify any methods of winning adherents to it.

The gradual deterioration of the word 'propaganda' was hastened by what politicians might describe as the 'exigencies' of the last war. Some of the Governments set up press bureaux to disseminate information with the double purpose of uniting the people in support of their policy and of presenting that policy in the most favourable light for the benefit of the countries that remained neutral. These bureaux were at first called 'Departments of Propaganda', but were later renamed 'Departments of Counter-Propaganda'. At this stage the deterioration of the word is completed. The word 'counter-information' does not make sense.

In this book we are concerned with propaganda as an obstacle that we may encounter in our efforts to think to some specified purpose. For the satisfaction of this purpose we often require information. We are effectively baulked if what we are given is propaganda. It is important to remember that the propagandist is the advocate of a cause; he wants to make other people do something. The cause may be worth while or not; that is a consideration that lies beyond the scope of this discussion. There are indeed occasions when we approve of a cause whilst disapproving of the methods used to advocate it.

There are three main ways of making other people support our aims: by compelling them, by persuading them to accept our views, by convincing them of the reasonableness of what we propose. In so far as compulsion involves a resort to brute force, we are not here concerned to discuss it. Men may, it is true, be bullied or tortured into behaving as though they accepted a belief which those who have power over them wish to impose upon them. Such outward conformity does not entail belief, nor would the use of force fall under the heading of propaganda. In distinguishing between *persuading* and *convincing*, as I propose to do, I recognize that I am to some extent departing from the most common usage of these words. There is, however, a clear and important distinction between the process of getting people to agree with us by using non-rational methods and the process of providing them with rational grounds for such agreement. There is not, I believe, any pair of words in common use which clearly mark this distinction. Accordingly, I shall adopt the arbitrary convention that 'convince' is to mean 'to satisfy by rational argument', i.e. by adducing evidence in support of the proposed conclusion. I shall confine the use of the word 'persuasion' to mean 'to bring about the acceptance of a conclusion by methods other than that of offering grounds for rational conviction'. Most people would, I think, say that 'persuasion' covers what

I have called 'conviction'. I have admitted that this is a correct usage, but it is inconvenient for my purpose.

I do not in the least wish to assert that in the actual formation of our conclusions we are always able clearly to distinguish between those occasions when we have been non-rationally persuaded and those when we have been convinced by rational argument. On the contrary, I am anxious to insist that we easily mistake persuasion for conviction. Nor do I wish to maintain that it is never right to allow oneself to be persuaded. All that I wish to assert is that there is a fundamental difference between holding a belief into which we have been persuaded and holding a belief as the outcome of a reasoned argument. It is upon persuasion that the propagandist relies.

Advertisers have brought the art of propaganda very near to perfection. A consideration of the devices employed in advertisements may help us to recognize the tricks of other propagandists and to understand how immense and insidious is their influence. The advertiser has something to sell; it would be unreasonable to expect him to be disinterested. He wishes to present his goods in the most favourable manner possible. Accordingly he is unlikely to provide us with all the information that would enable us to form an independent opinion of the value of the article advertised. Frequently he has to create in us a felt want for his goods. Accordingly he will seek to arouse our emotions, appealing to our desire to be healthier, or more beautiful, or better dressed than we are. At the same time the skilful advertiser will support this appeal with some show of evidence that his goods are able to satisfy these desires.

Look at the advertisements in any newspaper or magazine that is at hand. Following my own advice I select a few specimens, slightly camouflaged to prevent complications.

A man and girl gaze at each other. An inscription says that as long as men can see they will respond to beauty. Then follows the advice: *Use this cream and awake the response that she does.*

A patent medicine is offered as an infallible cure for a common chest complaint. A promise is made that even the most obstinate cases will yield to this treatment. There follow 'letters of gratitude selected from hundreds'. A woman writes that she had despaired of ever being well, but now she is 'a different woman'. Eminent medical men and well-known public persons (unspecified) are said to have praised the treatment. The reader is assured: '*Health is your right*'. He believes that he has been offered evidence that this medicine will enable him to attain this right.

Notice how often you see advertisements containing such captions as the following:

'They all swear by …'.
'Everybody is doing …'.
'We are going to do …. ARE YOU?'
'Trust the … baker.'
'Trust your dentist. He knows a good tooth-paste.'
'Some who know *good* … made this.'
'Good-bye to doubts when you see … trade mark.'
'Send them happy to school. Give them …'.
'You want a healthy baby, don't you? Then …'.
'Here's value you never saw before. Why don't you get a …'.
'This is the brand that is used by men of action, men who DO things.'
'This soap is different.'

These captions, often accompanied by pictures, are designed not only to arrest your attention, but also to appeal to your desire to do as others do or to obtain something which, it is suggested, would be good for you. Something is wrong with you and the advertisement tells you to trust the expert upon whom you must in the end rely. The advertiser reckons upon your not pausing to ask for any evidence that 'they all' swear by the goods offered, nor for evidence of the credentials of 'the expert' who hides so modestly behind the description. The purpose of the whole lay-out of the advertisement is to persuade you that you have been offered reliable evidence, although, in fact, you have not.

It is worth while to consider briefly the psychological causes of the success of such methods of advertising. Successful they undoubtedly are, otherwise firms with goods to sell would not expend large sums of money in exhibiting these advertisements.

Foremost among these causes may be placed the power of suggestion. It is an empirically discovered fact that when we have often heard, or seen, words expressing a certain statement we have a tendency to accept that statement as true. Advertisers take advantage of this tendency. The power of repeated affirmation to affect behaviour and inculcate beliefs is well known to public speakers as well as to vendors of goods, even though they may never have reflected upon this curious characteristic of human beings. It is, of course, 'curious' only if we forget that human beings are not for the most part rational. Oddly enough, we often do forget this. Advertisers perhaps show more knowledge of human nature.

Consider, for instance, the custom of placarding walls during an election with 'Vote for Jones'. It is recognized that if we see numerous placards saying 'Vote for Jones', it is not unlikely that we shall vote for Jones without asking ourselves what are the reasons for voting for Jones rather than for his rival Brown. In the same way, if we frequently see a poster saying 'Brunton's beer is best', we may come to believe that it is best, and refuse to drink anyone else's beer. There is hardly any need for me to multiply examples. You will see many examples if you pay attention to the advertisements on hoardings, in buses, in newspapers, and affixed to buildings in such a place as Piccadilly Circus. A slight variation in the manner of expressing the statement intended to move you to action, whilst not in any way diminishing the effect of repetition, may lead you to feel that here is an additional reason for acting upon the advice given. I purposely used the word 'feel' in the preceding sentence. Those who are a prey to the suggestion of repeated affirmation do not consciously reflect upon what is said; they are led merely to accept the statement. Considerable ingenuity is shown nowadays by some advertisers who produce a series of advertisements all of the same form, with regard both to the mode of expression and to the accompanying picture, but with variations in detail. I recollect, as I write, having seen three different beverages lately advertised in just this manner. Probably you have noticed these and many more.

Another cause of success in advertising is our need for expert guidance. In advertisements for patent medicine it is not unusual to find 'extracts from recommendations' by 'eminent doctors' designated only by a list of letters that are accepted as standing for medical degrees and other distinctions calculated to inspire confidence in the minds of the ignorant. We are apt not to notice that no evidence is provided to indicate that the recommendations are in fact made by qualified persons who desire disinterestedly to aid those who suffer from bodily ill. 'Doctors recommend' makes its appeal by what Professor Thouless has called 'prestige suggestion', that is, the authority of a recognized profession.[3] If we could be sure that doctors have made the recommendation, then we begin to have some evidence in favour of the article advertised.

We should not so easily accept these statements were it not for our pathetic faith in the accuracy and truth of anything we see 'in print'. 'In our own day', Professor Laski has said, 'it would not be an unfair description of education to define it as the art which teaches men to be deceived by the printed word'.[4] This is a hard saying, but I believe that it contains a considerable amount of truth. That this is so with regard to much of the practice of advertising I have already suggested. But the matter is more serious when we consider our dependence upon newspapers for supplying us with information about what happens in the world.

I do not desire to add to the number of books that have been written about the popular Press. I wish only to illustrate the way in which newspaper propaganda makes it more difficult for us to think effectively. I am not concerned with the dubious and, in my opinion, utterly vicious methods that have been adopted to increase a newspaper's circulation. Nor am I concerned to deny that the expense of producing a modern newspaper may necessitate an immensely large circulation if the newspaper is to pay its way, still more if it is to pay large dividends to its shareholders. Taking newspapers as they are now, we have to inquire to what extent we may look to them for help in our attempt to form reasoned opinions upon matters of importance to everyone who has the rights and duties of a citizen.

'Of all public transactions', wrote Samuel Johnson in 1773, 'the whole world is now informed by the newspapers.' With what greater accuracy, it might be supposed, could this remark be made to-day, so immense has been the development in the means of transmitting rapidly and from a distance what is happening. There is less cause for congratulation when we consider how this information is given, what information is withheld, what subtle means are adopted to suggest to the reader a distorted view of the facts reported. We must examine these considerations from two points of view – that of the provider of the news and that of the reader of what is provided.

'After all,' said the Prime Minister (Mr Neville Chamberlain), 'a newspaper is not primarily an institution for the gratuitous education of the public. It is a combination of a factory, commercial business, and a profession.'[5] There does not seem to be any ironic intention in this remark. Unfortunately the Prime Minister's statement is correct. For the most part our daily newspapers do not seek to educate the people who read them. They provide 'news', i.e. information about happenings which excite interest. I believe that the reports in our newspapers are usually accurate in the sense that they are not mis-statements. But these reports are very often not so presented as to be intelligible to the reader who needs to be informed of the context within which events occur. In Dr Johnson's time, no doubt, all who were able to read the papers were conversant with the state of affairs in those places about which information was given. To-day this is not so. Nor could it be so. When reporters range 'from China to Peru' there can be few people who are sufficiently well-informed of what has already happened to be able to see the significance of what is happening. The newspapers with the largest circulation rarely supply any commentary that would provide the context that is essential for understanding the significance of the 'news'. We should not expect a reporter, still less the editorial staff, of a newspaper to be unbiased. Each of us thinks and speaks from a point of view. A careful commentary and a reasoned discussion would reveal the bias and at the same time truly inform the reader by making the news intelligible. Instead of being thus informed the reader is given disconnected items; reports of matters of grave importance are printed on the same sheet as trivial happenings that have, it is true, 'news-value' but only in the deplorable sense that the phrase has come to have now that the newspaper is a 'commercial business'. Information of 'public transactions' – to use Dr Johnson's phrase – has 'news-value' to-day only when those transactions are at once recognized as having a direct bearing upon our own lives.

That a successful newspaper need not be 'primarily an institution for the gratuitous instruction of the public' had been clearly seen by the late Lord Northcliffe. According to the account given by his biographer, Mr Hamilton Fyfe, Lord Northcliffe, when he was still young Mr Alfred Harmsworth, was impressed by the success of Tit-Bits, the newspaper founded by George Newnes. 'The man who produced this Tit-Bits has got hold of a bigger thing than he imagines.'[6] Thus Mr Fyfe reports Alfred Harmsworth's reflections; he continues: 'He [Newnes] is only at the beginning of a development which is going to change the whole face of journalism.'[7] Tit-Bits had been founded in 1881. In 1870 the first School Board Act was passed. There were growing up a number of people who could read, but who remained extremely ignorant and almost incapable of concentration or of thinking seriously about public transactions. Mr Fyfe's description is worth quoting:

Once you start on the idea of exploiting the new class of readers, there is no end to it. There they are, millions of them, waiting with pennies in their hands. Anyone can get those pennies who will give them what they want. That's it, find out what the public wants. New idea that it wants anything! Easier to tell what it doesn't want. Evidently the new readers don't want the newspapers. They can't understand them. They haven't time for them. They can't concentrate their attention for long enough at a time to wade through their voluminous reports and immense three-decker articles. ... Their minds resembled Newnes's mind; they liked scraps, titbits. Well, why not give them scraps. News could be treated in a way that would please them; make them feel they knew all about everything, instead of suggesting to them, as existing newspapers did, that everything was very difficult to understand, that nothing could be discussed or reported except at very great length (pp. 18, 19).

Whether this be a true description of what passed in Harmsworth's mind, or not, it is an apt account of his reaction to the situation created by 'the millions' of new readers. It did not occur to Harmsworth that here was a means of continuing the education of these new readers and of helping to develop a well-informed interest in affairs of moment. Truly he may be said to have 'changed the face of journalism' and thereby set up an obstacle to the proper development of a democracy. To-day most of the newspapers read by 'millions of readers' give equal stress to items about royalties, film stars, racing news and sport, animal stories and beauty hints. Fashionable events – Society weddings, garden parties, elopements, accidents to titled persons, the birth of quintuplets, are given an amount of space and stress out of all proportion to their public importance. By way of example, consider the silliness of the following extract from the *Observer*:

The Queen's powder-blue dress and tilted wide-brimmed hat made the garden-party seem more real.

I am not protesting against the description of clothes worn by royal ladies at public functions. It may be only the limitations of my own point of view which render me unable to find such descriptions interesting. Nevertheless, I am depressed to find so odd a judgment of value in the *Observer*. It is indeed not a little disquieting that some readers do not find it 'odd' that the beautiful clothes worn by the Queen should be judged to make the party 'more real'. This debasement of the English language is evidence, I believe, of slipshod thinking.

There is no need to multiply instances of odd items that are regarded as having 'news-value'. Test for yourself the amount of space given in your own newspaper to trivial items compared with the amount allotted to reports of, and comments upon, affairs of national and of international importance. An examination of our newspapers shows that the great majority of them are extraordinarily uniform with regard to what news is included, what is omitted, and what comments are made. On those occasions when newspapers of rival political views take up strongly opposed sides there is very seldom any discussion of the views of the other side. Few newspapers report the opinions of foreigners about British policy, unless that opinion happens to be favourable. There are honourable exceptions, but those newspapers are not widely read. The lack of variety is not, on reflection, surprising. I was at first surprised when I began to study different newspapers. This was so because I had not reflected upon the fact that most of the newspapers with the biggest circulations are owned by a comparatively small group of men. Sixteen London newspapers (ten daily papers and six Sunday papers) are owned by five groups of proprietors. These groups also own a large number of provincial newspapers. Papers belonging to one group naturally give the same news in much the same sort of way. The owners of these newspapers have an almost unlimited power to form the opinions of the reading public. 'Almost', but not quite, for the owners are themselves to some extent controlled by the big advertisers who are relied upon to provide the main revenue of the newspapers. The advertisers would not advertise in a newspaper that tended to undermine 'the confidence of the public'. The advertisers want the readers to be ready to spend their money; the newspapers want the advertisers to spend large sums in advertising their goods.

That the Press should be thus controlled constitutes a serious obstacle to our obtaining the information we require in order that we should think to some purpose about public transactions. I have used the word 'controlled' because, in the ordinary sense of the word 'free', our Press is remarkably free, notwithstanding the laws of sedition, blasphemy and libel. These laws affect the Press neither less nor more than they affect the private citizen. Books, pamphlets, journals, supplements to newspapers, can be and are in fact published which criticize and condemn the Government of the day in a manner that would not be tolerated in many countries. This we all know, and are apt to congratulate ourselves thereon. But here lies a peculiar danger for the majority of the readers. We tend to believe that we have a 'free' Press because we know it to be legally free. But the Press is in fact controlled by a comparatively small number of persons. The danger lies in the fact that the majority of people are not aware of the ownership. Consequently, when they see different newspapers providing the same news and expressing very similar opinions they are not aware that the news, and the evaluation of the news, are alike determined by a single group of persons, perhaps mainly by one man – a Press Lord. Accordingly, the readers mistakenly believe that they have been provided with independent testimony whereas they have been provided only with repetitions.

Finally, in the most popular newspapers, the readers are definitely encouraged to indulge in potted thinking. The whole layout of the newspaper is designed to achieve this end. Startling headlines, every device of large and small block capitals and other variations of print are used to put the emphasis where the editor desires it to be put. Crude appeals to our emotions, sensationalism of all kinds, repetition in variety of expression, all these combine to create in us the response that the owners desire. Well might it be said – If the editor determines the headlines, he need not care who reports the news nor trouble overmuch what news is reported.

I select a single example of a startling headline. In the *Daily Worker* for May 13th, 1938, there appears in the largest size heavy block capitals the headline, *Chamberlain says he started truthful*. There follows a smaller-sized caption and then a report of a speech made by Mr Chamberlain in the Albert Hall, from which the following is reported: 'I was brought up in a household where we were taught the importance of telling the truth, even though we got into trouble for doing so.' Now this is a fair report of what the Prime Minister said. Many people, however, may read the staring headline, with its insinuation, and fail to read the speech. Papers of different political views will choose different headlines which are, from my point of view, equally objectionable.

These devices would not be as successful as they undoubtedly are were not we so frequently tempted to be lazy in thinking. We are too content to have our opinions thrust upon us instead of eliciting them by the effective opposition and careful consideration of possible views. Just as the advertiser seeks to form our beliefs and save us from the trouble of thinking, so that we may be ready to buy his wares, so the newspaper editors desire to furnish our minds with opinions of which they approve. This is, I believe, true of nearly all newspapers. They seek to persuade, not to convince. It is our fault if we are too lazy to be critical. Nevertheless, it must be admitted that editors and journalists for the most part do very little to help us to develop habits of critical thinking. On the contrary they seem to have learned Lord Northcliffe's lesson — that 'the millions of readers' cannot concentrate nor think for themselves. Accordingly, we are to be encouraged to jump disconnectedly from one headline to another, and to be content with ignorance. An amount of time and effort that it is surely unreasonable to demand of us must be expended if we are to have reliable and full information of public transactions and to be provided with good reasons for our political beliefs.

NOTES

1 This is the definition given in the *Shorter Oxford English Dictionary*, which states that this committee was founded in 1622.
2 Compare the use of the word 'cause' in "The Week's Good Cause'.
3 *Straight and Crooked Thinking*. I am, in common, I suppose, with most people who have written on this subject, much indebted to Professor Thouless's useful book.
4 *Liberty in the Modern State*, p. 168 (Pelican Books edition).
5 Speech on May 3rd, 1938, proposing the toast of the 'Newspaper Society', reported in *The Times*, May 4th, 1938.
6 *Northcliffe: An Intimate Biography*, p. 17.
7 *Op. cit.*, p. 17. It is not easy to tell whether Mr Hamilton Fyfe is reporting what Northcliffe said or merely suggesting what he may have thought.

8

DIFFICULTIES OF AN AUDIENCE

The art of persuading, exemplified in advertisements, in the lay-out of newspapers, and in the modes of selecting news that are practised by journalists, cannot be entirely neglected by a public speaker who aims at moving his audience to do something. The speaker must attract the attention of his audience, and he must, further, so hold their interest that they will continue to listen to him. Accordingly, he must enforce what he has to say by the method of repetition with variety of expression, since it is not easy to grasp any complicated matter at a first hearing. Finally, he must make his hearers feel that he has a right to be address-ing them. For this purpose, he must claim to speak with some

DOI: 10.4324/b22927-8

measure of authority. In the fulfilment of these needs lie great temptations for the speaker and grave dangers for the audience. If a speaker were to announce that he had no special competence in the problem to be discussed, if he were resolutely to refuse to make any point more than once, if he were to refrain from making any appeal to the emotional attitudes of his hearers, then they would become bored and inattentive. In that case the speaker might just as well stand silent in front of his audience. This, you will notice, would be a contradiction in terms. An effective speaker will gauge the response of his hearers. Some audiences deserve the speakers who exploit their suggestibility and ignorance.

There are many different kinds of audience and many different kinds of speakers. The latter include school teachers and university lecturers, at one extreme, and political speakers at election meetings at the other extreme. I have cited these as opposite extremes on the assumption that a lecturer who is speaking to his students is primarily concerned to help in their education, whilst a speaker to an audience of electors is primarily concerned to persuade his hearers to vote for himself or for the candidate whom he is supporting, even if he also hopes not only to persuade but to convince. Both these aims are honest and are worth pursuing in a democratic country. The character of an audience also varies between these extremes. The methods appropriate to attract and hold their attention must likewise vary.

I have used the convenient pair of words – 'lecturer' and 'speaker' – to mark the important difference between those whose primary object is to educate and those whose business is to persuade. An educator has two main objects: to impart information and to create those mental habits that will enable his students, or pupils, to seek knowledge and to acquire the ability to form their own independent judgment based upon rational grounds. A university lecturer necessarily speaks with the authority due to his having greater knowledge of the subject than is possessed by his students. Presumably he is appointed in virtue of his possessing the requisite knowledge, whereas the students are, at least at the outset, comparatively, and sometimes amazingly, ignorant. The student is there to be informed, the lecturer is there to inform him. I hope, however, that everyone would agree that the business of the lecturer does not stop with imparting information. Moreover, even a properly appointed lecturer is sometimes mistaken with regard to the facts. Further, no sharp distinction can be drawn between imparting information and inculcating opinions. This, so far as I know, is especially the case in the subjects of history, the social sciences and philosophy. Most lecturers, I think, would agree that a habit of qualifying every important expression of opinion, that the adoption of a hesitating manner, in short, the creation of the impression that the lecturer has no special competence to speak to his class, would make his lecture completely valueless. He must assume the authority due to his having special knowledge and having expended much effort in thinking out the topic on which he is lecturing. There his reasonable authority ends. An intelligent but not well-informed student may be capable of criticizing the lecturer's judgments and, be it noted, may even be correct in his criticisms. No one, not even a university lecturer, is infallible; even the youngest among us may see something that our blinkers have concealed from sight.

Sometimes the fault lies with the students; they sit, as Carlyle said, 'like buckets waiting to be filled'; they have an exaggerated respect for the authority of the lecturer; they are too lazy to wish to make the effort of thinking for themselves. Fortunately, the respect for lecturers as such is, I believe, on the wane. On the other hand, it is well for the student to remember that 'even the youngest among us may be mistaken'. There is no getting away from the fact that the teacher does start with an initial advantage over the taught, and may further be presumed not only to have more knowledge but also to be more intellectually alert than some of his class – unless that class be very small and quite unusual in composition.

Lecturers to adult classes may be confronted with peculiar difficulties due to the special temptations to which some adult students are exposed. Not infrequently such students attend these classes in the hope of obtaining information that will help them to establish a conclusion which they have prejudged.[1] Their minds are made up; all that they ask for is information supported by the prestige of a competent lecturer. An adult student's comment on his tutor may serve to illustrate this point. He said:

> He is an able man who often says things to provoke dissent. My ideal would be a man who speaks with conviction. There are times when a casual opposing remark will make our tutor say, 'Yes, that may be', in such a way that one would think there is as much to be said for the opposing view as the one he has put forward.[2]

This student expected his lecturer to have weighed the evidence in favour of the opposing views and to have thereby come to a decisive judgment in favour of one of the possible conclusions; further, he expected the lecturer to make clear that one of the opposed views was indubitably correct. This is not always possible. I agree that it is an ideal which we may well wish were more often capable of attainment. Nevertheless, it is true that there are many topics of importance about which there is much to be said on both sides, so that it is not reasonable, having regard to all the evidence, to assert that one of the two opposed views is indubitably correct. To admit this is not incompatible with the assertion: 'For my part, I am convinced that this is the correct view.' It is important to notice the distinction between saying: 'This conclusion is indubitable' and saying: 'I do not doubt that this conclusion is true.' The former statement implies that no reasonable person can doubt the conclusion. If this were so, then anyone who does entertain doubts is thereby held to be unreasonable. The latter statement merely implies that at least one person, namely the speaker, has resolved his doubt and is prepared to bring forward evidence in support of his belief.

The adult student whom I have quoted would, in my opinion, have been making a justifiable criticism of his tutor if it were the case that the tutor had 'put forward' one view only and had nothing to say with regard to the opposed view except that it might be true. I am not sure, however, whether this was the point of the criticism, since the student evidently desired the lecturer to be a man who spoke 'with conviction' and did not 'provoke dissent'. But an audience of students is a special kind of audience since it is composed of people who desire to be educated and not converted. At least, a lecturer hopes that this is a correct description of his hearers' state of mind. Confronted with such an audience it is a positive gain if a lecturer sometimes makes mistakes and lets his hearers realize that he has not been divinely inspired to be always right.

It is a far cry from the peaceful atmosphere of a lecture room to the emotionally turbulent atmosphere of a political platform. Nevertheless, in the former case we may be able to discern, in miniature as it were, some of the temptations that beset the public speaker and some of the difficulties that confront the audience. I say that the speaker has 'temptations' and the audience encounter 'difficulties' because I am thinking of the speaker as a person who desires to win his audience to accept his point of view and to move them to action, whilst I think of the audience as persons who desire to have reasonable grounds for the decisions they will be called upon to make. From this point of view the language I have used seems to me to be convenient. I do not, however, deny that the speaker may have difficulties in his own thinking which honesty of purpose does not in itself suffice to remove. Again, the audience may be, and, I am afraid, very often is, tempted to indulge in potted thinking, the outcome of lazy mental habits. Neither of these is my present concern. Further, I shall assume that the speaker is an 'honest politician', that is, a person who desires to make his views acceptable because he is sure that these views are right.

What, then, are the temptations to which such a public speaker is exposed? Clearly he has to 'get a grip' upon his audience; he comes before his audience with a halo due to his public importance, possibly reinforced by the presence of a distinguished chairman. His purpose is to persuade; he has hardly time to educate his hearers. He may expect to be 'heckled', to be beset by irrelevant and often ill-natured interruptions. Although I have been regarding the audience as composed of persons who desire to attain rational conviction, I do not wish to deny that such an audience would be found only in a logician's dreams. On the contrary, I am anxious to insist that it is in no small part the fault of the audience that political speakers are subject to such strong temptations that only a 'political saint' of the type of John Stuart Mill would not fail at times to succumb.

I shall try to make clear the nature of some of these temptations by examining certain speeches addressed by politicians to the electors at the time of the 1931 election. After the time that has elapsed since that date it may not be too difficult for us to consider with some measure of detachment what was then said and the manner of its saying. But it is important to bear in mind that neither are you nor am I capable of complete detachment. The issues then at stake are not yet by any means all settled. We may hold strong views with regard to these issues; we are, perhaps, strongly attached to one political party. It is for this reason that I assume that we shall not achieve more than some measure of detachment. My own opinion is that most of the politicians who took a prominent part in that election sincerely believed that their party alone could save the nation from disaster. This is not so silly as it may sound. The disaster from which one party offers to save us is not the disaster for which the other party puts forward its remedy.

Without further preamble I shall quote first, at some length, from a speech made by Baldwin at Leeds, on October 20th, 1931, and reported, as follows, in the *Manchester Guardian* the next day:[3]

> Mr Stanley Baldwin received a great welcome when he addressed a big audience at Leeds to-night. It was the first of a number of speeches he is to make in the North of England and Scotland ... Mr Baldwin said:
>
> 'It is with the fullest confidence that I am starting my campaign in the industrial North. I put my faith in the good, sound common sense of Yorkshire men and women.(*a*) They are far too level-headed to be bamboozled by the crazy promises of the Socialists or deluded by the hypocritical talk about tariffs.(*b*)
>
> 'If they want any evidence of this they have only to read what Mr Philip Snowden, himself a good Yorkshireman, has said during the last few days on the subject of his former colleagues,

who left them in the lurch at the hour of the nation's crisis. (c) Workers up and down the country are tired of parties which can do nothing but promise more and more doles when they know full well that the money is not in the till. What we want is a Government which will honestly try to bring back work in the mines, the mills, and the workshops. (d)

'That is why they will give their support in overwhelming numbers to the National Govemment. (e) ...

'They were told that the election was a Tory ramp and the whole crisis was a banker's ramp. For the first statement we have no less an authority than Mr Lloyd George,' said Mr Baldwin. Mr Lloyd George had accused them of astute electioneering. 'I am not astute (f), or not reputed so', Mr Baldwin remarked with a smile. 'I think that had we been astute we should have gone to work in a very different way. When the financial storm arose and when the Labour Government saw nothing but shipwreck ahead, shipwreck for itself and shipwreck for the country, had we been astute politicians we should have refused to co-operate in saving the ship. We should have made party capital out of the distress which had occurred to the nation and forced an election then and there. (g)

'We were in a strong tactical position. ... But life, even political life, is more than tactics. There is something in this country a great deal more precious than the Labour Party or the Liberal Party or the Conservative Party. In this old country of ours there are tens of millions of quiet, decent folk. We were bound to think of them, and no decent man could help thinking of them, and they came first, before all the parties in the country.' (h) [Loud cheers.]

[Mr Baldwin proceeded to point out that there was arduous work ahead and that the National Government must seek a mandate from the country to do this work. He stated that the Socialist Party were bad losers. He admitted that there had been a flight from the pound but no flight from the banks. He paid a tribute to the bankers, especially to the Governor of the Bank of England. He stated that, in his view, the remedy for the adverse balance of trade was to be found in tariffs.]

'There has been something said lately which I cannot quite fully understand about the right of this Parliament to impose a permanent tariff. (*i*) Parliament cannot impose anything that has a permanence. Every Parliament has a perfect right, if it thinks fit, to rip up the work of its predecessor. No Parliament could pass a law saying that this or that shall be permanent.'

[He proceeded to urge that there should be a scientific adjustment of tariffs by a non-political commission. He pointed out that he was here in disagreement with other members of his side in this election.]

The fundamental issue was not Socialism; it was not individualism; it was not Free Trade; it was not Protection. But it was whether they would, in the hour of their country's need, entrust their destinies to a Government selected from all the great parties in the State, who were willing to work together harmoniously in the interests of the country and were trying to pull together to pull the country through that disaster, or would they prefer to hand back the conduct of affairs to the men who only a few weeks ago deserted the ship and left the passengers to their fate, and who, in the words of Mr Snowden, ran away because they were not willing to lose their political souls in order to save the national soul. (*j*) [Cheers.]

'The crisis,' concluded Mr Baldwin, 'is not past. There are hard days in front of us, and we need to keep steady and keep united. It is no time for apathy. Let there be no shirkers. Let everybody go to the ballot-box determined to do his or her best for the country in its hour of need.'

Let us suppose that we had listened to this speech with a view to deciding whether or not we should vote for the National Government. Our first need would be to have made as clear to us as the brief time would allow what exactly were the issues at stake and what proposals Mr Baldwin had to make with regard to them. I think that this need was in no way met by this speech. It would be unreasonable to expect a full and comprehensive statement dealing with large issues, some of which are not capable of being simply explained. But we look in vain for any clear statement with regard to what had happened. We are given scarcely any information with regard to the party's programme; instead, we are told that the policy of scientific tariffs, favoured by Mr Baldwin himself, is not acceptable to the National Government.

What, then, is the technique of this undoubtedly successful speech? The answer to this question is, I believe, to be found by paying attention to those statements to which I have affixed letters. I will consider them in order.

(a) Flattery, designed to establish happy relations between the speaker and his audience, and thus to put them into a receptive mood.

(b) Continuation of flattery, combined with denunciation of the other side, expressed in strongly toned emotional language with complete absence of information.

(c) Skilful arousing of patriotic emotion against those who differed from the National Government. Such denunciation is skilful because it makes a charge of dastardly behaviour without specifying in what that behaviour consisted.

(d) Suggestion that his own party will work honestly for the welfare of the nation whilst imputing dishonesty to the other party.

(e) Using a form of words that suggests that a reason has been given, although no reason has been given.

(f) Appeal to the mental habits of his audience. Most Englishmen like simple-minded people. 'Stupid but honest' is by no means a term of abuse in our everyday vocabulary. Baldwin was frequently so described, and no doubt was not ill-pleased with the description. Accordingly, he is likely to win assent when he disclaims astute practices. It should be noted that (if we can trust the *Manchester Guardian* reporter) Mr Baldwin smiled as he repudiated the notion that he was astute. I think his impulse to honesty came out when he added, 'or not reputed so'. But by that time we may assume that the trick had worked.

(g) Appeal to patriotic emotion by representing his own party as having come to the rescue of the State even to their own disadvantage.

(h) Appeal to feeling of fellowship and of sympathy with quiet people whose distress has not been thought of by the other side. The appeal is made more effective by the use of 'this old country of ours', and 'decent folk', language calculated to evoke unreasonable emotional attitudes.

(i) False affectation of ignorance, followed by a deliberate evasion of the point, since there had been discussion in the previous Cabinet with regard to the alternatives of imposing a 'temporary tariff' so as to avoid cuts in unemployment grants and the policy of adopting tariffs as a normal procedure for safeguarding British industries against foreign competition. The latter alternative might be not inappropriately described as 'imposing a permanent tariff'. In my opinion, it is difficult to acquit Baldwin of insincerity here. At no time had he concealed his own desire for a protectionist policy.

(j) Pretence that now the fundamental issue was to be plainly stated, followed by reiteration that the National Party will save the country whereas the other side are no better than cowardly deserters. Whether these statements were correct or not, no grounds were offered to the audience to support their claim to truth.

Perhaps the best commentary on this speech may be taken from another speech of Baldwin's, when he was talking frankly and sincerely to an audience of university students at St Andrews on 'Truth and Politics'. I have already quoted part of the following statement but, in fairness to Baldwin, it is worth while to repeat and extend the quotation: 'The political audience is not dishonest in itself, nor does it desire or approve dishonesty or misrepresentation in others, but it is an audience only imperfectly prepared to follow a close argument, and the speaker wishes to make a favourable impression, to secure support for a policy. It is easy to see how this may lead to the depreciation of the verbal currency and to the circulation of promises which cannot be cashed.'[4] The fault, then, lies with the audience? In my opinion this is to some extent true. But I do not think that the intellectual incompetence of the audience deserves to be so flagrantly exploited. 'Rhetoric', said Baldwin on another occasion – this time at the University of Oxford – 'is meant to get the vote of a division or at an election, but God help the man who tries to think on it!'[5] If this be so, the tricks of public speaking that were used by Baldwin in his election address at Leeds must have been designed to hinder the audience from thinking.

I do not want to suggest that no appeal should be made to the emotions of the audience; on the contrary, such an appeal must be made. It seems to me to be fitting for a politician to arouse his hearers' love of their country and their fellow-men. It would no doubt be utopian to suppose that they need not vilify their political opponents. But I do not believe that we can absolve a speaker from dishonesty or from twisted thinking who professes to be informing his audience so that they may be enabled to make a wise decision but who nevertheless contents himself with encouraging them to indulge in emotional mental habits and to take refuge in potted thinking.

My second example must be stated more briefly from Mr Ramsay MacDonald's address to his constituents at Seaham, on October 23rd, 1931. At the beginning the meeting was plainly hostile, feeling that Ramsay MacDonald had deserted the cause of the Labour Party. I will quote the report given in the *Manchester Guardian*.

> Thrusting out his hand defiantly, Mr MacDonald cried, 'I have no apologies to make. None whatever. I have no excuses to offer.' Tentative cheers were raised. 'We are Labour and will remain Labour.' With uplifted finger and against some jeering interjection, he reaffirmed that what they had done was to maintain the standard of life of the working people. 'We are doing it,' he said, 'because we continue to be Labour men, and when this is over, and you have seen the effect of our action, you will come to bless us for having stood by you.'
>
> Now the audience cheered without reserve.

In this way Ramsay MacDonald won over his audience until he had them completely under the spell of his words and his personality. A man of Ramsay MacDonald's type – emotional, handsome, gifted with an attractive voice – could hardly avoid putting his audience into a docilely receptive frame of mind – until the moment came when he had been utterly discredited before he stepped on to the platform. Such a person is likely to be strongly tempted to exploit the suggestibility of his hearers, whilst they will encounter difficulties in resisting such exploitation. It would be absurd to maintain that the speaker must refrain from arousing their suggestibility; they will accept what he says, whether he gives them reasons or not. All that he can do is to make every effort to state only what he would be prepared to assert in his own study, and to avoid the dishonest tricks that we have previously considered.

We must face the unfortunate fact that we are moved to the acceptance of beliefs by factors that are wholly irrelevant to their truth. Asquith relates that Kinglake, the author of *Eothen*, sat for eleven years in the House of Commons and sought frequently to make impressive speeches but without success. On one occasion he delivered a peroration, which Mr Justin McCarthy described as 'remarkably eloquent and brilliant'. It failed to make any impression, for he had 'a thin voice and poor articulation'. The next night, Sir Robert Peel (the second), with Kinglake's consent, 'wound up his own speech with Kinglake's peroration'. The result was that he brought the house down. 'Probably', comments Lord Asquith, 'a unique incident in the life of the House of Commons.'[6] Certainly it is an incident that shows how great is the power over an audience of a speaker possessed of a commanding presence, a fine voice and expressive gestures. These characteristics may be possessed by a man who is intellectually honest and does not aim merely at persuading his audience. I do not think that intellectual honesty is incompatible with making public speeches. But to preserve it requires a very rigorous examination by the speaker of the methods he employs to arouse interest and to present his views. He must be especially careful not to adopt a commanding manner and confident tone of voice when he is putting forward a statement which he knows to be extremely doubtful. In short, such a speaker would seem to be under an especial obligation to refrain from exploiting his personality and subduing his hearers without convincing them. He is most fortunate if it should happen that his audience is alert and critical and if at least some of his hearers should have trained themselves to distinguish between sound and unsound thinking, no matter how that thinking may be presented to them.

NOTES

1 See p. 39.
2 *Learn and Live*, p. 110.
3 The report is too long to be quite fully recorded: the paragraphs in square brackets are my condensations of the *Manchester Guardian*'s report in indirect speech. Those passages in inverted commas are reprinted, as given in the *Manchester Guardian*, as full quotations from Baldwin's speech. I have affixed small letters in parentheses to those statements upon which I shall proceed to comment.
4 See *On England*, p. 96.
5 *Ibid.*, p. 101.
6 *Memories and Reflections*, vol. 1, p. 55.

9

ILLUSTRATION AND ANALOGY

'Money is like muck, not good unless it be spread.' Thus tersely
Bacon conveys in a line as much as a less able writer might have
told us in several lines. The apt use of a definite comparison in
the form of a simile may not only delight but also enlighten us.
Bacon is a master of this style. Examples might be drawn from
almost any one of his *Essays*. I shall please myself by quoting two
more:

He that hath wife and children hath given hostages to fortune;
for they are impediments to great enterprises, either of virtue or of mischief.

DOI: 10.4324/b22927-9

Suspicions amongst thoughts are like bats amongst birds, they
ever fly by twilight.

These comparisons are not, I think, used for the sake of explanation or persuasion; they are meant to be enjoyed for their own
sake. Dr Johnson maintained that 'a simile to be perfect must
both illustrate and ennoble the subject'. The three examples I
have given from Bacon seem to me to meet this demand. He is
not always so successful when he proceeds to draw conclusions
from a comparison between things in most respects unlike one
another, as we shall shortly see.

Metaphor, simile, parable and allegory, all involve implicit
or explicit comparison. A metaphor is an implicit comparison
in which the notion compared replaces the notion that could
be illustrated by the comparison. Thus we speak of 'weighing
the evidence' although there is no explicit comparison between
the process of weighing bodies and evaluating evidence. We can
hardly think of 'weighing the evidence' as a metaphorical expression, for it is at once too familiar to attract attention and not
easily to be replaced by any other expression that is as brief and
convenient; nor are we aware of any implied comparison when
we speak of 'balancing one consideration against another'. Our
language abounds with metaphors that are − metaphorically −
'dead', that is, have been used so often that the speaker and
hearer are unaware that the words used are not literal. This is not
the place to discuss the fascinating subject of the ways in which
language has been enriched by metaphors that were once alive
and are now dead. The reader may not have great difficulty in
finding many examples in the preceding sentence. A 'metaphor'
has sometimes been defined as a 'compressed simile'. No doubt
a simile is sometimes compressed into a metaphor, but I think

that metaphors are older than similes. Were this not so, then the use of metaphorical expressions in our language must have been preceded by recognition of the literal usage and by awareness of the comparison involved. I do not think that anyone would wish to maintain that this is the case.

A metaphor may be expanded into a deliberate comparison, that is, into a simile. A simile may be worked out at some length, involving detailed comparisons between several points of resemblance. When such words as 'like' or 'as' are used, the comparison is rendered explicit. This explicit use of comparison constitutes an analogy. No sharp line can be drawn between an explicit use of comparison and an implicit reliance upon a comparison that is *felt* rather than thought out. Nevertheless, they are very different in the way in which they enter into our thinking. Analogy forms the basis of much of our thinking; we notice that two cases resemble each other in certain respects important for our purpose and thereby infer an extension of the resemblance. This mode of reasoning has been extremely fruitful in scientific thinking, notwithstanding the dangers to which it is exposed. These we shall presently consider.

There are two quite different ways in which we may use an analogy to help us in thinking effectively. We may use an analogy for the sake of making some difficult topic easier to understand or as an argument designed to lead us to some definite conclusion. The first way is naturally used by an expositor who understands what he is talking about and wants to explain it to those who are unfamiliar with the notions involved. A skilful expositor will select notions with which we are presumed to be familiar in order to draw a comparison between these and those other notions which lie outside our experience. The use of such illustrative analogies is very common in popular expositions of science, since the aim of the expositor is to enable the common reader to understand a theory involving unfamiliar concepts. Professor Andrade, who is a master of such expository devices, explains to the common reader the difference in the form of a solid, a liquid and a gas by means of a detailed comparison. Having explained that every compound body (i.e. a body that is not an 'element' in the chemical sense) is made up of the combination of atoms into 'knots', or 'molecules', and that these molecules are in ceaseless agitation even in the case of a solid, he proceeds:

> We can form a rough human picture of what is going on in the following way. In a solid, the molecules can be pictured as a crowd of men all doing physical exercises – 'the daily dozen'– without moving from the spot where they stand. If they have taken up their positions at random, we have a so-called amorphous or non-crystalline solid, such as glass or glue; if they are neatly drawn up in rows by a drill instructor, we have a crystalline structure, such as quartz or rock salt or washing-soda. In a liquid the molecules can be pictured as a swarm of men gathered together in a hall at a crowded reception; they are tightly wedged, but each one works his way through the others, with many a push and apology, and we cannot expect the same two men to be near each other all through the evening. (If we want two kinds of atoms, we may take men and women; if dancing starts we have chemical combination, two atoms combining to form a molecule.) For a gas we have to think of a large open space on which men are walking without looking where they are going; each man continues in a straight line until he bumps into someone else, when he abruptly starts off again in a different direction.[1]

Professor Andrade, it should be noted, introduced this illustration as a rough 'picture' of what is going on in a body. This picture is designed to make something we do not see more vivid to our understanding than it would be without such a device. If he had gone on to suggest that in the formation of a crystalline substance there is some person who commands the molecules to form rows as a drill instructor commands his men, then he would have made an unwarrantable extension of his analogical illustration, an extension that would be fraught with misleading associations. Such an unwarrantable extension has in fact sometimes been assumed. Again, if he had said that two atoms combining to form a molecule 'chose each other' as a man and a woman may choose each other to be dancing partners, then he would have misled us to make a false inference. But so long as we are content to use the analogy simply as an illustrative picture, then we are helped in trying to think about what is not at all familiar to us. Scientists have been considerably helped in their construction of scientific theories by making 'pictures', or constructing 'models', based upon the behaviour of perceived bodies. The chemist's use of the word 'affinity' is an example of an implicit analogy. The original meaning of 'affinity' is 'relationship by marriage'. It is then extended to mean 'kinship generally'. The tendency of chemical elements and of their compounds to unite and form new compounds was quite naturally expressed in the eighteenth century by saying that these elements (or their compounds) have 'an affinity for one another'. The origination of the theory of the molecular structure of matter was aided by the 'picture' of bodies moving about in a space.

I have no doubt (said Professor Poynting) that the atomic hypothesis was first imagined to escape the necessity of taking the expansion and contraction of solid and liquid matter as simple, inexplicable, ultimate facts. Were matter *continuous* they would have to be so taken. But imagine that matter consists of separated atoms, and contraction is merely a drawing together of the members of the group, expansion is merely a separating out. We have explained them by likening them to what we observe every day in a crowd of men or a flock of birds.[2]

'Imagine' here means 'make a mental picture'; 'explain' means 'make intelligible'. The picture affords us an explanation because it makes us understand something we did not previously understand. We are made to understand by being shown a likeness to something with which we are already familiar.

We must not underrate the value of analogy in the construction of scientific theories; it plays indeed an indispensable part in the art of discovery. Molecules, atoms and electrons were thought of as extremely tiny solid balls; their behaviour could then be likened to the behaviour of billiard balls which we can touch and see and observe in motion. Again, light was thought of as a wave travelling through an elastic medium. These were fruitful analogies, since they guided scientists in making experiments and in interpreting the results in an intelligible way. Nevertheless, in each of these cases a point was reached at which the likeness was more misleading than helpful. The tiniest ball has some colour or other, but it is meaningless to speak of colour in connexion with an atom or an electron. The experimental investigation of the properties of light revealed absurdities in the conception of an elastic medium filling all space. We cannot go into details here; it must suffice to say that physical science has now reached a stage of its development that renders it impossible to express observable occurrences in language appropriate to the behaviour of what is perceived by our senses. The only appropriate language is that of mathematics. To those who cannot use the symbolism of mathematics such scientific theories must remain largely incomprehensible. It is dangerous to ask that anything should be explained in the terminology of a language that is inappropriate. Scientists have themselves been misled by being unable at times to free themselves from familiar associations.[3]

Since most of us can think only in terminology appropriate to what we can perceive by sight and touch, it is not surprising that ordinary languages abound with dead metaphors. As our intelligence develops and our knowledge increases, we become more able to discriminate likenesses and distinguish differences that were previously unnoticed. This is true both of the child as compared with the adult and of primitive peoples as compared with those who are more developed. An experienced but not consciously recognized likeness between being struck by a falling bough and being hit by another person may lead a child or a savage to feel anger against the tree and to behave to it as though it were a person. In civilized people this mode of behaviour survives the explicit denial of the belief that an inanimate object merits wrath. An example of it is provided by the man who damns his recalcitrant collar stud. The use of the word 'recalcitrant' further illustrates our point. This attitude to an inanimate object does not necessarily presuppose a personification of that 'offending' object, although reflection arising out of the experience may give rise to a deliberate attribution of personal qualities either to the inanimate object itself or to something 'dwelling within it'. It was considerations of this kind that led me to say above that the use of metaphors precedes the use of similes.

If you select any short passage from a book on some serious topic – such as politics, history or philosophy – you would easily recognize how numerous are the metaphors we use and how indispensable they are. Read the passage carefully and note each expression the meaning of which is metaphorical rather than literal. You are very likely to find many words originally metaphors, but now so familiar in the transferred sense that it is difficult to realize that they ever had any other sense. These are the dead metaphors with which we cannot dispense. Some words may be said to be 'half-dead' metaphors, that is, their metaphorical significance passes unnoticed unless some incompatible metaphor be used in the same sentence. Then these 'half-dead' metaphors revive; the result is either amusing or merely silly. You will have noticed that to speak of 'half-dead' metaphors is to use a metaphor. An example of a metaphor that may be regarded as quite dead is 'examine'; it is derived from the Latin word *examen*, which means 'the tongue of a balance'. Perhaps the expression 'weigh the evidence' is not a completely dead metaphor, but it is at least nearly dead. Examples of expressions that have almost, or quite, lost their literal significance are: 'going to the root of the problem', 'falling into mistakes', 'a well-founded theory', 'a conclusion based upon sound evidence', 'to coin a new expression', 'filling the mind with facts', 'a forcible argument'.

I deliberately coined the metaphor 'potted thinking' in order to state briefly and (I hoped) present vividly a certain very common mode of thinking. At the beginning of Chapter 6 I elaborated the metaphor, but I did not seek to draw any conclusions from the metaphor, nor to expand the metaphor into an analogy. Had I done so, the results would certainly have been disastrous, since the points of unlikeness between our minds and our bodies are as important as the points of likeness. An argument derived from a metaphor will necessarily be a bad argument if the metaphor is at all apt. An apt metaphor resembles that for which it is substituted only in a single point. The elaboration of a metaphor involves a set of comparisons of single points. An analogy, on the contrary, involves many points of likeness; it is indeed the logical counterpart of an extended simile.

I said, some pages back, that there were two ways of using analogies for the purpose of thinking effectively. The second way consists in using an analogy for the sake of deriving some conclusion. This is known as argument by analogy. The logical form of argument by analogy is as follows:

X has the properties $p_1, p_2, p_3 \ldots$ and f;
Y has the properties $p_1, p_2, p \ldots$
Therefore, Y also has the property f.

In representing the logical form I put dots after the p's (each of which was supposed to represent a definite property of X, and of Y), in order to indicate that both X and Y had other properties that were not taken into account in deriving the conclusion. The force of the argument depends upon the resemblance between X and Y with regard to the p's. If Y possesses some property incompatible with the property f, then the analogy is unsound. In such a case the argument that Y has f because X has and X and Y are alike in respect of the p's is fallacious, no matter how much we may extend the number of p's which both X and Y possess. Things alike in some respects are unlike in other respects; we must be careful to take note of their unlikeness as well as of their likeness if we wish to conclude that what is true of one is true also of the other. I do not suppose that anyone would disagree with this remark; on the contrary, it is more likely to be regarded as a boring commonplace. Nevertheless, we are most of us apt to forget it at times and to draw a conclusion from an analogy which a little reflection would have shown us to be unsound. To bear this in mind need not lead us to belittle the useful part played by thinking in terms of an analogy. We have seen the use of analogy as a guide to scientific investigation, and we have briefly noticed the danger of carrying the analogy too far. An analogy that is carried too far is said 'to break down'. Sooner or later all analogies break down, so that the careful thinker is on the lookout for the point at which this breakdown occurs. We are sometimes warned not to carry an analogy 'to its logical conclusion'. This mode of speech seems to me absurd. To press an analogy farther than it will properly apply is to carry it to an illogical conclusion. It is true that no precise logical principles can be laid down from which may be derived rules telling us how far a *given* analogy may be carried. But the detection of the point at which the analogy has broken down involves logical thinking.

Argument by analogy is mainly used to persuade *other* persons to accept a conclusion or to enlighten the *hearer* so that he may come to see the situation in a new light. The advantages and the dangers of this mode of arguing will best be seen by considering definite examples.

The first example is taken from the *Second Book of Samuel*. It may be remembered that David desired the wife of Uriah. Accordingly, he planned to have Uriah set in the forefront of the battle, in order that Uriah might be killed. The plan was successful and David married Bathsheba, who had been the wife of Uriah. Thereupon the narrative continues:

> But the thing that David had done displeased the Lord. And the Lord sent Nathan unto David. And he came unto him, and said unto him:

There were two men in one city; the one rich, and the other poor. The rich man had exceeding many flocks and herds: But the poor man had nothing, save one little ewe lamb, which he had bought and nourished up: and it grew up together with him, and with his children; it did eat of his own meat, and drank of his own cup, and lay in his bosom, and was unto him as a daughter. And there came a traveller unto the rich man, and he spared to take of his own flock and of his own herd, to dress for the wayfaring man that was come unto him; but took the poor man's lamb, and dressed it for the man that was come to him.

And David's anger was greatly kindled against the man; and he said to Nathan, As the Lord liveth, the man that hath done this thing shall surely die: And he shall restore the lamb fourfold, because he did this thing, and because he had no pity.

And Nathan said to David, Thou art the man. ... And David said unto Nathan, I have sinned against the Lord.

Nathan's object, it may be presumed, in putting forward to David this story of an action in one respect similar to his own, was to elicit from David a disinterested judgment. The considerable unlikeness between the action of David and the action of the rich man who stole the poor man's one ewe lamb enabled David to judge the action without personal bias. When the point was brought home to him, he was enabled to see that what held in the case of the man he had condemned held also in his own case.

The parables in the Old and the New Testament are, we find, frequently used in this way. Such a device may help us to avoid the fallacy of special pleading, since we are called upon to pass judgment first and are then shown the application to our own case. To achieve this aim the resemblance implied in the parable must be striking as soon as it is pointed out but not sufficiently detailed to indicate the moral from the start. Since the conclusion to be drawn is directed to a single point, it is not a defect that the resemblance should be slight; all that is required is that it should be a relevant resemblance. A parable may, I think, be regarded as a concealed analogy explicitly used for a didactic purpose. Obviously this mode of instruction is liable to serious abuse. Further, its use is confined to instruction; it is not a form of argument. Nowadays public men – those who seek to educate us through the medium of the evening newspapers, didactic playwrights, and politicians – do not inform us that they are speaking in parables. Like Nathan they tell us a story and leave us to jump to its application. Unlike Nathan, however, they do not usually adopt the form of a story; they present us with an analogy, or even a metaphor, under the guise of providing us with a reasoned argument. The examples we shall now consider can scarcely, in my opinion, be regarded as examples of *argument* by analogy; they are rather suggestions of an analogy that could not withstand a moment's quiet reflection.

Sir John Simon, in his broadcast speech in November 1935, said:

> You cannot build a superstructure without preserving the foundation. The National Government has provided the foundation – the foundation of confidence instead of crisis; and it seems to me that our duty now is to preserve and strengthen that foundation, and to do nothing to weaken it, for if it is weakened, the only result will be that our industrial and social progress will be obstructed and prevented.

Now it is true that you cannot build a superstructure unless the foundations be preserved; they cannot be preserved unless they have been laid. To this Sir John Simon's listeners must unhesitatingly have assented. The point at issue, however, is whether the National Government had indeed provided that foundation.

It is not without significance that election speeches should be full of analogies, sometimes barely suggested, often imperfect, occasionally so obviously unsound that we are inclined to marvel at their indisputable appeal. The following examples are taken from election speeches made in 1931 or in 1935. Both these elections were, it will be remembered, held at a time when the electors were aware that the situation was critical. I shall first quote the analogies, then comment briefly upon their logical imperfections, and shall finally inquire the reasons for their undoubted appeal to electors.

(i) 'A doctor's mandate', suggested Lord Dawson of Penn ... was a phrase of good omen for 'the coming election'; for if that meant 'that the ills of the body-politic should be handled on the lines of sound investigation, orderly diagnosis, and treatment based on realities rather than on vain fancies, we should be able to look forward with confidence to our recovery.'

(*Manchester Guardian*, October 5th, 1931.)

(ii) Sir Godfrey Collins said that while the ship of State was nearly on the rocks, Arthur Henderson and his crew took to the lifeboats, leaving only a few officers behind. They left 'Ramsay' on the bridge, Philip Snowden at the wheel, and plucky 'Jimmie' Thomas at the bow looking out for breakers ahead.

While Arthur Henderson and his crew pulled away in lifeboats, others clambered up the ship's side. 'Ramsay' met them on deck with a smile, did not stop to ask their views, but asked Stanley Baldwin to go to the stokehold to keep the pressure up in all boilers while the ship was riding the storm. Another he invited to go to the pantry, another to get in touch by wireless with other boats and nations; another he asked to look after the women and children who had been left behind. So those men rode the storm while Arthur Henderson pulled away to land in some safe place.[4]

(*M.G.*, October 16th, 1938.)

(iii) Mr Runciman said the issues and dangers were more grave than any by which this nation had been faced since the war. ... Whatever criticism had to be offered of the Labour Government might very well be left to Mr Philip Snowden, who saw the red light before many of his colleagues and did not funk making economies and adopting a policy which he knew would be unpopular. He had the courage to face up to the facts and make recommendations which he knew were necessary in the interests of national safety.

The truth is that the ship is on fire. I am not disposed to enter into any controversy on the name of the pump that is to be used or the length of the hose. The main thing is that we should save the ship, and I have no doubt we shall do it.

(*M.G.*, October 22nd, 1931.)

(iv) Sir John Simon, speaking on October 24th, 1931, said:

The only question is: 'Shall we sink or swim?' When Mr Arthur Henderson threw up his hands and disclaimed responsibility, Mr Ramsay MacDonald struck boldly out for the shore. The National Government is keeping hold of the life-line, and the nation can be saved only by saving itself. Away with party-labels and let us pull together.

(*Observer*, October 25th, 1931.)

(iv) Sir John Simon, speaking on October 14th of the same year, said:

We were in a ship that was sinking. If the ship was sinking, it is no good arguing with one another as to who is to stop the hole. It has got to be stopped at once.

(M.G., October 15th.)

(vi) Ramsay MacDonald, speaking on October 11th, 1931, said:

When the country is on an even keel again and the accounts are balanced, we can go on building up what we were striving to build before. Without foundation no house can stand, without financial security no policy of progress can endure.

(M.G., October 12th, 1931.)

(vii) Mr Ramsay MacDonald, in a broadcast speech in November 1935, said:

I began with a reference to the contrast between the state of the country in 1931 and its state to-day. The ship then near to the rocks is again floating, and has been made seaworthy. There is rough and trying weather ahead. How can it most wisely be encountered?

(Listener, November 13th, 1935.)

It is perhaps a straining of language to say that these extracts from speeches contain analogies, but so far as they can be regarded as putting forth any argument at all, the argument is by analogy. Mr A. P. Herbert has made fun of the habit, so freely indulged in by political speakers, of using nautical terms. He points out that these terms are frequently misused and may rouse mirth rather than conviction in the minds of the hearers. This misuse of terms is not, however, our concern. We have to inquire whether the analogy between a ship in danger and a nation in a time of crisis is a sound analogy. If any speaker offers us an argument based upon the analogy implicit in the figure of speech, 'the Ship of State', then the whole logical force of his argument depends upon the soundness of the comparison between the position of the Government and the position of the officers and crew of a ship, on the one hand, and between the position of the electorate and that of the passengers of the ship on the other hand. It does not seem to me that there is any relevant likeness between the things compared. That this is so is, I believe, clearly shown in Sir Godfrey Collins's argument (example ii). If Arthur Henderson 'pulled away to some safe place', are we not entitled to ask why the others remained behind? Again, from what place did those others come who 'clambered up the sides', apparently prepared to take the places of those who had gone to safety? That these questions could receive no answer from the speaker suggests at best that the analogy was so imperfect as to be useless for the purposes of an argument, and at worst that the analogy was never intended to provide an argument at all.

Perhaps the most convincing way of showing the logical defect of this analogy is to point out that it could just as well have been used by Mr Arthur Henderson and his supporters. He might have replied (although, so far as I know, he did not) as follows:

The Ship of the Government is going on to the rocks, owing to the lack of skill of the Captain and the absence of an efficient lookout. 'Ramsay', the Captain, greeted with a smile those who came on board, at the same time keeping his place on the bridge. He sent Stanley Baldwin to the stoke-hold, another to the pantry – presumably to overhaul the stores – and another to look after the women and children who cowered in their cabins. Meanwhile, I and those of the officers and crew who remembered that there were life-boats and that our paramount duty was to save the passengers, persuaded them to enter the life-boats which provided their only hope of safety. We then pulled away to port. It is to be regretted that the ship and those who stayed on board went down. It was magnificent, but it was not seamanship; it was folly, seeing that there were life-boats enough and to spare and men able to row them to safety.

Had Mr Henderson thus replied, he would have given the electors no reasons whatever for supposing that the Labour Government (or, let us say, his own Party) was fitted to govern the nation in a time of crisis. Nor did any of those politicians who used this analogy give any reasons. Nor did Lord Dawson of Penn (example i) provide any reasons for supposing that his Party could heal 'the ills of the body-politic'. There is certainly a resemblance between a diseased body and a nation in difficulties. We have Mr Baldwin's word for it that 'the whole world is sick'. This is again a resemblance that cannot be pressed very far, but it is not unreasonable to hold that just as a diseased body stands in need of a competent doctor, so a distressed nation stands in need of a competent Government. What has to be established, however, is which of the alternative parties (if any) is capable of giving us that competent Government. Unfortunately, most politicians do not seem aware that this is the conclusion to which their arguments must be addressed. Reluctantly we may be compelled to accept the view that politicians pleading with electors can aim only at persuading them to support a policy without giving them any reasons to suppose that that policy will satisfy their desires.[5]

It is not, I think, so difficult to understand how these inept analogies and metaphors suffice to persuade the electors. They have the psychological effect of a good slogan or of repeated affirmation – the stock-in-trade of advertisers. The analogy used is of the sort to call up a vivid picture in the minds of the hearers. Consider, for instance, example iii, given above. The device used and the effect upon the hearers may be exhibited as follows:

'The ship is on fire,' says the speaker.
'Something must be done at once,' respond the hearers.
'To enter into controversy on the name of the pump that is to be used or on the length of the hose would be to waste time,' hints the speaker.
'Of course, of course, what do names matter, what does the length of the hose matter? All that matters is that the ship should be saved,' respond the hearers, in growing agitation.
'The main thing is that we should save the ship,' says, the speaker, 'and I have no doubt that we shall do it,' he adds.
'How thankful we shall be to have the ship saved,' the hearers feel.

The trick is simple enough, but it works. It seems to be the case that most people will accept a vivid argument by analogy without pausing to reflect whether there is any relevant likeness between the things compared. Since we find it difficult to think about complicated matters, we are, owing to mental laziness, prone to accept any argument of the form: X is Y, just as A is B, where X and Y are abstract and unfamiliar whilst A and B are familiar matters of fact. We fail to notice that the only reason for believing that X is Y is that there is a proper analogy between the relation of X to Y and the relation of A to B.

I have dealt with this topic at great length because I am convinced that one of the gravest difficulties of an audience lies in this habit of the uncritical acceptance of imperfect analogies. One possible remedy is to ask oneself whether the analogy could just as well be used to establish the opposite conclusion. I gave an example of this procedure in the speech I attributed to Mr Arthur Henderson (who would not, I believe, have stooped to make it). This remedy is clearly applicable to examples (i), (iii), (iv) and (v), as well as to example (ii). It is also applicable to Sir John Simon's argument that you cannot build a superstructure without preserving the foundations. On the other hand, it is not relevant to our purpose to stress the extraordinary mixture of metaphors in example (vi), since Ramsay MacDonald's metaphors of 'an even keel' and 'balanced accounts' simply illustrate the psychological effectiveness of repetition in variety, whilst we may admit that a 'house' can be 'built' on a ship, since we speak of 'the wheel-house', and that, too, must have secure foundations. We may be content to dismiss this extract as a string of commonplace platitudes.

Another possible remedy for dealing with an argument by analogy is to form the habit of asking whether the assumed comparison is correct, and, if so, at what point exactly the comparison holds, for it is at that point that the analogy breaks down. Let us ask these questions with regard to the following example, taken from Francis Bacon's *The True Greatness of Kingdoms*:

> No body can be healthful without exercise, neither natural body nor politic; and, certainly, to a kingdom, or estate, a just and honourable war is the true exercise. A civil war, indeed, is like the heat of a fever; but a foreign war is like the heat of exercise, and serveth to keep the body in health; for in a slothful peace, both courages will effeminate and manners corrupt.

The comparison between a State (Nation, or 'Kingdom') and a human being is old; this analogy of the State to an individual citizen was used with – in my opinion – disastrous consequences by Plato in the *Republic*. Bacon limits his argument to a 'natural body' and a 'political body' – i.e. a State. Using modern terminology we may set out the argument in the following form:

Just as my body, in order to be healthy, needs exercise, so does the State;
Foreign war is to the State as bodily exercise is to my body;
Civil war is to the State as fever is to my body (i.e. it generates the wrong sort
     of heat).

It is to be noted that Bacon first asserts that 'the true exercise' of the State is a 'just and honourable war'; but this qualification is then dropped in favour of 'foreign war' as opposed to 'civil war'. The comparison between the generation of heat in my body by bodily exercises and 'health' in the State by war is so far-fetched that one might almost suspect that Bacon was making a pun upon the word 'heat'. This, however, is not to be imputed to Bacon. I conclude that the extent to which the comparison holds is limited to the fact that 'my body' is a unity of a certain kind and that 'the State' is also a unity, but of quite a different kind. It is essential to bear in mind that any argument based upon the analogy between a State, or a Nation, on the one hand, and an individual citizen on the other ought to be subjected to the most careful criticism.

The application of the second remedy for being misled by imperfect analogies may be finally illustrated by reference to the well-worn comparison between the brain and a telephone-exchange. This 'mouldy old metaphor', as Professor C. D. Broad has lately called it, was first, I believe, used by the late Professor Karl Pearson.[6] It has lately been revived, in other forms, by Sir Arthur Eddington, who finds an analogy between *my mind* and a *newspaper office*, also between *the mind* and *a central wireless station*. It must suffice here to quote one statement of this analogy:

> The inside of your head must be rather like a newspaper office. It is connected with the outside world by nerves which play the part of telegraph wires. Messages from the outside world arrive in code along these wires; the whole substratum of fact is contained in these code messages. Within the office they are made up into a presentable story, partly by legitimate use of accumulated experience but also with an admixture of journalistic imagination; and it is this free translation of original messages that our consciousness becomes aware of.[7]

It is instructive to compare this analogy with the analogy quoted from Professor Andrade, at the beginning of this chapter. Eddington does not use his analogy purely for the sake of illustration; he uses it in order to draw conclusions with regard to the nature of the external world and the nature of our knowledge about the external world. The comparison, it seems to me, fails at every relevant point. Objects in the external world (which is, presumably, the world 'outside' my head) are compared to reporters; these reporters (or objects) send messages in code; these code messages are compared to the transmission of nervous impulses; those who receive the messages (i.e. the editor and sub-editors?) correspond to my mind; their 'free translation' of these messages corresponds to what my consciousness is aware of. Perhaps it is enough to point out the complete breakdown of the analogy in the last point, I am said to receive 'messages', but what I am conscious of is only 'a free translation' which bears no resemblance to the message that was handed in. This is serious enough, but when we go on to consider that the analogy is used, first, to explain the process of perceiving objects in the world, and secondly, as a basis for the conclusion that these 'messages' are the products of my own mental (but unconscious) activity, we must, I think, conclude that the analogy is singularly unenlightening and completely unconvincing as a basis for the conclusions that Eddington wishes to assert.

It is only too easy to multiply examples of analogies. We could draw them from the writings of sociologists, psychologists and philosophers with equal ease. Thinking by analogy is much more common than we are likely to recognize until our attention is called to it. Such thinking may be, as we have seen, useful for the purpose of understanding an unfamiliar topic and also as a guide to further investigation. Nevertheless, we need to remember that it is a guide whose reliability must constantly be tested. Further, although argument by analogy may be used to suggest a conclusion, it is incapable of establishing any conclusion at all. The suggested conclusion stands just as much in need of testing as though it had never been arrived at by the process of thinking by analogy. Even in the case of a good analogy there is always a point at which the analogy breaks down. Our tendency to forget this is exploited by those who aim at persuading us to accept their views without offering us any grounds that would be acceptable to a reasonable thinker. I am afraid that it is sometimes the case, as in some of the political speeches we have examined, that there are no reasonable grounds that could be offered.

NOTES

1   *The Atom* (Ernest Benn, Limited), p. 18.
2   *Collected Scientific Papers*, p. 680.
3   An allied difficulty will be discussed in the next chapter.

4   Lord Nuffield now (Nov. 19th, 1938) urges us to 'cease criticizing the man at the wheel.' (Further quotations from the *Manchester Guardian* cited as *M.G.*)

5   Cf. Baldwin: *On England*, pp. 94–6.

6   *Grammar of Science*, Chapter II, § 3.

7   *New Pathways in Science*, pp. 3–4. I have dealt at length with this analogy, and allied metaphors, in *Philosophy and the Physicists*, Chapter V.

10

THE UNPOPULARITY OF BEING MODERATE

In writing the previous chapters I have several times been tempted to assert 'No one could believe so and so', or 'Everyone will admit such and such'. Sometimes I have refrained from making these sweeping statements. I knew that I should want to point out a common defect in our thinking arising out of a not unnatural dislike of sharing the condemnation of the Church of Laodicea. To be willing to admit that there is much to be said on both sides of a question lays one open to the charge of being lukewarm in cases where vigorous action is needed. To be content to say, for instance, that not all one's political opponents are self-seeking is sometimes regarded as a sign of academic detachment from

DOI: 10.4324/b22927-10

the realities of social evils. Anyone who habitually speaks with moderation tends to be regarded either as an ignorant fellow or as incapable of effective action. We have already seen that there is no incompatibility between care in reaching conclusions which we may be ready to revise under the influence of fresh evidence and acting vigorously and decisively in support of them so long as we see no reason for adopting the opposite conclusion. If we realize that our conclusion though not indisputably true is nevertheless the most reasonable conclusion to hold in face of the evidence, then we should be behaving unreasonably if we were to refrain from acting in accordance with it.

I am aware that the preceding paragraph is likely to make but a tepid appeal to most readers. It may be remembered that Lord Selborne, having praised 'our glorious incapacity for clear thought', went on to recommend the advantages of saying 'often and loudly and clearly' – whatever it is you want to say – in order to convert your hearers. Sweeping statements may be regarded as a device having the same effect both in arresting attention and persuading others to accept our views. Consider the following example:

> Among average respectable women envy plays an extraordinarily large part. If you are sitting in the Underground and a well-dressed woman happens to walk along the car, watch the eyes of the other women. You will see that every one of them, with the possible exception of those who are even better dressed, will watch the woman with malevolent glances, and will be struggling to draw inferences derogatory to her. The love of scandal is an expression of this general malevolence: any story against another woman is instantly believed, even on the flimsiest evidence.

When I first read this statement, in 1930, I tried to test the truth of the generalization about the behaviour of women who see a well-dressed woman in the Underground cars. Unfortunately I was not able to detect any malevolent glances, possibly because I did not recognize the 'well-dressed' woman when she appeared. The form of this reasoning is worth noticing. The author, Bertrand Russell,[1] first makes a statement about 'average respectable women'; then he proceeds to assert that 'every one' of the women in the car will feel envy and be malevolent. I am not sure how the word 'average' is used in this context, but I assume that we may interpret the statement as asserting that in the case of *most* respectable women 'envy plays an extraordinarily large part'. So far as my experience goes, this does not seem to me to be true, but possibly I am missing the significance of the qualification '*respectable* women'. However that may be, it does not justify the inference that whenever you see a well-dressed woman enter a car on the Underground you will see *every* one of the less well-dressed women turn malevolent glances at her. Perhaps Mr Russell's first statement is not offered in evidence of the second but as a conclusion from it. It is difficult to know. Possibly he is generalizing from his own experience uncorroborated by other evidence. It is more probable, however, that he is deliberately making a sweeping generalization simply for the sake of attracting attention. His laudable desire in writing the book from which this passage is quoted was to point out to us how often the causes of our unhappiness lie within ourselves. He says 'all' when, so I am assuming, he means 'most'; perhaps 'half' (or even less than half) would have been all that was justifiable. To speak thus moderately would not be so effective for his purpose. Russell often, in his popular books, uses this trick of attracting attention, much in the way in which Macaulay was inclined to say: 'Every schoolboy knows' what, indeed, most of us do not know, and what, indeed, is sometimes not even true.

There are serious dangers in indulging in such a habit of loud speaking, as advocated by Lord Selborne and practised by all of us at times. It encourages us to turn aside from contrary evidence, to oversimplify important issues, to attribute to other people an unwarranted extension of what they have been asserting. We have already seen how potted thinking about Fascism, Socialism, Pacifism, and so on leads us to make sweeping statements that are not justified and to turn a moderate statement into an extreme statement which had not been put forward. These forms of twisted thinking tend to go together, and are partly responsible for our use of tied epithets. The dislike of being moderate and the desire for certainty are at the root of these mistakes. We want to condemn or praise wholeheartedly; we then make judgments about a whole class. Frequently we substitute an abstraction for the members of the class. Thus, instead of speaking of 'All capitalists', we talk about the abstraction *Capitalism*.

In reflecting upon the preceding paragraph I am led to ask myself whether I seriously wish to maintain that we *all* want to condemn, or praise as the case may be, wholeheartedly. It may be that not everyone does, but I believe that the statement '*most* people so want' is true. It may, again, be an over-statement to say, as I said, that we *all* of us at times use the device of speaking loudly. But I leave the paragraph as I have written it. I believe the statements to be true; if you believe that they are not, then you have grounds (so I assume) for thinking that I have supplied you with an example of lack of due moderation. It is difficult to be moderate. On the other hand, regarded as an attempt to attract attention and win agreement, exaggeration may fail of its effect, just as shouting may. We saw that the exaggerated claims made by some advertisers for their wares seem to have led other advertisers to adopt, at least in appearance, a more moderate tone.

It is only too easy to find examples of this form of twisted thinking. You will find them scattered in reports of speeches, in newspaper articles, in books written about the 'burning topics of the day'. I give some examples that I have found in this way.

'You all know that the Socialist Party are purely predatory,' said Dr Inge, as reported in *The Times*. This statement contains three sweeping generalizations: we *all* know, the Socialist *Party* without discrimination, and '*purely*' predatory,' that is, are motivated by nothing but predatory aims.

In the debate on the Budget, in the House of Commons, May 4th of this year (1938), in discussing the proposed increase in the tax on tea, the member for Colchester's speech is reported in *The Times* as follows:

> There would not be much murmuring anywhere except among those who had so far absorbed the principles of Socialism that they expected somebody else to bear all their burdens.

Some time ago Ramsay MacDonald protested against this habit of generalizing from the opinions expressed by some members of the Socialist Party to statements about all Socialists, and thus to statements about the principles of Socialism. In his book on *The Socialist Movement*, he pointed out that at the birth of Socialism its exponents were pioneers challenging the established order. They were passionate in defence of their cause and immoderate in their attacks on those who opposed it. Mr MacDonald continues:

> He [the Socialist pioneer] grouped all his enemies in one crowd, all their creeds and professions in one bundle, and he

condemned them in the bulk. This happened in other directions, with the result that to-day the opponents of Socialism try to make Socialism itself responsible for every extravagance, every private opinion, every enthusiasm of every one of its advocates. The logic is this: Mr Smith writes that the family is only a passing form of organization; Mr Smith is a Socialist; therefore all Socialists think that the family is only a passing form of organization. This method of controversy may offer for itself a shamefaced justification when it is resorted to for the purpose of a raging and tearing political fight in which the aim of the rivals is not to arrive at truth but to catch votes, but it cannot be defended on any other or higher ground, and it requires only the slightest knowledge of the history of opinion in this country to see what havoc would be played with our critics if we were to apply such a perverted logic to them and their creeds.[2]

This seems to me to be well said. Ramsay MacDonald makes clear the logical fallacy involved in this form of reasoning. He also recognizes that this fallacy may be deliberately employed for such purposes as that of winning support for a policy or inducing people to reject a creed. A speaker who knowingly presents this fallacy to his hearers is not himself the victim of twisted thinking; on the contrary, he is deliberately using a crooked argument for the sake of persuading his hearers. He relies upon their not observing the fallacy. It might, however, be the case that a speaker who uses such an argument is stupidly generalizing from a *single* case to *every* case of the same kind. This involves an error so obvious that I suppose no one would fall into it unless he had not reflected upon what he is saying. A dishonest speaker, using such a form of argument, might be trying to establish his conclusion by selecting instances favourable to his contention whilst ignoring those that conflict with it. Later, we shall consider this form of dishonest argument. This mistake is less obvious if an assertion about *several* is twisted into an assertion about *all* of a certain class. Mr H. G. Wells, in his recently published book, *World-Brain*, has called attention to an error of this kind.

In an address given to the Educational Section of the British Association for the Advancement of Science, Mr Wells made certain demands for the improvement of education in this country. He insisted:

> Everything I am saying now implies a demand for more and better teachers – better paid, with better equipment. And those teachers will have to be kept *fresh*. It is stipulated in most leases that we should paint our houses outside every three years and inside every seven years, but nobody ever thinks of doing up a school teacher. There are teachers at work in this country who haven't been painted inside for fifty years. They must be damp and rotten and very unhealthy for all who come in contact with them. Two-thirds of the teaching profession now is in urgent need of being reconditioned or superannuated.[3]

This criticism provoked a large number of indignant replies which seems to have surprised Mr Wells. In *World-Brain*, which contains the original address, he adds an appendix entitled 'Ruffled Teachers', in which he makes the following comment:

> I say that there are teachers who are not up to their job, that some of them have not been done up inside for fifty years. They are as damp and rotten as old houses. And surely every teacher knows that that is true. 'Some' is not 'all'. But will they admit it? Instead they flare up. 'You say *we* are all damp and rotten!'

I don't. And when I say two-thirds of the teaching profession is in urgent need of reconditioning or superannuation, I mean two-thirds and not the whole.

This incident is instructive for our present purpose in three ways. First, it shows that an attack upon *some* members of our own group (in this case a professional group) is easily twisted into an attack on *all*. Secondly, Mr H. G. Wells in replying seems to me to be somewhat disingenuous. It is true that he had condemned two-thirds of the teaching profession, not the whole profession. But he had committed himself to the statement that all who had been teaching (i.e. 'not painted up inside') for fifty years were in need of being superannuated or reconditioned. He did not offer any evidence to support the implication that there were any teachers at all who had been teaching (or not 'painted up inside') for fifty years. To me it is not credible that any school teachers should have been teaching for fifty years, since they would hardly begin to teach before the age of eighteen, and would not be teaching at the age of sixty-eight. Possibly, however, Mr Wells did not say this. His metaphor, at this point, is not very clearly used. Thirdly, Mr Wells used decidedly immoderate language, which provoked some members of the teaching profession to repudiate the statement as wholly untrue. So far as Mr Wells's attack on the teaching profession is concerned this incident does not illustrate the unpopularity of moderation. On the contrary, this reaction to his immoderate use of language provides an example of the difficulty of keeping one's head when one has lost one's temper. If someone attacks our own group we are tempted to retaliate by an immoderate extension of what was said. *Two-thirds*, as Mr Wells truly says, is not *all*. The replies seem to have assumed that *two-thirds* may be replaced by *all*, and then to have gone to the extreme of denying that *any* teachers needed 'reconditioning' (to quote Mr Wells's unpleasant word). In my opinion we might question whether Mr Wells was not himself guilty of twisted thinking in using so precise an expression as 'two-thirds'. It suggests that a very careful examination of the total number of teachers had been carried out. Possibly it had been, but there was nothing in the address to suggest that this was the case.

The failure to be moderate in statement occurs not only in cases when we are defending our own group, but also when we are pleased to hear attacks on other groups. You have probably heard arguments of this form:

> 'Here is another vicar who has been convicted of immorality. That just shows you that the whole Church is corrupt.'

A recent very popular novel contained, so I was told, an attack on the medical profession. I heard someone say: 'Yes, it is quite true. Doctors are venal and incompetent'. Some doctors certainly are, but we are indulging in twisted thinking if we allow ourselves to pass straight to the conclusion that, since *some* are, *all* are. We are very unlikely to fall into this mistake if the statement, upon which we base our conclusion, is in the form *Some doctors are incompetent*; but if the qualifying *some* be left out, then we are apt not to notice the omission, so that we are hardly aware that any inference has been made. Again, when we hear that 'the heroic Republicans (in Spain) are holding out against Franco's forces', we may too hastily assume that *all* Spanish Republicans are heroic. Similarly, if it is asserted that 'the Republicans burn and desecrate churches', we easily fall into the mistake of supposing that the statement has been made about *every* one of the Republicans.

It is not necessary to multiply examples. We are not concerned with judgments about teachers, or doctors, or Spanish Republicans. Our concern is with a form of unsound argument that is very common and is sometimes used with deliberate dishonesty. This argument is of the form:

Some A is B,
therefore, All A is B.

As thus stated the fallacy is obvious. It is much less obvious when we use the expression 'A is B' instead of the expression 'Some A is B' or when we use the expression 'The A's are B' instead of the expression 'Some of the A's are B'. Yet, in each case, it may be that only the latter expression 'Some A is B' is appropriate to the evidence, whilst our argument requires the statement to be in the form, All A is B. This mistake crops up in many ways, one of which is so common that logicians invented a name for it, calling it 'the fallacy of undistributed middle'.[4] To see wherein the mistake lies we may begin by paying attention to an example of the syllogism in which the conclusion is correctly drawn:

All cows are quadrupeds,
All quadrupeds are vertebrates,
therefore, All cows are vertebrates.

I do not happen to know whether the second statement is true, but, if it is, and if the first statement also is true, then the conclusion is true. We have already formulated the principle of reasoning of which this argument is a special instance.[5] Let us contrast this argument with two other arguments:

(1) All cows are quadrupeds,
      All mules are quadrupeds,
      therefore, All cows are mules.

(2) All Europeans are civilized,
    All Frenchmen are civilized,
    therefore, All Frenchmen are Europeans.

It is not difficult to see that in neither of these cases does the conclusion follow from the premisses. The conclusion in (1) is false, in (2) true; the premisses in both cases are, I assume, true. But in each case the truth of the premisses does not justify our inferring that the conclusion is true. Let us now use letters of the alphabet to stand for the classes about which an assertion is made in one, or other, of the premisses. We then represent the forms of these arguments by,

(1) All A is B   (2) All A is B
    All C is B   All C is B
    therefore, All A is C   therefore, All A is C

You will notice that the form of both arguments is the same. Let us (using a similar device) represent the form of the argument stated on page 139; we obtain,

All A is B
All B is C
therefore, All A is C

This is a valid form. In saying that it is valid, we are saying that, *no matter what classes we may be talking about*, the conclusion must be true provided that the premisses are true. To deny it would be equivalent to asserting that it would be logically possible for one circle to be *wholly included* in a second, and the second circle *wholly included* in a third circle, without having the first wholly included in the third. Now, in the arguments (1) and (2) we are informed only that both the classes A and C are contained in B. This information does not enable us to connect A and C through their relation to B. We cannot, therefore, tell whether A and C are coextensive in membership, or overlap, or wholly exclude one another. Any one of these possible relations between A and C would be consistent with our information.

In exemplifying this fallacy I have used trivial examples of the type usually provided in elementary textbooks of logic. I did so because it was important for us first to concentrate upon the form of the argument without thinking about the topic. Very few people, I hope, would commit this fallacy if the argument were stated in this bare way, freed from emotionally toned language, and dealing with topics about which we are not strongly moved. I add, however, three examples which, I am told, are taken from actual discussions.[6]

'His generosity might have been inferred from his humanity for all generous people are humane.'

'We respect those that keep us in order, and we respect those that shine at games; hence, it is a reasonable assumption that those who are good at games should be good disciplinarians.'

'Of course, the U.S.A., though a mixture of races, is an Anglo-Saxon nation. All Anglo-Saxon nations are devoted to freedom, and devotion to freedom is nowhere more evident than in America.'

The reader should have no difficulty in seeing that each of these arguments involves the fallacy of undistributed middle. We are most often tempted to fall into this fallacy when we are arguing about a topic on which we feel strongly and about which our minds are already made up. In such cases it often happens that we have in mind a statement of the form *All A is B*, even though we might actually say 'Some A is B,' or more probably, 'Only B is A'. It is easy to slip into the mistake of supposing that to assert 'Only B is A' is equivalent to making an assertion about *every* B, and is thus of the form *All A is B*. This is not so. To say 'Only those who were unprejudiced were convinced' is not equivalent to the assertion that every one who was unprejudiced was convinced. It is equivalent to saying 'All who were convinced were unprejudiced'. If we forget this we might argue as follows; 'Only those who were unprejudiced were convinced, and since he was not convinced it follows that he was prejudiced'. This does not, however, follow. In this argument a mistake similar to the fallacy of undistributed middle has been made, for a conclusion has been drawn that makes an assertion about *all who were unprejudiced*, namely the assertion that the man in question is not to be found among them. This goes beyond the evidence provided by the original premiss. It involves once more the illegitimate process of replacing a statement about *some* of a class by a statement about *all*. This process is illegitimate if we are maintaining that since *Some A is B* it must be true that *All A is B*; it may be true, but we are not justified in saying that it must be so.

We must remember that in ordinary discussion we do not generally use such bare statements as 'Only those who were unprejudiced were convinced.' We use emotionally toned language and involved statements which conceal from us what the form of our argument is. Thus we might meet such an argument as the following: 'If these Conservative Ministers are not Fascists, then tell me what they are. They openly deride the League of Nations and so do the Fascists. If that doesn't prove that the whole lot of them are Fascists, I don't know what's what.' The last sentence would seem to be true, for this argument, cleared of its rhetorical devices and emotional language, reduces to the form:

These Conservative Ministers deride the League of Nations.
Fascists deride the League of Nations:
therefore, These Conservative Ministers are Fascists.

Stated in this form the fallacy is openly revealed.

I have not been asserting that every statement of the form *All A is B* is false; on the contrary, that assertion would itself involve a statement of that form, and it would certainly be false. I have been concerned to maintain the moderate statement that *some* statements of the form *All A is B* are false, and I have been anxious to point out that we sometimes (not *always*) fail to notice their falsity because the qualifying word 'all' has been omitted. I remember being told when I was a child that people with china-blue eyes were untrustworthy. It seems difficult to believe that anyone could credit such a statement if it were explicitly asserted that *all* people with china-blue eyes were untrustworthy. One often hears people say: 'Naturally she is bad-tempered. Hasn't she got red hair?' I am indebted to the entertaining column 'This England', in the *New Statesman and Nation*, for the following example: 'Red-haired people are poor at history, according to an Oxford History Examiner.' (I hasten to add that, so far as I know, the *Yorkshire Evening Post*, from which the statement is taken, is responsible for the attribution of this odd view to an Oxford History Examiner.) I am not personally prepared to admit that red-haired people are poor at history, since one of the most brilliant professors of history I have known had dark-red hair. Moreover, so many false generalizations have been made about red-haired people that I have become sceptical about their accuracy. Again, I have frequently heard it said that people with receding chins are weak. This is a belief encouraged by Mr P. G. Wodehouse's hero, Bertie Wooster, who has won such fame as to be described in a newspaper as 'the opisthognathous hero'.

Now it may not be false to say that there is some connexion between *red hair* and *hot temper*, or between *being chinless* and *being weak*, although it may be false to maintain that *all* red-haired people are hot-tempered, and that *all* chinless people are weak. The truth may be (to confine ourselves to the last example) that chinless people have a tendency to be weak. This is equivalent to saying that in proportion to the total number of chinless people compared with those who have not receding chins, we shall find a greater number who are weak. We have indeed to consider the connexion between four classes, namely, (1) those who are both chinless and weak; (2) those who are chinless and not weak; (3) those who are weak but not chinless; (4) those who are neither chinless nor weak.

Let us suppose that we urgently desire to find out whether there is a risk that a chinless person will be weak. This, in fact, is not an absurd proposal; I have heard a headmistress of a school discussing the risk of appointing a candidate to a vacant post because she had a decidedly receding chin. The question we have to consider is whether there is any reasonable method of testing the suggestion that chinless people are weak. The proper method to use is the statistical method of association. In this chapter I shall indicate only very briefly the correct procedure.

We shall assume that we are able to study a random selection of one thousand people. We shall further assume that we have some means of ascertaining with regard to each of these people into which of the four possible classes he, or she, falls. Let us further suppose that we have divided the 1,000 people into two groups: (i) 200 who were chinless, (ii) 800 who were not chinless. Let us next suppose that we divided class (i) into those who were and those who were not weak, and proceeded to make the same sub-division in class (ii). We will suppose that the results were as follows:

(a) Chinless and weak 50
(b) Chinless and not weak 150
(c) Not chinless and weak 100
(d) Not chinless and not weak 700

We have now all the data we require for answering the question whether a chinless person is more likely to be weak than someone who is not chinless.

If you examine the above table, you will see there are twice as many people who are weak and not chinless as there are people who are weak and chinless. It does not follow that it is not more likely for a chinless person to be weak than one who is not chinless, since there are a greater number of people who are not chinless than of those who are chinless. The result of the investigation might be summed up in this way: the proportion of weak people among the chinless is greater than that of weak people among those who are not chinless. We may therefore safely assert that there is a tendency for chinless people to be weak. This is a moderate statement, but it is not necessarily an indefinite statement. Assuming the figures given to be correct (they are, in fact, chosen merely for the sake of illustration) we could say quite precisely how great is the tendency for chinless people to be also weak. We are not then confined to saying either *All chinless people are weak* or *Some chinless people are weak*. We find that there is a statement of a totally different form from either of these, namely, the statement *A tends to be* B. This is a form of statement that is peculiarly appropriate in the discussion of topics concerned with politics, psychology, economics and sociology. It is to be regretted that this form is so rarely used in everyday discussion. No doubt the reason for this is partly to be found in the difficulties involved in providing evidence sufficient to enable us to state precisely how great the tendency is. Some of these difficulties will be considered in the next chapter. I think that one reason why we so seldom say that two characteristics *tend* to be associated is that we do not really want to be moderate.

NOTES

1 *The Conquest of Happiness*, p. 84.
2 *Op. cit.*, pp. x–xi. (This book was published in 1911.)
3 *Op. cit.*, p. 81.
4 This name has not much significance apart from the technical vocabulary of traditional logic. To distribute a term is to take it in its whole extent, i.e. to refer to every member of the class for which the term stands.
5 See Chapter 2, p. 22.
6 I owe these examples to Mr Rex Knight.

11

ON BEING MISLED BY HALF, AND OTHER FRACTIONS

The discussion at the end of the last chapter should have shown us that, even if we knew, for instance, that 90 out of every 100 bus drivers have gastritis some time between the ages of thirty and forty, nevertheless we should not be justified in concluding that there is any special connexion between driving a bus and having gastritis, *provided that that was all that we knew*. We should require further information with regard to the incidence of gastritis, between the ages of thirty and forty, in men who are not bus drivers. In selecting samples of this latter class we should be wise to take men engaged in somewhat similar occupations, say lorry drivers, and others engaged in quite different occupations, say

DOI: 10.4324/b22927-11

Members of Parliament, teachers and solicitors, and also others of no definite occupation at all, say unemployed men and the 'idle rich'. This procedure commends itself to plain common sense; it is also good logic. If it were found that among those men who are not bus drivers the proportion of those who did not have gastritis was lower than in the class of bus drivers, then it would be reasonable to conclude that there was a special connexion between the conditions involved in driving a bus and having gastritis. This would not mean that *all* bus drivers have gastritis; it would mean that bus drivers *tend* to have gastritis. The point of introducing the brief discussion, in the last chapter, of a similar problem was to emphasize the fundamental difference of form between the statement *A tends to be* B as compared both with *All A is* B and *Some A is* B. By saying that the difference of form is fundamental I am saying that 'A tends to be B' gives us information of a different kind both from 'All A is B' and from 'Some A is B'. If we say 'A tends to be B' we are providing more information than if we were to say 'Some A is B', although the former statement entails the latter. Again, 'A tends to be B' is not equivalent to 'All A is B'. If we use our words carefully, then, to say 'A tends to be B' means 'Although some A's are not B and some non-A's are B, yet there is a larger proportion of A's that are B as compared with the proportion of non-A's that are B'. A little reflection will, I hope, convince anyone that this sort of information is useful and is often the only kind of information we can obtain about the association of characteristics with regard to matters that are of interest and importance in human affairs. Very few statements that are both true and relevant to our ordinary purposes can be stated in the form *All A is* B, when 'A' stands for such variable things as human beings, or forms of Government, or kinds of trades, or kinds of punishment – to select a few examples.

When we speak of an occupational disease we are saying that there is a tendency for persons engaged in the given occupation to develop that disease. Such a discovery should lead us to investigate the conditions upon which the disease is causally consequent. It might be found that these conditions could be so altered as to eliminate the tendency, or at least to lessen it, without withdrawing people altogether from that occupation. It is hardly necessary to elaborate examples of cases in which we need to find out whether two characteristics are connected in a special way or are merely fortuitously conjoined, whilst, owing to the fact that these characteristics cannot be isolated from a medley of circumstances, we are unable directly to study their connexion. This was the case with regard to the problem raised by the prevalence of gastritis among bus drivers. In this problem we were confronted with a complex state of affairs and were uncertain whether these men would be as likely to have gastritis if they had not followed the occupation of driving a bus. To deal with problems of such a kind it is necessary to use statistical methods. In problems of this kind we can neither observe all possible cases nor can we experiment. In order to perform an experiment, the experimenter must be able to so control the relevant conditions that he can vary a single factor at a time. When this cannot be done, the effects of changes in one factor are upset, so far as our observations are concerned, by the effects of various other changes. Statistical methods are devised to enable us to deal effectively with such a multiplicity of causes. There is, indeed, no other means of unravelling them.

It does not lie within the scope of this book to expound the nature of statistical investigations in any detail, still less to discuss the technique of statistical methods. We are concerned wholly with some of the difficulties involved both in the statement and in the interpretation of the results of statistical methods. Much ineffective thinking arises from a failure to recognize that certain precautions must be observed if we are to draw correct conclusions from statistical statements, and if we are to avoid being misled by the way in which statistical results are often presented.

One of the obstacles to thinking effectively is our failure at times to recognize that our conclusion is based upon incomplete data and that we ought to have used an elementary form of statistical method. Such was the problem, touched upon in the last chapter, of the tendency of chinless people to be weak. We are tempted to generalize from a single instance, or a few instances, in which A is observed to be B, to the rash conclusion that A is always B. We forget to take any notice of negative instances, and thus lay ourselves open to being contradicted by a single instance of an A that is not B. Yet, as we have seen, although there are A's that are not B, we need not be content with the weak statement 'Some A's are B and some A's are not B'. There may be a tendency for A to be B. It will be remembered that to establish this contention we must take account of four classes. Using the letters, A, B, these classes can be presented as follows: AB; A non-B; non-A B; non-A non-B. If the proportion of A's among the B's is the same as the proportion of A's among the non-B's, then the two classes are said to be independent. In that case there is no tendency for A's to be B or not to be B. So far as I know there is no tendency for blue-eyed people to be sweet-tempered, or the reverse. If this were so, then we should say that there is no correlation between having blue eyes and being sweet-tempered. I have heard it said that naval men tend to be blue-eyed. I suspect that this belief is born of the association between naval men and the blue sea, and that it is fostered by fiction. If, however, this belief were correct, then we should say that there is some degree of positive correlation between being in the navy and having blue eyes. The

association of two characteristics may vary between perfect correlation and complete absence of correlation, i.e. independence.

There is always a danger of committing a fallacy when we fail
to take account of the four classes AB, A non-B, non-A B, non-A
non-B. The following provides an instance:

> Vaccination does not prevent smallpox or render it milder if con-
> tracted. More young children die from vaccination than from
> smallpox, according to the Registrar-General's returns.
>
> (*Peace News*, April 23rd, 1938.)[1]

Let it be granted that more children die from vaccination than
from smallpox. This does not establish the conclusion stated
above, since more children are vaccinated than are exposed to
infection from or actually develop, smallpox. The writer of the
above passage has failed to take into account those who have
not been vaccinated and have had smallpox and have died, in
relation to those who have been vaccinated and have been exposed to infection from smallpox and yet have not developed
that disease.

It is the purpose of statistical investigations to enable us to
discover and to state connexions between groups of characteristics, or – which comes to the same thing – the interdepend-
ence of classes of individuals. Vital statistics are concerned with
the comparison of the birth-rate, death-rate, etc., during one
period with the birth-rate, death-rate, etc., during some other
period, or in different localities. Data are collected with regard
to the number of accidents in some industrial occupations and
the amount of fatigue involved in this occupation in order to
ascertain the connexion, if any, between them. To express these
results we use the convenient language of *averages*.

I assume that everyone is familiar with usages of the word 'average', but not everyone is aware that there are different sorts of averages used by statisticians. Which sort is used depends upon the type of the data and the purpose for which the statistics are to be used. The most familiar is the arithmetic mean average. Suppose, for instance, that a candidate in an examination is told that he has obtained 60 per cent of the marks. How is he to know whether that is a good mark or not? There is considerable variation in the marks given by different examiners and by the same examiners in different examinations. If the candidate were told that 60 per cent is 'well above the average', he will probably be content. Here the average would probably be the arithmetic mean. It is obtained by adding together the marks of all the candidates and dividing the total thus obtained by the number of candidates. Thus an average is a single number representing a set of numbers; it may be regarded as expressing the central tendency of the set. The arithmetic mean may be very misleading, since it does not supply any information with regard to the way in which the items are dispersed; they may be clustered together round the centre or be widely dispersed, or evenly distributed from the lowest mark to the highest mark. If we want to compare two different occupational groups with respect to the average income attainable in these groups, the arithmetic mean may be very misleading. Suppose that we wish to compare the salaries obtained by a set of teachers with the salaries obtained by a set of employees in Egohill's Stores. Let us suppose that we select twenty instances from each set; I will call the first set A and the second set B. It is found (I am supposing) that in set A eight individuals have a salary of £300 per annum, three have £325, four have £350, two have £400, one has £425 and two have £500. The average income of this set is £350. It is found that in set B, two have a salary of £150 per annum, four have £200, four have £250, four have £250, two have £300, one has £350, one has £400, one has £450, one has £500, one has £600, two have £800, and one has £1,000. The average income of this set is £380. But although the average income of set B is higher than that of set A, it would be a mistake to conclude that there is a greater tendency for people in set B to have larger incomes than those in set A. On the contrary, ten individuals in set B have lower incomes than any individual in set A; that is, half the members of set B have less than any member of set A. The fact that the 'joint incomes' of members of set B amount to £7,600, whilst the 'joint incomes' of members of set A amount to £7,000, is no recommendation to an individual member of set B, who has very little chance of rising above the amount of salary received by half the members. The much larger incomes at the higher end 'pull up' the average. But the incomes are not jointly possessed, so that the thought that some individuals are getting much larger incomes than most of those in set A is not likely to be consoling. Thus, if we use the arithmetic mean to compute the average income of the inhabitants of the United Kingdom, we are liable to get a very false impression, since the amount of wealth is very unevenly distributed, owing to the fact that there are millionaires at one extreme, and people without any income at the other extreme, whilst the majority have an income of less than £250 per annum. We should find it more useful in this case to use the sort of average that is called the 'mode'. The mode is the item in the group that occurs most frequently. For this reason the mode is often regarded as the *typical* representative of the group. When the variation between the extremes (which is called 'the range of distribution') is considerable, then the mode represents the group better than the arithmetic mean does, since the mode indicates the largest sub-group in the whole group; it thus indicates what is most likely to be the case. It is not affected by being pulled up, or pulled down, by extremes on one side or the other, as the arithmetic mean is. This characteristic of the mode is sometimes very useful. For instance, if we wish to determine the nature of a very large collection from which we have taken fair samples, then the mode is a useful sort of average to use just because it is not affected by wide divergencies at the extremes. On the other hand, this may be a defect for some purposes, since several items could be eliminated without affecting the mode. Another sort of average is the *median*. This is the middle term of a series of items when the items have been arranged in order of magnitude. In a series containing an odd number of terms, there must be a median in the set, and the median will be that term which has as many terms below it as there are terms above it. If there are an even number of terms, then the median is the arithmetic mean of the two terms in the middle of the series.

I have attempted to give only a very elementary and sketchy account of averages. A full discussion of averages and of statistical methods can be found in many textbooks. My concern is with certain difficulties, often unsuspected, which ordinary readers of newspapers may encounter. We may notice first, that the arithmetic mean does not give us information about any *one individual* of the group. It may be that no individual exactly fits the mean; even if it did, the statement of the mean would not be a statement about that individual; an average represents *group* characteristics. Thus, for example, if we know that a cricketer's batting average is 50, we must not conclude that there is any occasion at all when he makes exactly fifty runs. On the contrary, he may be a nervous man, who will get out in the first over or so, but, if he 'gets his eye in', may be safe to score a hundred.

Another danger is to be found in trying to be more precise than the facts warrant. For example, a student may be asked to state the number of hours he has worked each day for a week. He may give the numbers, 8, 7, 7, 5, 6, 8, 7. The arithmetic mean is $6\frac{6}{7}$ hours. This might be expressed in decimal form as 6.8571. The arithmetical work is correct, but it would not be safe to conclude that the expression is accurate. The student provided the data in 'round numbers', i.e. an exact number of hours. Thus he may have said '7 hours' when he had actually worked for 6 hours 52 minutes. This is a trivial example, but it serves to show the absurdity of relying upon exact numerical results unless the data, upon which the numbers were based, have been carefully observed with the same degree of precision. It is important not to allow ourselves to be misled by a fictitious precision. We too easily assume that we can take statistical results on trust, because we have confidence in the mathematical ability of the statisticians. But, as Professor A. N. Whitehead has said, 'There is no more common error than to assume that, because prolonged and accurate mathematical calculations have been made, the application of the result to some fact of nature is absolutely certain.'[2]

The following is perhaps an example of spurious accuracy: 'Between 1930 and 1935 the number of inhabitants of Japan proper increased from 64,450,005 to 69,254,148. Births exceeded deaths in 1935 by more than 1,000,000.'[3] One wonders whether the author drew the line accurately between those (if any) who were born at one minute to midnight on December 31st, 1930, and those born at one minute past midnight on December 31st, 1935. If not, it would be interesting to know how he obtained the '5' in the unit place. Averages for population statistics are not of much value unless the inquiry is carried over a considerable number of years. Common sense shows us that we are not justified in asserting that the birth-rate of a country is declining if our investigation has been limited, say, to three or four years. There may have been special, non-recurrent causes, operating to produce a decline during the selected period. Common sense – which is, unfortunately, too rare – suggests the rule that an average is more reliable in proportion as the number of observations upon which it is based is greater. Further, given an average based upon a certain number of observations, then the average is more reliable, for the purposes of inference, in proportion as the data observed are not widely dispersed at the extremes. It must be borne in mind that an 'average' is 'a measure of variation between extremes'. It may be regarded as a representative number.

Although, I believe, most people who have not studied the subject would say that 'average' means 'the arithmetic mean', I think that in popular speech 'the average man' must be taken as meaning 'the *mode*' – or 'model man', by which is presumably meant the 'typical' man. This must, I think, be the sense in which Bertrand Russell uses the word in his statement about 'average women', which we discussed in the last chapter. No doubt the 'typical woman' (if there be one) is the woman having those characteristics that are most often associated with women. This explanation does, I assume, fit Russell's usage. Possibly, however, he did not mean to say anything so precise. As a character in *Punch* once remarked: 'It is my belief there ain't more than one average woman in fifty.' When the divergences between the extremes are great, it is sometimes difficult for comparatively uneducated people to realize that nevertheless there is *an average*. It is sometimes difficult for all of us, except professional statisticians, to bear in mind exactly what, and sometimes how little, information we are given in terms of averages, or, generally, in the statement of statistical results.

Most people know that important conclusions are sometimes drawn from the statistical results obtained from the data derived from answers to questionnaires. This method was used in the famous Peace Ballot of 1935, and a few years previously in an investigation, undertaken by two London newspapers, to ascertain whether religious belief was on the decline. It should be obvious that no very reliable information could be obtained in this manner. The questions were mainly supposed to be answered by an unqualified 'Yes' or 'No'. It is almost impossible to frame questions on such topics in so precise a manner as to permit of this simple answer. Further, only a certain type of people would be likely to answer these questions; others might refuse to do so either because this method was distasteful to them, or from laziness, or from preoccupation with other concerns. Under these circumstances it is extremely difficult to delimit the field of investigation. This, however, is the first essential of a correct use of statistical methods. So much depends upon the precise way in which each question is framed, the ground covered in these questions, and the type of people whose replies constitute the data, that, in my opinion, very little reliance can be placed upon the questionnaire method, especially when conducted through the medium of a newspaper or by personal canvassing. In order to be of use the questionnaire method must be employed only under conditions subject to some measure of control by the investigator.

I will give an illustration taken from Dame Millicent Fawcett's *Woman's Suffrage*,[4] published in 1912. She states that stress has been laid by the Anti-Suffrage League in England upon the number of petitions and protests obtained from women municipal voters declaring their antagonism to women's suffrage in Parliamentary elections. But she points out that the results obtained when the Suffragists 'conduct a canvass of the same people on the same subject is entirely different' from that obtained by the Anti-Suffragists. To support this statement she quotes 'the canvass of women municipal electors in Reading made respectively by the Suffragists in 1909 and Anti-Suffragists in 1911.' The results were as follows:

Suffragists in 1909:

In favour	1,047
Against	60
Did not answer and neutral	467

Anti-Suffragists in 1911:

In favour	166
Against	1,133
Did not answer and neutral	401

Dame Millicent concludes: 'With such disparity as this between the two returns, no conclusion can possibly be drawn from either without further investigation of the methods pursued.'

A mistake of a different kind is made sometimes in speaking of the percentage of a group without specifying the numbers contained in the group. If, for instance, a teacher claims that a hundred per cent of his pupils have been successful in passing an examination, whereas a rival teacher has only had sixty per cent successes, we may be impressed. We should, however, revise our opinion if we discovered that the first teacher had prepared only one pupil whilst the second had prepared ten pupils. Unlettered people sometimes fall into amusing mistakes in dealing with percentages, of which the following story is a grotesquely extreme example. The *Manchester Guardian Weekly* (May 27th, 1938) quotes, from a French paper, an account of the experiences of a French traveller in Scotland. He concludes with 'the typically Scotch story':

> The captain of a little paddle-steamer was selling postcards. 'Tuppence', he said. 'I am content with only a very small profit of 1 per cent. You see, I buy it for one penny and sell it for two.'

I do not vouch for the truth of this story, but it has a point in connexion with this chapter.

An opposite mistake was made by the schoolboy who boasted that he had missed his train for school only once, whereas the boy next door had missed it five times. The first schoolboy had been going to school for one term only, but the other boy had been attending school for two years.

Great care is needed not to be misled by pictorial presentations of the comparison of figures. I have before me such a picture, published in a London newspaper (*Evening Standard*, March 28th, 1938). The picture is designed to present the comparative amount (1) of goods imported by Britain from Russia; (2) of goods re-exported from Britain to Russia; and (3) British goods imported by Russia. The amount in pounds is given for the three cases, namely: (1) £29,096,536; (2) £16,432,557; (3) £3,083,025. The picture is headed: '*Ten to one against.*' It must be admitted that a pictorial presentation helps us to grasp the comparison between the amounts. This picture gives a flat-drawn diagram of three ships, each labelled with the appropriate sum. The ship, in each case, is very broad in proportion to its height, somewhat in the fashion of the *Europa* type of ship; the hull is in heavy black. Now, the height alone is relevant for presenting the comparison between the three amounts. The eye of the spectator must inevitably take note of the area as well as the height.

Unless he is on his guard, he will assume that the *whole* of each figure is relevant to the comparison. The height of the tallest ship (presenting the amount of Russian goods imported by Great Britain) is 66 millimetres: that of the smallest ship is 6 millimetres. This is good enough for a rough comparison between the amounts given in pounds beside each ship, viz. £29,096,536 for the largest, and £3,083,025 for the smallest ship. The spectator, however, who does not pay careful attention to the figures will be influenced by the area, and possibly, if interested in ships, by the volume. The resulting impression would be somewhat as follows:

	Smallest Ship	*Largest Ship*
Height	*6 mm.*	*66 mm.*
Area	$\propto 6^2$	$\propto 66^2$
Volume	$\propto 6^3$	$\propto 66^3$

Any reader of the newspaper glancing at the ships will probably have an implicit impression of 100 times the difference from the areas, and if he happens to be thinking of the carrying capacity of the ships, his impression will be that the smallest ship is 1,000 times smaller than the largest, instead of 10 times. It is true that he is given the actual sums involved, but presumably the picture is to aid him to grasp the relation between these sums. It fails signally to do so, suggesting, in the case of the area, an exaggeration of 100 times, and in the case of the volume, an exaggeration of 1,000 times.[5] This is a very unskilful pictorial presentation of comparative numerical data. Or, is it, perhaps, *too* skilful?

ADDENDUM

Note to pages 155-156: Since the above was written the *News Chronicle* has begun to publish the results of the British Institute of Public Opinion, which aims at finding out 'what the people of England think'. The method used is that of the questionnaire. So far as I have been able to judge, the questions set are so framed as to admit of precise answers. A sample in proportion to the whole population is taken. Since accuracy in the results depends rather upon proper cross-sectioning than upon the number of items considered, care is taken to make the sample properly representative. It is known that accuracy to within 3 per cent can be secured with a random sample of 2,500.

The British Institute has no connexion with the *News Chronicle* except with regard to the framing of questions and the subsequent publication of the results. (See *News Chronicle*, October 15th, October 28th, 1938.)

NOTES

1   I am indebted to Susan Miles for this example.
2   *Introduction to Mathematics, p. 27.*
3   W. H. Chamberlain: *Japan over Asia*, p. 21.
4   Millicent Fawcett: *Woman's Suffrage*, pp. 51–52.
5   I am indebted to Mr A. F. Dawn for this illustration.

12

SLIPPING AWAY FROM THE POINT

There are so many ways of being slipshod in our thinking that it would be impossible for us to attempt to examine them all. Nor is it possible to discuss in an orderly manner the mistakes into which we are prone to fall in our efforts to think to some definite purpose. These failures are evidence of disorder in our thinking; they cannot be rigorously isolated nor classified in a neat logical manner. There are many ways of being wrong, but only one way of being right. To think effectively involves knowledge of the topic, dispassionateness in weighing the evidence, ability to see clearly what follows from the premisses, readiness to reconsider the premisses if necessary, and, in short, courage

DOI: 10.4324/b22927-12

to follow the argument 'to the bitter end', if the end be indeed bitter. Some of our failures are due to causes we have already noticed – our prejudices which lead us to distort the evidence, our keeping our minds in blinkers and thus closed against criticism and incapable of further reflection, our habit of using words repeated parrot-fashion, and our fear of being dragged from the shelter of comforting beliefs.

In this chapter we are concerned with certain recurrent mistakes in reasoning which, just because they are very common, have been singled out by logicians and labelled with more or less appropriate names. The word 'fallacy' has unfortunately often been used in different senses. It is used sometimes as a synonym for 'error of fact', as in the statement: 'It is a fallacy to suppose that aeroplanes can be built by mass-production.' This is, in my opinion, a plainly erroneous use of the word. The speaker meant that aeroplanes cannot, in fact, be produced by methods suitable to the production of, say, motor-cars. I shall assume without further discussion that the speaker, in using 'fallacy' in this sense, was simply showing his ignorance of the correct usage of the word. There remains to be noticed an ambiguity that is more important for our present purpose. If we say: 'He is guilty of a fallacy', we sometimes mean to imply that he is guilty of a deception. The *Shorter Oxford English Dictionary* gives as a meaning of 'fallacy', now obsolete, 'deception', 'trickery'. This obsolete meaning does, I think, influence our modern usage. It would certainly be an advantage if we recognized that to accuse a person of having committed a fallacy is not to accuse him of intent to deceive. A fallacy is a violation of a logical principle; 'to fall into a fallacy' is to slip into 'an unsound form of argument', that is, to make a mistake in *reasoning*, not in what is *reasoned about*. If we mistakenly suppose that we have premisses adequate to establish our conclusion, then we are reasoning illogically and thus committing a fallacy.

If we think of a fallacy as a deception, we are too likely to take it for granted that we need to be cautious in looking out for fallacies only when other people are arguing with us. We come to suppose that a fallacy is a trick and, thus, as involving deliberate dishonesty. Thinking along these lines, we are apt to assume that where there is no dispute, and so no disputant, there is no danger of fallacies, so that honesty of intention will suffice to keep our reasoning sound. This is a profound mistake. You and I, engaged in solitary meditation, have great need to be on our guard against drawing a conclusion that does not follow from our premisses. In speaking of 'solitary meditation', I am thinking of myself (or you) as labouring to elicit from what is already known some conclusion that will be useful for the purpose that initiated the meditation. In such cases we are not seeking for any argument, good or bad, to establish a conclusion at all costs. We are not willing to accept the cost of having unsound beliefs. On the contrary, when we are thus meditating in solitude we are genuine investigators in search of true answers to questions prompted by our needs, whether these needs be intellectual or practical. It is not enough to be honest; we need also to be intelligent; it is not even enough to be intelligent; we need also to be well informed.

This last consideration – the need to possess sufficient information about the topic – must be borne in mind. Logicians have been wont to regard Logic as the art of thinking. One of the most famous works on Logic, *The Port-Royal Logic* (published in Paris in 1662), had for its sub-title 'The Art of Thinking'. Consistently enough, its opening sentence runs as follows: 'Logic is the art of directing reason aright, in obtaining the knowledge of things, for the instruction both of ourselves and others.' The authors of a recently published work on Logic state, 'The goal of logic in a word is to show how true propositions can be distinguished from those that are false. The logician is also charged with the task of showing how the truth or falsity of some propositions can be inferred from the truth or falsity of other propositions.'[1] The first statement makes an amazing claim. It is not from studying logic that we can find out whether dodos are extinct, whether there are any unicorns, whether water expands or contracts as it freezes, whether the best means of securing peace is to prepare for war, whether capital punishment is needed for the protection of society. The task with which these authors assert that the logician is *also* charged, is indeed, the only task that the logician can perform. Given that certain propositions are known to be true or are known to be false, then, under certain conditions, the logician can determine whether certain *other* propositions are true or are false. But the logician cannot, in his capacity as a logician, decide whether these propositions are, or are not, true. The logician says: *If such and such propositions are true, then such and such a conclusion is true;* or he says: *If such and such propositions are true, then such and such a conclusion is probably true, or may be asserted with such and such a degree of probability.* That is to say that the logician is concerned with the validity of the argument. We have already seen that an argument is valid provided that the relation between the premisses and the conclusion is such that the premisses cannot be true and the conclusion false.[2] This relation is a formal relation. Hence, the validity of an argument is independent of the truth or falsity of the premisses. Nevertheless, given (i) that the premisses are true, (ii) that the argument is formally valid, then the conclusion is necessarily true. The logician is concerned with studying the various kinds of formal relations that suffice to secure the validity of an argument. We have already seen that the special form of argument, called a syllogism, is familiar to us all. People untrained in logic can detect a formal fallacy in a syllogistic argument once the argument is clearly set out. But a fallacious argument that would not mislead so intelligent a child as Emily,[3] provided that the argument is stated barely, in a few sentences, may mislead all of us when stated at length in a long book, or when wrapped up with much verbiage, or when combined with appeals to our passionate interests. Some practice in detecting these fallacious modes of reasoning may enable us the more easily to notice them when we are not actively engaged in fallacy hunting. A knowledge of the formal conditions of valid arguments thus has its uses, but it would be a profound mistake to conclude that a knowledge of these conditions alone would suffice to guard us from error.

In this book no attempt is made to deal with all the modes of argument the fallacies in which would be obvious to anyone were the arguments to be set out clearly and at length. The reader will find full discussions in many text-books of logic. Here we shall consider a few fallacious forms of arguing that are of very common occurrence. We have already (in Chapter 10) noticed that a syllogism may be fallacious owing to the fact that the middle term is undistributed, so that there is no guarantee that the other two terms are connected through the relation they bear respectively to the third term. There is an allied fallacy, of which the following argument provides an example:

> 'Since he said that he would go to Paris if he won a prize in the sweepstake, I infer that he did win a prize, for he has gone to Paris.'

It is convenient, but not in the least logically necessary, to restate this argument in a shape that makes its form evident at a glance:

'If he won a prize in the sweepstake, he would go to Paris.
'He has gone to Paris.
'Therefore, he won a prize in the sweepstake.'

This argument is fallacious; he might have had a legacy, or been sent to Paris on business, or he might have grown tired of waiting to win a prize in a sweepstake and gone to Paris whether he could afford it or not. The fallacy committed in this argument is known as 'the fallacy of the Consequent'. This name is due to the fact that the first premiss is a combination of two statements connected by the logical conjunction If … then …. The If-statement is called the Antecedent, the then-statement is called the Consequent. (In popular speech the word 'then' is, as above, often omitted, but it is understood to be implied in the form of the whole statement.) It hardly needs to be emphasized that it is fallacious to conclude, from the affirmation that the consequent is true, that the antecedent can likewise be asserted to be true. The same consequent may have many different antecedents. It may be true that, if there are too many cooks, then the broth will be spoilt; it is also true that a single inefficient cook may spoil the broth. Again, it is true that if a man takes cyanide of potassium, he will be poisoned; but from the fact that he is poisoned we cannot infer that he has taken cyanide of potassium. By using P to stand for the antecedent, and Q for the consequent, of a statement, we can represent the bare form of this fallacious mode of argument as follows:

If P, then Q,
Q,
Therefore, P.

It is easy to see the resemblance between the fallacy of affirming the consequent and the fallacy of undistributed middle. For example, the argument

All weak people are sometimes tempted to lie; and
He is sometimes tempted to lie,
Therefore, he is weak,

might have been stated in the form:

If a man is weak, he is sometimes tempted to lie,
This man is sometimes tempted to lie,
Therefore, this man is weak.

Either form of stating this argument reveals that it is fallacious owing to the fact that the conclusion goes beyond the evidence. A strong man may be tempted to lie in order to secure his ends, whereas a weak man may be tempted to lie because he is afraid, as well as for other reasons. Thus, *being weak* is a sufficient but not a *necessary* condition for *being tempted to lie*, provided that the premiss is in fact true. The point of our (supposed) argument was to establish that *this man is weak*. We have slipped away from the point if we bring no other evidence than that *weak people* have some characteristic which *this man* also has. Suppose, however, that we had asserted *Only weak people are tempted to lie* and also that *This man is tempted to lie*, then the premisses would justify the conclusion. I shall assume that we all know that it is not true that none but weak people are tempted to lie, so that the conclusion is not established as true, since one of the premisses is false. It may be true, but a false premiss cannot provide evidence of the truth of any conclusion based upon it.

I have purposely selected trivial examples, and have set out the arguments in full in order to reveal their fallacious form. Usually we state our arguments less fully, omitting a premiss that is tacitly assumed. Thus the above argument would (if used in ordinary conversation) assume some such form as 'He is weak, as is shown by his being tempted to lie'. The speaker may be assuming the premiss: 'All weak people are sometimes tempted to lie', in which case his argument is invalid; or, he may be assuming the false premiss, 'Only weak people are tempted to lie', in which case he has not established his point, since the premiss is untrue. We do not know of which sort of error he is guilty – a formal fallacy or an error in fact. But if I, the thinker, am trying to establish a conclusion, then by discovering a formal fallacy I may be led to ask whether I can establish as true a premiss that would remedy the invalidity.

From the affirmation of the antecedent we may validly infer the affirmation of the consequent. This is obvious to common sense, since the antecedent states a condition from which the consequent follows. We may exhibit this form by

If P, then Q,
P,
Therefore, Q.

After what has been said above, it is not difficult to see that from the denial of the consequent there follows the denial of the antecedent. That is, the form

If P, then Q,
Not Q,
Therefore, not P

is valid. To assert that if *wishes were horses, then beggars would ride*, but that *beggars do not ride*, justifies us in concluding that *wishes are not horses*. The speaker who says: 'If X does not win that match, I'll eat my hat', is emphatically asserting his belief that X will win the match, since he takes it for granted that his hearers will deny the consequent and thus deny the antecedent.

It should also be clear that from the denial of the antecedent it does not follow that the consequent can be denied. That is, the form:

If P, then Q,
Not P,
Therefore, not Q

is invalid. To assert that *if we prepare for war, then we shall preserve peace*, and that *we have not prepared for war* does not justify us in asserting that *we have not preserved peace*. To establish this conclusion we should have to maintain that *only if* we have prepared for war, shall we preserve peace. Whether this latter statement be true or not, it is not what was asserted as a premiss in the argument, which, as it is given, involves the 'fallacy of denying the antecedent'. I do not think it is quite so common a fallacy as that of affirming the consequent, but no doubt we all slip into it at times. You may have met an argument to this effect: 'If the employees of a business co-operate in its management, then the business will flourish. But since the employees in this business have had no share in its management, it is not surprising that it has not flourished.'

There are two fallacies into which we may slip from a failure to remember that what is true of the whole is not necessarily true of the parts, and conversely. Thus it is sometimes argued that if a given restriction is not beneficial to some sections of the community, it cannot be for the welfare of the community as a whole. This conclusion does not follow. An opposite mistake would be made if it were argued that, since the economic welfare of the country would be promoted by subsidizing *certain* industries, therefore it would be for the good of the country that *all* industries should be subsidized. Again this conclusion does not follow. It is possible that some gamblers may be influenced by fallacious reasoning of this kind; they may argue: 'Since it is not uncommon for large prizes to be won for small stakes, it is not unreasonable for me to expect to have such a prize.' This conclusion would follow only if the premiss asserted that it is not uncommon for a *given* individual to win a large prize for a small stake. But this is not the premiss which is asserted. These fallacies are, I believe, of frequent occurrence, though often in disguised forms. Some listener to the 'Week's Good Cause' might leave himself in poverty if he sent a donation (large in proportion to his income) every week, although he might have afforded to do so a few times; another listener might be too careful of his pence if he argued that he could not afford to contribute to *any* 'good cause' because there are so many of them.

We may slip away from the point because we forget that circumstances alter cases. The fallacy of special pleading (considered in Chapter 4) might be considered as arising out of a false claim that circumstances have altered the case; the falsity consists in the claim that the circumstances are relevantly different, whereas, in fact, the differences are not relevant. Whenever there are relevant special circumstances which we have failed to take into account, then our reasoning is necessarily fallacious. We may commit the fallacy of arguing from a specially qualified case to a conclusion that ignores the qualification. Thus, suppose it were agreed that to kill a man for private gain is wrong, we should commit this fallacy if we thereby concluded that to kill a man in warfare is wrong. That there is a relevant difference between these two cases is recognized in our common usage of words. We say that the first case constitutes 'murder', i.e. 'wrongful killing', whereas the second does not. Hence, to assert that 'killing an enemy in warfare is murder' is not to utter a tautology. There would, however, be no fallacy if we were to argue that killing enemies in warfare *ought* to be regarded as just as wrongful as killing murderously. This contention may be (and in my opinion is) mistaken; its point lies in the recognition that the two cases are different, although both are to be condemned. Accordingly the *ought* in the above statement is not the logical *ought*; the contention is a statement involving a moral judgment.

We should fall into a fallacy, that may be regarded as the converse of the above, if we were to argue from an unqualified statement to a statement about a special case. This fallacy is sometimes committed by writers on social science, who argue, for example, that, since democratic institutions are the best, they must work well in India.

The last five forms of fallacy we have been considering are not always easily distinguishable. I doubt whether we can draw a sharp line between the various ways in which we ignore relevant differences between whole and part or between essential and non-essential characteristics. My failure to apply a general rule to my own case may be due to my failure to see that I am not justified in regarding my own case as 'privileged': I may honestly believe that there is something 'special in my case', even when there is not. We can guard against such mistakes only by remembering to look out for relevant differences. As we have seen, we may need to change 'I' into 'You'. No laying down of logical rules will enable us to derive any criteria for determining when circumstances do alter cases and when they do not. For this purpose we need to be well informed about the facts of the case. To claim that a study of logic would either provide us with this information or would enable us to dispense with it is manifestly absurd. If we accepted the first of these alternatives, we should be committed to the assertion that logic includes both history and all the sciences. No one has ever made this claim – so far as I know. If we accepted the second alternative, we should fall into the absurdity of maintaining that it is possible for us to draw conclusions and assert them to be true without having knowledge of what it was that we were asserting.

From the two premisses

No hangalars are circular,
All mimetones are circular,

you could deduce: No mimetones are hangalars. But what is it that you know from this deduction? What are you asserting? You have never heard of hangalars and mimetones, since these have made an appearance in this book, never to be heard of again. I have invented these words (if so they may be called) in order to bring out the distinction between apprehending the validity (or invalidity) of a deductive form and drawing a true conclusion from true premisses that jointly entail that conclusion. The truth of a conclusion is not secured by validity of form. Whenever we use such words as 'therefore', 'and so', 'thus', 'accordingly', 'hence', we claim to assert the conclusion to be true whilst dropping the premisses from which we derived our knowledge of the conclusion. Certainly the following compound proposition is true: If no hangalars are circular and if all mimetones are circular, then no mimetones are hangalars. But this is not a true statement about hangalars and *mimetones*: it is a true statement about a form of implication. It is a single statement; there are no premisses and no conclusion. The separate sentences in it are combined in the If ... *then* ... form. We might just as well – and, for all other purposes, much better – have used letters, e.g. X, Y, Z, instead of combinations of letters that look not unlike English words.

The above remarks are apposite to the consideration of a most dangerous defect in our thinking – a defect that often leads us into slipping away from the point. This is the defect of using words ambiguously. A word is used ambiguously when the speaker (or writer) uses it first with one meaning, then with another meaning, without noticing the change in meaning. Words taken in isolation are not ambiguous. This, at least, is my opinion. Ambiguity arises from difference of usage; there is ambiguity only so far as the difference of usage is not noticed. Words are used in a context. The context may be a bodily gesture, a tone of voice, a frown or a smile. We can limit our discussion to the consideration of words used in the context of other words, that is, in sentences. A conversation does not consist of single sentences but of sentences more or less linked together by the topic of discussion. I say 'more or less' because our conversations are often desultory, or are interrupted by utterly irrelevant interjaculatory sentences. Always, however, there is a topic with reference to which the words used by the speakers are to be understood.

'They exchanged drivers.' Suppose that you heard this isolated remark made by one person to another on the top of an omnibus. You would not know whether the speakers were talking about golf-clubs or about motor-cars. Some logicians say that the word 'driver' is ambiguous. To dispute this involves a dispute about what the word 'word' means. However this dispute may be decided, I think we can all admit that there is no harmful ambiguity in the usage of the word 'driver'. In a seventeenth-century book we might find 'driver' used to refer to a certain kind of boat. The context would show us that it is so used; if we did not know what 'driver' in that context meant, we should have resort to a dictionary. I cannot believe that we should be left uncertain whether the writer was speaking of cab-men or of golf-clubs. Ambiguity is harmful when there is an un-noticed shift of meaning; it is not harmful when there is a clear change-over from one meaning to another or, if it be preferred, from one word to another. The difficulty arises from the fact that words used ambiguously are used with allied meanings. It is for this reason that we so easily fail to notice the shift in meaning and thus we fall into serious blunders.

In the context of discussions about the civil war now going on in Spain, is the word 'non-intervention' used ambiguously or not? It might well be argued that, in this context, 'non-intervention' is a question-beggar, since we should ordinarily understand it to mean 'not intervening at all', and thus, as the contradictory of 'intervening'. Whereas, so it may be contended, it has come to be used as equivalent to 'neutrality with regard to two bel-ligerents'. Those Members of Parliament who would like to se-cure the victory of the Republican forces seem to think that the Government's policy of 'non-intervention' is a policy of helping General Franco. Those who desire General Franco to win the victory seem to mean by 'non-intervention' what would more clearly be designated by 'neutrality'. This harmful ambiguity is well brought out in the exchange of letters between the Duchess of Atholl and the Prime Minister, published in The Times, April 29th, 1938. The Duchess of Atholl complained that the Non-In-tervention Committee's scheme of control had placed 'a terrible handicap' upon the Republican forces; she argued that it was not consistent with a policy of non-intervention to agree to the withdrawal of Italian troops only after the fighting is over. In her opinion (if I understand her statements correctly), the non-intervention policy of the Government has 'deprived a recognized Government of its right under international law to buy arms with which to defend its people against invaders assisting a military rebellion'. The Prime Minister replied that the 'policy of non-intervention was originally, and has since been continuously, applied by His Majesty's Government in an entirely impartial manner.' 'To non-intervene impartially' seems a curious combination of words. I shall not attempt to extract their precise meaning. Readers of the parliamentary debates on this controversial topic will easily discover that there is a tendency for the *word* 'non-intervention' to be used differently by different political parties, and that this difference in usage corresponds to a difference in their views with regard to what they consider is, and what ought to be, the attitude of the Government with regard to the Spanish Civil War. We saw in Chapter 4 that the plea for non-intervention may be urged by one political party when one of the opposed forces in Spain seems to be gaining the advantage, and by another political party when the position is reversed. Presumably the word 'non-intervention' is intended to be used in the same sense in both cases. If this be so, then it looks as if 'non-intervention' has come to be used as meaning 'intervening on the side that I support'. I do not suggest that these politicians have noticed that there has been a shift in the meaning of the word. On the contrary, I assume that they are able to believe themselves to be consistent only because they have not observed this change in sense. I am reminded of the suggestion that the verb 'to be impartial' should be conjugated as follows: 'I am impartial', 'you are obstinately prejudiced', 'he is pig-headedly convinced'.

To take another example. There is much discussion just now about the need for political and economic appeasement. The phrase 'to appease' is commonly used to mean 'to bring to peace'. I have no doubt that anyone, asked to define this word in isolation from a context, would give this definition. But as 'appeasement' is now being used in political circles, it seems to mean sometimes 'mollify X by giving him whatever he desires', and sometimes to mean 'establish friendly relations with the most powerful nations'. To seek to achieve what either of these two meanings suggests may possibly be a wise policy, but to use a word which does not commonly bear either of these interpretations is confusing to ordinary people. I find an apposite comment on this point, in *The Times*' report to-day (June 4th) of Colonel Wedgwood's speech in the debate on 'Economic Peace':

> Colonel Wedgwood said that the trade treaty being negotiated between U.S.A. and this country was a practical outcome of the method of the Van Zeeland report, and showed the world that two sensible peoples could tackle the appeasement problem and get us back a little in the direction of free trade. But let members clear their minds of words. Whom did they want to appease and at whose expense? If it was a vague attempt to appease the dictators, it would only lead to further demands. It was essential to establish international law and reliance on treaties.

This is a timely reminder that 'appease' needs a context: *someone* appeases *somebody*. The word 'appease' is likely to shift in meaning according to what is substituted for *someone* and for *somebody* respectively.

We have often been told 'to clear our minds of cant'. Wise advice, though hard to follow. We can hardly 'clear our minds of words'. All that we can do is to see that we understand clearly the words we use in our own thinking, and to try to convey to our hearers what precisely it is that we are using these words to convey. As Francis Bacon remarked: 'Men imagine that their minds have the command of language; but it often happens that language bears rule over their minds.'

I have chosen controversial examples of the danger of using words ambiguously, because I believe that it is of great importance for us to be constantly on guard against this danger. It is an insidious danger, not to be remedied by looking at a dictionary, but only by asking ourselves what exactly it is we are saying *in the given context*. This, I take it, is the point of Colonel Wedgwood's advice, however unfortunately he may have expressed himself. We easily slip away from the point by using language that begs the question. In Chapter 5 we considered some examples of question-begging words. We shall now consider how the use of such words depends upon an unnoticed ambiguity.

Suppose that two people A and B are discussing modern poets. A complains that there are no poets nowadays, or at least, only a very few. B says: 'What about Stephen Spender, W. H. Auden, T. S. Eliot, C. Day Lewis and Louis MacNeice?' A replies: 'Oh! well – most of those aren't poets at all. I don't mean people who are called, or who call themselves, "poets". I mean *true* poets'. 'But what', asks B, 'are "true poets"?' 'Well', replies A, 'true poets are those who write poems that are poems, and not the stuff that the so-called "modern poets" write at all.' This conversation is so much condensed that the fallacy is at once evident. A is arguing in a circle. He has accepted, without recognizing that he has done so, a definition of 'poets' which *excludes by definition* those about whom the discussion is supposed to be. We do not usually fall into this fallacy in so flagrant a manner; perhaps we never do so in our own thinking. Still, I believe that we do not always avoid vicious circles even when we are not engaged in the heat of controversy. I will take as a possible example the belief that suicide is a crime. This may be defended upon the ground that murder is a crime and that 'suicide' means 'self-murder'. If this were accepted as its meaning, then it would follow from the definition that suicide is a crime, provided that it be admitted (as I am here supposing to be the case) that *murder* is a crime. It is true that the *Shorter Oxford English Dictionary* gives 'self-murder' as a meaning of 'suicide'. Let us grant (as the White Knight in *Alice Through the Looking-Glass* might say) that that is what *suicide* has been called. The point remains that so to *call* it is to beg the question, since murder is essentially killing *someone else* whereas suicide is killing *one's own self*. If it be argued (as I conceive that it might fairly be) that I have myself begged the question by contending that 'murder is essentially killing someone else,' then I should reply that we have here a danger of confusing two essentially different actions by referring to them both by means of the same word. I suspect that suicide has been called 'self-murder' because it has been regarded as a sin of the same kind as murder, since both involve the wilful destruction of a human personality. It would conduce to clearness if we recognized the distinction I have made above. The way would then be open to discuss the question whether suicide should be regarded as a crime, independently of the question whether it be a sin or not. This is not an idle question. The House of Lords recently decided that 'on grounds of public policy a policy of insurance is not enforceable where the assured has committed suicide, for suicide is a crime, and no man, nor his estate, may profit by a crime.'[4] As the correspondent to *The Times*, from whose letter this quotation is taken, points out, the view that suicide is a crime is a relic 'of the old ecclesiastical law and of the times when the suicide's goods were forfeit to the Crown'. There may be good reasons for regarding suicide as a crime (although I do not personally think so), but these grounds cannot be rested upon the definition of 'suicide' as 'self-murder'.

A final example of the danger of begging the question by using words defined in an unusual way may be taken from another current controversy. In a discussion on Christianity and Communism by various authors, Dr Ernest Barker raises the question: 'But is Communism, in any real sense of the word, a faith?' He replies:

> Faith demands some affirmation of belief in things apprehended but invisible: it is a venture of spiritual courage, which leaves the pedestrian ground and takes to the wings of flight. The whole philosophy of Communism is resolutely opposed to faith. It is a philosophy of material causation; and its devotees are vowed to the study of material causes and the production of material effects.

To this Mr Hamilton Fyfe replied:

> Dr Ernest Barker limits unduly the meaning of 'faith' when he says 'the whole philosophy of Communism is opposed to faith,' and defines 'faith' as 'belief in the invisible'.
>
> Communists have faith in human nature, faith that Right will triumph over Might (though they do not leave Right unarmed), faith in the emergence of justice and comradeship from the welter of struggling and selfish cut-throat competitors, faith that equality of chances in life will give better results than the harsh and undeserved social distinctions of our present system.[5]

This discussion seems to me to bring out three points of importance. First, Dr Barker distinguishes between 'a real sense of the word' and, presumably, some unreal sense. This distinction is surely meaningless, or else a flagrant begging of the question in favour of some 'sense of the word' that suits one's own argument. This is a temptation to which we are all liable to succumb. Secondly, Mr Fyfe, in calling attention to Dr Barker's definition of 'faith', protests that its meaning is unduly limited if it be defined as 'belief in the invisible', but he at once goes on to maintain that the Communists have faith in what I, at least, should have supposed to be also 'the invisible'. Thirdly, we can detect in this argument a senseless controversy involving an ambiguity in the middle term of a syllogism. Dr Barker's argument may, I suggest, be formulated as follows:

'The philosophy of Communism is *resolutely opposed to faith*,
A doctrine that is *resolutely opposed to faith* must be condemned;
therefore, The philosophy of Communism must be condemned.'

The cogency of this argument depends upon freedom from ambiguity in the middle term (italicized in the argument). If the middle term is used in the same sense precisely in both premisses, then the argument is valid; if it is not so used, then the conclusion does not follow. If the claim that it is so used is based upon a distinction between 'faith' in any real sense of the word and 'faith' in some non-real sense, then the argument begs the question. In that case, the thinker has slipped away from his point. This is all the more to be regretted since Dr Barker is one of those opponents of Communism who sees that 'there is a soul of goodness in Communism', and believes that there is that in 'the Christian inheritance' which would enable us 'to lay hold on this soul of goodness.'

In the same volume we are provided, by Dean Inge, with an extreme example of the absurdity to which we may go if we attempt to settle controversial issues by resort to definition. 'Marx,' the Dean says, 'was not exactly a Communist, if we accept Sidgwick's definition.' To this Mr John Strachey replies:

> This is delightful. Marx, the founder of the world-wide Communist movement, is ruled out by Mr Sidgwick and Dean Inge. It is a little as if in a controversy on the nature of Christianity I adopted a definition of that religion which made it necessary for me to admit that its founder was 'not exactly' a Christian.

You may well be prepared to admit that Christ was not a 'Christian', but if so, you must state clearly what the word 'Christian' means. So with the contention that 'the founder of the world-wide Communist movement' was not a 'Communist'. The truth or falsity of these contentions cannot be established until we have clearly understood what the words we are using *mean*, and have succeeded in keeping steadily to this meaning. To do this is difficult, not only in the heat of controversy, but also when we are trying to think in the quiet solitude of our own study.

There are other fallacies dependent upon our imperfect apprehension of the meaning of words. I was told the other day by someone upon whose statements I can generally rely that there are people who like to listen to lectures, sermons, or speeches that they do not properly understand, that these people prefer a speaker who uses some words the meaning of which they do not know. I confess that I found it difficult to credit this statement. On reflection I am disposed to believe it. How else can we explain the willingness of an audience to listen to speeches full of words which, in the context, have no precise reference? We might say that the explanation is that the audience is polite. This, however, can hardly be the explanation, since, knowing what to expect, the same people listen again to the same speaker and are sometimes moved to enthusiastic agreement. The difficulty is to know with *what* there is agreement.

Consider the following extract from a speech made by Ramsay MacDonald on the problem of unemployment:

> Schemes must be devised, policies must be devised if it is humanly possible to take that section [i.e. those unemployed who are shortly to be reabsorbed into industry] and to regard them, not as wastrels, not as hopeless people, but as people for whom occupation must be provided somehow or other, and that occupation, although it may not be in the regular factory or in organized large-scale industrial groups, nevertheless will be quite as effective for themselves, mentally, morally, spiritually and physically, than, perhaps, if they were included in this enormous mechanism of humanity which is not always producing the best results, and which, to a very large extent, fails in producing the good results that so many of us expect to see from a higher civilization based upon national wealth.
>
> That is a problem that has got to be faced.[6]

A considerable amount of effort must be expended by the hearers of such a speech if they are to know what exactly is the problem that has to be faced. After reading and then rereading it I am not clear exactly what the problem is beyond the bare fact that there is some problem or other concerning the reabsorption of the unemployed.

An even more extreme case of using many words to say nothing at all is provided by one of Ramsay MacDonald's statements on the policy of the National Government. In 1934 he said:

> The modification of the past as quickly as possible to meet the circumstances of the future is the one policy which is going to bring us as a Government and as a nation up, up, and up, and on, on, and on.

Let us examine this second statement. We can, I think, extract from it the notion that, if the Government is to be brought 'up and up' and 'on and on', it must be prepared 'to meet the circumstances of the future'. But what is 'the one policy' that is to achieve this? Mr MacDonald said that it was 'the modification of the past as quickly as possible'. As it stands, this sentence is, I believe, nonsensical. The past cannot be modified. It may be objected that I am indulging in idle quibbling. I do not think so. I am anxious to admit that Ramsay MacDonald did not say what he meant to say. I will suppose that what he meant was: 'Present conditions, which have grown out of conditions that are now past, and which are not suited to what is likely to happen in the near future, must be so altered as to make them suitable'. I am not at all sure that this is what he did mean, but that is the only sense I can extract. It does not seem to say anything much worth the saying. An example or two of what sort of conditions and what sort of modifications he had in mind would surely help us to understand. As for the latter half of the statement – well, I suppose we may assume that 'up and up' and 'on and on' are used to indicate 'progress towards something worth attaining'.

It is not to my purpose to pursue further the meaning (if any) to be extracted from speeches like these. I wish only to call attention to the dangers we run if we allow ourselves to fall into the habit of supposing that something important has been said because some public person has made a grandiloquent speech. We should not be too modest. If what we hear *sounds* nonsense, then the fault may be ours. On the other hand, it may not. We must ask what is the 'cash value' of the sentences used. That is a convenient metaphor. The 'cash value' of a word is what it is used to refer to; this, in Chapter 5, I called its 'objective meaning'. A sentence that cannot be understood by the hearer as referring to an objective meaning is either strictly nonsensical or else merely an incitement to an objectless emotional attitude.[7] I hope it will be agreed that a speaker who sets out to state the policy of a Government – with regard, say, to the problem of unemployment – is professing to provide his hearers with information. His statement will be useless for this purpose unless he says, for example, that *such and such* are the conditions, *such and such* are the difficulties, *such and such* are the actions to be taken. Now the italicized words are used here, i.e. in my statements, for the sake of their indefiniteness. It is suitable for my present purpose to be indefinite. I am not concerned to lay down a policy of action. We should, however, expect Ramsay MacDonald to *specify* the conditions, the difficulties, and the actions to be taken. The conditions could be specified by giving a *sample* of the conditions that have to be taken into account. Similarly, a *sample* of the difficulties, and a *sample* of the sort of actions to be taken, could be provided. We should then know what *sort* of problem had to be faced and what *sort* of policy was being proposed. There are degrees of indefiniteness; we cannot expect absolutely definite information with regard to the policy of a Government. To admit this does not, however, entail the conclusion that '*nothing* can be said'. It seems to me that Ramsay MacDonald came, at times, very near to saying nothing. I suggest that the statement of his, quoted above, had no more meaning for him than for his hearers. This suggestion, I admit, may be mistaken.

We do certainly sometimes string words together which sound well enough, or which may convey some vague suggestions of unformulated ideals, but which say nothing at all. This is possible because, once we have learned the habit of using language, we can put words together in accordance with the rules of syntax, and feel ourselves to be talking sense. But when we are asked – or better still, ask ourselves – what we have been saying, we may not be able to reply. Consider this declaration, made at a critical moment, by a public man:

> I hope that we may all see and approach the light at the end of the tunnel which some are already able to point out to us. I myself see it somewhat indistinctly, and different directions are pointed out to us, all of which I hope will lead us where we wish to go. But I must admit for the moment that the way is not clear. We have not yet emerged from difficulties through which we have been passing.

It would be profitless to discuss such verbiage in detail. The main thought it arouses in my mind is that, if all the different directions pointed out to us may be hoped to lead us where we want to go, then we need not be worried as to which direction we should take. As I write this last sentence it occurs to me that perhaps that is the thought the speaker wishes to convey. But that is hardly likely. I think that we must admit that this and some other statements, quoted from Ramsay MacDonald's speeches, provide us with examples of the expansion of the minimum amount of thought into the maximum amount of words. We are the more likely to fall into this mistake when we are using abstract words and are thinking in terms of abstractions.

The chief danger of getting into a habit of thinking in abstractions is that we take the words to have meaning and yet do not know what it is these words stand for. This may seem incredible; it is in fact horribly true. I say that it is 'horribly true', since, for example, human individuals are prepared to die or be tortured and to kill or torture other individuals for the sake of liberty without knowing what 'liberty' means. To know what 'liberty' means is to know how 'having liberty' will make a difference to me and to you, whosoever I and you may be. It is to know in what ways I am free and in what ways I am hindered from being free, and to know wherein these ways differ from being unfree. Some people hate and fear Communism; others hate and fear Fascism; others again are ready to suffer and to inflict suffering in order to save (or to destroy) Democracy. 'Nations hate one another'. But a Nation is not the sort of thing that can hate; a Nation is not a person. Individually the men and women one meets in one's own country can be loved or hated; individually a Frenchman, a Russian, a Jew, a Japanese, etc., can be loved or hated. Most of us, I imagine, have many interests in common with individuals who are foreigners, i.e. members of some other nation. The interest of one individual may conflict with that of another. These are commonplaces. They are important commonplaces of which we need to be reminded when one nation confronts another nation with hostility. To illustrate the danger I am discussing, I will consider the last sentence: 'One nation confronts another nation with hostility.' We know what it is for one person to confront another person with hostility. But a nation is not a person, so that the word 'confronts' cannot be used in the same sense when the word 'nation' is the grammatical subject as it is when the words 'one person' are the grammatical subject. 'A nation' is a convenient expression for referring to a set of individuals standing in certain relations to one another. (This is not a definite statement, since I have not specified the relations; but to do so is not relevant to my purpose.) We fall into mistakes when we speak, and thus think of, a nation as a person.

'Nationalism is different from Internationalism.' This sounds a harmless remark. It does, indeed, say very little, but it is easy to slip from this into 'Nationalism is incompatible with Internationalism'; it is then easy to slip from this to the conclusion 'Anyone (i.e. some *one* definite but unspecified person) who loves his nation cannot accept Internationalism, i.e. cannot co-operate with these and those specifiable *individuals* in this, that, and the other country.' I believe that philosophers who have written about the philosophy of society have often bemused themselves with words. In this they have been followed (or preceded?) by statesmen, who set up the nation as an entity whose welfare can be secured, although not a single member of that nation is in any way benefited. 'Who dies if England live?' comes perilously near to nonsense. But it is not nonsense if it means 'Who would not die if *he* (or *she*) could thereby secure more worthwhile conditions for *them*?' The 'State' is another abstraction, and one that is too often confounded with the nation. We speak, for instance, of a nation as declaring war. It is true that, at least under modern conditions, every member of a nation is implicated in a war once that war has begun; it is not true that 'the whole nation' decided upon war, or took any part in its preparation. Certain agents of the State decide for war or peace; in thus deciding, these agents may not be consulting the interests of even the greater number of those individuals in whose name they act. *Nationalism* and *Internationalism* are abstractions in terms of which we can think effectively only when we could, if we so desired, say precisely which and which sets of individuals we are referring to in any sentences in which the words 'Nationalism' and 'Internationalism' occur.

'Either you are for Nationalism or for Internationalism. But if you love your country, you cannot hesitate for a moment.'

This argument is only a little sillier, because more shortly stated, than many an argument I have heard. We must ask: 'What does it *mean* to be "for Nationalism"?' and 'What does it *mean* to be "for Internationalism"?' If we can answer these questions, then, but only then, can we think clearly whether we are for, or against, and what precisely it is that we are for or against.

The distrust felt by some people for logic – which we noticed in Chapter 1 – is, I believe, partly due to the mistaken belief that we are being peculiarly hard-headed and logical when we think in abstractions, opposing or connecting 'clear-cut ideas'. There is, as Sir Austen Chamberlain dimly saw, a danger in these clear-cut ideas, for we may be substituting them for ideas about matters of fact that are not clear cut. This, it seems to me, is what M. Painlevé prided himself upon doing. There is a well-known logical principle to the effect that there is no middle term between two contradictories. 'Either it is your birthday to-day or it is not.' This is true, no matter whether you happen to be ignorant on which day your birthday falls. Now, for example, Nationalism is not the same as Internationalism, but these are not logical contradictories. It does not follow that the welfare of *this nation* is logically incompatible with the welfare of *other nations*. It may be incompatible but there is nothing in the meaning of 'one nation' and 'all other nations' that necessitates such an exclusion. It is illogical to attempt to draw a hard-and-fast line between two things that are different, or opposed, by treating them as though they were logical contradictories when they are not.

The logical principle which I just mentioned is called 'the Law of Excluded Middle'. An instance of it is provided by the White Knight's remark: 'Either it brings the tears into my eyes or it doesn't'. There is no middle term between 'having tears in my eyes' and 'not having tears in my eyes'. But there is a middle term between 'having my eyes full of tears' and 'not having my eyes full of tears'. Indeed, there are a number of intermediate states, a whole range, between *being full* and *being empty*. Again, 'neutral' and 'not neutral' are logical contradictories. But there is a difference between being 'neutral' and 'benevolently neutral' and between 'not neutral' and 'benevolently neutral'. For the purposes of International Law 'neutrality' may be so defined that 'benevolent neutrality' is not 'neutrality' at all. The abstraction *neutrality* has to be interpreted in terms of quite definite sorts of actions. It is by no means easy to lay down criteria determining what actions are to be regarded as consistent with observing neutrality and what actions are inconsistent with it. To recognize this difficulty is to be logical; to ignore it is to run the risk of substituting contradictories for contraries admitting of a mean between extremes. In former chapters we have met examples of absurd statements about *neutrality, bias,* and *open minds.*

There are some words that are properly vague, i.e. words that can be correctly used to apply to a characteristic that may be possessed in varying degrees. The word 'bald' provides a good example. '*Bald*' is a vague word, since it may be correctly applied to a person who has no hair on his head and to a variety of other persons who have *some, but an indefinite number of,* hairs on their heads. 'Intelligent', 'grey', 'sweet', 'expensive', 'profit-making' are other examples. We use the word 'bald' to denote the opposite extreme to 'having a fine head of hair', but we also use it to denote a number of intermediate stages. It makes sense to say:

'He is becoming balder' and also to say of the same person at the same time: 'He is bald.' Likewise with the property of being intelligent, and the other properties I gave as examples, and a host of others that will probably occur to you.

A common mistake in logical reasoning is made by those who demand that a sharp line should be drawn between those who are bald and those who are not. It is true that 'bald' and 'not bald' are logical contradictories. They are logical contradictories because we have made them so; we have the convention that prefixing *not* to a word yields its logical contradictory. But this convention does not in the least help us to draw a sharp line between those who may be said to be bald and those who are not bald. Suppose we could arrange a set of men in a row beginning with a man who has not a single hair on his head and ending with a man who has a regular thatch of hair, whilst any man nearer the first has fewer hairs than his neighbour on the other side. It is theoretically possible that between any two men next to each other the difference in the amount of hair possessed is imperceptible. Nevertheless, there is a great difference between one at one end and another at the other end. It is not logical to ask us to draw a sharp line between them.

Failure to recognize that it is not logically possible to draw a sharp line between those who possess and those who do not possess a property capable of being present in any one of a continuous series of intermediate degrees leads us into making either of two serious logical blunders. On the one hand we may deny that there is any difference between the extremes just because they are thus connected. On the other hand, we may illegitimately demand that a sharp line should be drawn. In Ancient Greece some philosophers were fond of setting puzzles of this sort: a single stone is not a heap, nor are two stones, nor are three stones. How many stones must there be in order that there should be a heap of stones? The answer is not difficult: there is no *definite* number constituting a heap.

I will take another example. Black is different from white. What is black cannot be white. But black is a property that surfaces can have in varying degrees. It is possible to arrange a series of pieces of paper beginning with a piece that is unmistakably black and ending with a piece that is unmistakably white. In between there will be a range of varying degrees through a set of papers some of which are unmistakably grey. We could, if we chose, *define* 'black' as the property of a surface which reflects zero per cent light; 'white' as the property of a surface that reflects a hundred per cent light. This would not be convenient. You would unhesitatingly say that this page is white and the print is black; but this would not be in conformity with our arbitrary criterion for the distinction between black and white.

The mistake of demanding that a sharp line should be drawn, when in fact no sharp line can be drawn, I call 'the fallacy of *either black or white*'. It is a disastrous mistake in some circumstances, for example, when we demand that a sharp line should be drawn between the sane and the insane, or between the intelligent and the unintelligent. Our readiness to make this mistake may be taken advantage of by a dishonest opponent, who insists that we should 'define precisely' that which does not admit of such definition. For, in common usage, 'defining precisely' means 'setting out sharply distinguishable characteristics'. If we can make clear and precise a notion that we had not clearly apprehended, then well and good. It is very useful at times to give a precise definition. But we create an obstacle to thinking clearly if we try to mark off sharply a characteristic that is not in fact capable of being thus sharply marked off. If we do make this mistaken attempt we are very likely to substitute clear-cut abstractions for untidy facts. We may be able to play intellectual games with these abstractions and to give rigorous definitions that would meet with the approval of logicians, but we shall run the danger of losing contact with those matters of fact about which we desire to think effectively.

I have dealt with this mistake at somewhat tedious length because it seems to me that both statesmen, such as Sir Austen Chamberlain and Lord Baldwin, and many logicians have been misled by it. They have assumed that *unless* we are dealing with precisely definable characteristics we cannot be logical. This is a profound mistake. I have already dealt with the statesmen. I will now briefly refer to the mistake made by a logician, namely, Professor G. C. Field. In his chapter on 'Gear Thinking', published in the useful little book *Education for Citizenship*, Professor Field suggests that we may fall into 'False Clear Thinking'. He gives as an example this familiar problem presented by the 'Where-are-you-to-draw-the-line?' argument. To return to my own example. You ask whether a man with only one hair is bald, then whether a man with two hairs is bald, and so, by stages through the number series until you reach, say, fifty thousand hairs. Since it is impossible to assign a definite number of hairs which a man may have and yet be bald whereas the addition of one more hair makes him not bald, it is assumed that the decision whether a man is or is not bald is a decision that does not conform to logical principles. I have deliberately given again this trivial example. We are not likely to be excited about it. Professor Field takes the example of drawing the line between profit-making and profiteering. In order to stop profiteering at the end of the Great War, an Act was passed drawing the line between legitimate and illegitimate profit-making at $33\frac{1}{3}$ per cent. Certain critics made merry with the suggestion that a man who made 33 per cent profit was not a profiteer, whereas one who made 33⅓ per cent profit was. For practical purposes, namely, for the purpose of administering an Act of Parliament, it was necessary to draw a sharp line, and that sharp line had to be drawn at an arbitrary point. Consequently the *legal definition* of a 'profiteer'[8] could be made quite precise. But we do not use the word 'profiteer' in accordance with this legal definition. It does not follow, however, that we cannot make a clear distinction between excess profits and reasonable profits, i.e. between 'profiteering' and 'making legitimate profits'. We shall all, I hope, agree that there is a *clear* distinction, and further, that it is *in the nature of the distinction* that no sharp line can be drawn between the extremes, except in an arbitrary manner for the practical purposes of administration. The distinction is clear between 'excess profits' (or 'profiteering') and 'legitimate profits', although it is not a sharp distinction. We are thinking clearly when we recognize that the demand for a sharp line to be drawn is an illegitimate demand. Professor Field, however, says that the demand for a sharp line to be drawn is 'an illegitimate demand for clear thinking.' That is a shocking blunder, which is made worse by his statement that those who make this demand are 'indulging in false clear thinking'. The blunder is shocking because there cannot be an illegitimate demand for thinking clearly, and to speak of 'false clear thinking' is nonsensical. I am afraid that Professor Field has fallen into the statesmen's mistake of confusing *thinking clearly* with *drawing sharp distinctions*. When the topic concerns a characteristic which is such that it does not permit of being sharply demarcated, then we are thinking clearly in recognizing that no sharp line can be drawn. I believe that Professor Field has made a mistake about the application of the Law of Excluded Middle, and a more important mistake about the nature of thinking logically. The latter mistake consists in supposing that thinking logically is confined to thinking about clear-cut abstractions. We think logically when we reject contradictory statements and draw from our premises only that which they entail. We think illogically when we ignore the conditions set by the problem about which we are thinking and thus slip away from the point.

NOTES

1   D. Luther Evans and Walter C. Gamertsfelder: *Logic, Theoretical and Applied*, p. 111. (New York, 1937.)
2   See Chapter 2.
3   See p. 22.
4   B. A. Levinson, *The Times*, May 13th, 1938. The reader may notice in this sentence the unpleasant repetition of 'policy'. Though unpleasant, this repetition of 'policy' with two different meanings is not in the least ambiguous.
5   *Op. cit.*, p. 4, and pp. 10–11.
6   I quote this from John Gunther's *Inside Europe*, p. 281.
7   I have an objectless emotional attitude when I am afraid, although there is nothing of which I am afraid. So, too, in the case of other emotions.
8   Strictly, what was defined was 'excess profits'. I am here using 'profiteer' to mean 'one who makes excess profits'. This is, I believe, in accordance with common usage.

13

TAKING ADVANTAGE OF OUR STUPIDITY

In the foregoing chapters I have for the most part been concerned with difficulties that we may encounter in our own attempts to think to some purpose. I say 'for the most part', because I have in some places considered examples of twisted thinking which it is difficult to believe that the thinker himself did not know to be unsound. Further, I have given examples of certain habits of thought and of speech – such, for instance, as the use of emotionally toned language – in which we may fancy we detect evidence of crooked arguments. I adopt the phrase 'crooked argument' from Professor Thouless's book, *Straight and Crooked Thinking*. I wish, however, to draw a distinction between

DOI: 10.4324/b22927-13

what I have called 'twisted thinking' and what I shall call 'using crooked arguments'. My thinking is twisted when I believe that I am thinking effectively and have discovered sound reasons for my conclusion but am mistaken in this belief. The twist may be due to my supposing that I am in possession of all the relevant information, but in fact I am not. It may be due to my failure to see that my argument is invalid. It may be due to my inability to rid myself of some habit of thought that keeps my mind in blinkers. When I use a crooked argument I am in a quite different frame of mind. Then I am trying to persuade you to accept a conclusion, although I know that I have not offered you reasonable grounds for its acceptance. I try to persuade you by a trick, that is, by some dishonest device calculated to impress you.

This distinction between twisted thinking and using crooked arguments can be very sharply drawn by me at the moment, since I am thinking of two very sharply distinguishable mental attitudes. But it is not always possible for me to know whether I am using a crooked argument or whether I am the victim of twisted thinking. In trying to think out some problem which concerns me deeply it is very easy to slip from one attitude to the other. This is what we must expect to be the case if thinking involves our whole personality. That is the assumption upon which this book is based. Since I may find it difficult at times to know when I have slipped into a crooked argument, I must admit that it may be impossible for me to be sure when you are using a crooked argument and are not the victim of twisted thinking. This difficulty should be borne in mind. We are only too ready to accuse those who disagree with us of being 'scoundrels', 'lying jades', 'ignorant fellows', and so on. Even when we are convinced, after due reflection, that the other man's argument is crooked, we may sometimes need to admit: 'Perhaps he[1] is stupid and not dishonest'. Certainly many of the arguments presented to us must be regarded as evidence that the speaker is either 'stupid though honest' or 'dishonest and cunning'. If the latter, then he deserves to be shown up; if the former, then he needs our pity. In both cases it is desirable he should be refuted. But *quis custodes custodiet?* Our anxiety to refute must be so controlled that the refutation is neither dishonest nor stupid.

In this chapter I shall examine some very common forms of crooked arguments. You are fortunate if you have never been tempted to use any one of them. I doubt whether I can say as much for myself. It may even be that you can find in this book some evidences of my having used crooked arguments. Certainly I am not aware of having done so, but in that I may be self-deceived. I cannot hope to have avoided altogether the defects of twisted thinking.

As in the discussion of fallacious modes of thinking, so in considering the devices used in crooked arguments, it is not possible to proceed in an orderly manner. These devices are so numerous that we cannot hope to enumerate them all; they are so illogical that it is difficult to find a principle that would enable us to give a neat list. No importance is to be attached to the order in which I deal with these devices. In our consideration of twisted thinking we have already had occasion to examine some arguments that might very well be used crookedly. The question may be begged, not only through sheer stupidity or want of care, but also deliberately by the speaker in order to impose a conclusion upon his hearers. A dishonest speaker may take advantage of our stupidity in deliberately using ambiguous words, or letting his meaning shift as the argument progresses, or in constructing a circular argument in the hope that his hearers will not notice the circle. He might even try to impose upon us by using an argument involving the fallacy of undistributed middle. This device, however, is not very likely to succeed between two or three disputants, if the other disputants are at all mentally alert. The fallacy of special pleading (discussed in Chapter 4) may also be used dishonestly. If we should find this to be the case, we can deal with it as we do in our own thinking, namely, by pointing out that the speaker has failed to apply to this special case the rule that he has just been insisting upon as a general rule.

The attempt to establish a conclusion by appealing to selected instances is a common device of dishonest disputants. Its success depends either upon our want of attention or upon our ignorance that a selection has been made. The former defect we can remedy if we will; the latter defect is not so easily avoided. We can, however, develop the habit of noticing the form of the argument, and be ready to press the speaker to show us whether his selected instances are in fact representative, i.e. fair samples. A disputant who uses this device lays himself open to the possibility of being dishonestly refuted by an opponent who selects other, but conflicting, instances. Thus, for example, two people may argue whether the thirty-mile speed limit in built-up areas has been an effective measure in reducing the number of road accidents. One man may cite instances in which the accident was admittedly due to fast driving. The other may reply by citing instances in which an accident was averted just because the car shot by so rapidly. (This answer may surprise some readers, as it did surprise me. I quote it from a conversation I had with a man who was addicted to driving at sixty to seventy miles an hour, but had not himself ever been involved in an accident.) By selecting instances and counter-instances, neither disputant can establish his point. There is an appropriate method for obtaining a reasonable answer to the original question. The first step is to collect statistical data from reports of road accidents; the second step requires a careful statistical analysis of the conditions that are most prevalent in cases of road accidents. An analysis of these conditions might suffice to establish the conclusion that a speed limit does (or does not, as the case may be) tend to diminish the number of accidents. No arm-chair discussion could contribute anything of importance for establishing this conclusion. You have probably heard discussions on this topic in which people who are normally sensible make wild assertions with regard to the cause of road accidents. Such assertions proceed from prejudice or from a failure to take into account relevant data such as, for instance, that not all drivers of cars are as expert or as courteous as the speaker, and that many pedestrians are careless or foolhardy or ill-adjusted to the conditions of modern road traffic. I assume that it is admitted that there are various causes of road accidents. This being so, it is tempting to use crooked arguments and only too easy to slip into twisted thinking on this topic. The disputant who has been maintaining that the enforcement of a speed limit 'would not help to reduce the number of road accidents' can easily appeal to cases where neither of the two cars involved in a collision has been travelling at over 30 m.p.h. This selection of instances does nothing to disprove the moderate statement that the imposition of a speed limit in built-up areas tends to reduce the number of accidents. Nor does it contribute to establishing his own extreme position that no accidents are due to driving at high speeds. An unwary and prejudiced opponent, instead of pointing this out, may retort: 'So you think that all accidents are due to inefficient driving', and thus lay himself open to the reply: 'No, I think that most accidents are due to inefficient driving, such as giving wrong signals or no signals at all, but none are due to high speeds.' This leaves the argument where it began.

I remember that just after the speed limit had been re-imposed, one of my guests, who had driven from a town just over fifty miles away, was complaining bitterly of 'the utter idiocy of these 30-mile limits'. I, not being a motorist, inquired whether it was not worth while to try them in order to see if the number of accidents would be reduced. He replied: 'Oh, well, if you want us all to crawl about at 5 m.p.h., then no doubt there wouldn't be any accidents, barring the old women who step off the pavement sideways in front of the car'. Now, I was not defending any such reduction in speed, but the remark was no doubt intended as a diversion; first by substituting for my statement one that I had not made and could not perhaps defend, and secondly, by suggesting to our hearers that I had made a ridiculous proposal.

Diversion from the point at issue is a source of much fallacious thinking and the secret of much crooked arguing. It is difficult to keep to the point. The difficulty may be the intellectual difficulty of keeping the main point fairly in mind despite complexity of details. Resolute hard thinking is our only remedy. In carrying on a discussion with other people we may allow ourselves to be diverted if our opponent succeeds in making us look ridiculous, with or without justification. On such occasions it is important that we should keep our tempers. An angry man is not likely to argue effectively, still less to think clearly. There are exceptions to this statement. An angry man may be put on his mettle and stimulated to rapid thinking. I am inclined to think, however, that this is not usually the case. If a prejudice which we hold as peculiarly dear, or 'sacred' to us, is attacked, and we find ourselves unable to refute the attack and equally unable to surrender the prejudice, then our wisest course is to admit that some things that we hold to be true by authority, or by inward conviction, are beyond the reach of argument. In such a case argument is powerless both for defence and attack. I suspect that most people have some convictions belonging to this class. Some bitter and fruitless controversy might be avoided if we could bring ourselves to acknowledge that this is so.

There are some forms of diversion that could hardly be used other than dishonestly. For instance, if the speaker says that not all is well with our public school education, his opponent may reply: 'So you are an advocate of sending your boys to these namby-pamby crank schools, are you?' The original speaker must refuse to accept this diversion, pointing out that his moderate statement does not entail either the travesty of it presented by his opponent, or even the denial that our public schools are better than any other schools in the country; the assertion was merely that they are not as good as they conceivably might be. It is, I think, surprising how often this trick occurs. To admit that there is anything to criticize in, say, our marriage laws may be distorted into the contention that we don't believe in marriage at all. To recognize that there are some things that are better done in the United States than in this country may be regarded as equivalent to denying that *anything* is better done here than in the United States. The attitude of mind that makes such distortion possible is perhaps expressed in the slogan: 'My country, right or wrong.'

Diversion from the point of a contention may not be due to deliberate dishonesty. There are many fallacies of irrelevant conclusion that proceed from twisted thinking. Indeed, we might have considered some of them in the last chapter. I reserved fallacies of this type for discussion now, as there can be little doubt that the same form of argument is more often due to dishonesty than to stupidity. Logicians have been in the habit of discussing 'the fallacy of irrelevant conclusion' under its mediaeval Latin name, '*ignoratio elenchi*', i.e. the mistake of disregarding the opponent's contention. De Morgan defines it as 'proving something that is not contradictory of the thing asserted'.[2] He says: 'It is, of all the fallacies, that which has the widest range.' This is true. I shall have to be content with giving a few examples of arguments in which this mistake is made. I do not profess to know, in all cases, whether the disputants are stupid or dishonest. Incidentally, these are not incompatible attributes, but a disputant who is both stupid and dishonest need give us no trouble.

De Morgan's definition covers the arguments by deliberate diversion, discussed above, only in the sense that the opponent's diversion threw upon the original speaker the burden of proving something he had not maintained, unless he refused to accept the diversion.

An examination of the correspondence on some disputable topic, carried on through several issues of a newspaper, shows how easy it is to wander from the point. The topic of fox-hunting is still discussed in the correspondence columns. It is a matter about which people feel keenly. I wonder sometimes whether either side ever converts one of the other side. For it is a question in which people 'take sides'. Those who have hunted from their youth up, who know the exhilaration of hunting and the delight of a good seat, are naturally enough disinclined to ask whether there are any sound reasons against this sport. Those who have had no experience of hunting may be too ready to condemn it without considering whether there is, perhaps, something to be said in favour of it. A fresh batch of letters on this topic appeared in the *Manchester Guardian*, between the dates November 30th and December 10th, 1937. The arguments I am going to discuss are taken from this correspondence.

Two main objections had been made against fox-hunting: (1) that it was an extremely cruel sport, (2) that it involved much damage to farmers, both because foxes, preserved for the hunt, are destructive to chickens, and because the cross-country run often involved damage to the farmer's fences and land.

There are, it would seem, two ways of meeting these objections; either by refuting them or by admitting them but urging in defence that there are advantages to offset these evils. With regard to the first objection, it has frequently been maintained that 'foxes enjoy the hunt'. This amounts to a simple denial of the disputant's contention that fox-hunting is cruel, so that unless evidence be offered in support of it, the reply is a *petitio principii*, i.e. it assumes the point in dispute. Recent defenders of the sport seem to admit that it is cruel. One correspondent makes merry with the suggestion that the 'antis' must have had conversations with a fox in order to know what the feelings of a hunted fox are. He argues that to hunt foxes is to follow 'Nature's way', whereas to exterminate them (in the interests of the farmer's poultry) is to adopt a method fostered by an anthropomorphic way of regarding animals. This argument involves an undue assumption, since artificial means are admittedly used to prevent the escape of the fox. He replies to the objection that fox-hunting damages the property of farmers by the argument that the loss to the farmers is small in amount compared with the 'annual turnover' in the fox industry. This correspondent's reply to the objections brought by 'the antis' amounts, then, to admitting that the sport is cruel, but not as cruel as is supposed, and that it is 'Nature's way'; whilst, he urges, the farmers' loss is the huntsmen's gain. But he is not content with these considerations, which are certainly relevant whether justifiable or not. He suggests further that 'the antis' are like the Puritans (according to Macaulay) who 'objected to bear-baiting, not because it gave pain to the bears, but because it gave pleasure to the spectators'.

This accusation, even if true, is irrelevant to the point at issue, for the point is whether pain is felt by the fox. It is as crooked an argument as that often urged (but not by any of these correspondents) by 'the antis', that those who condemn fox-hunting have 'no guts'. The point of such accusations is to cast unpleasant aspersions against the arguer whilst ignoring his argument.

The device of reiterating what has not been denied and ignoring what has been asserted has been painfully evident, from time to time, in discussions concerning the private manufacture of armaments. I do not think anyone is likely to deny that this is a topic of great political importance, whatever may be the right decision. This topic has again been brought to the notice of the House of Commons in speeches made by the Opposition during the recent Budget debates.[3] The mounting profits of armament firms were commented upon both by Sir Archibald Sinclair and by Mr Stokes. (The latter had also raised the question on March 7th.) I shall select two replies, made on different occasions and in different years, to the contention that the private manufacture of armaments creates conditions that make war more likely.

On March 27th, 1935, Lord Marley protested:

There are a great many officers who go from important positions in the Services to the private employment of these armament firms. I have a long list here, which I do not propose to read out, of officers holding most important and responsible positions in the Admiralty, the War Office and the Air Ministry who have left these important positions, dealing with the Ordnance Department and with the purchase of arms and munitions, and have stepped straight into lucrative positions in private armament firms.[4]

To this Lord Halifax replied:

> I do not profess to any professional knowledge, but having per-
> haps some little knowledge of human nature, I do not suppose
> myself that people who trade in armaments are very much better
> or very much worse than any other ordinary business men, and I
> do not suppose that business men are very much better or very
> much worse than many politicians.

This reply does not meet the difficulty raised by Lord Marley,
although it was offered as doing so. First, Lord Halifax seems to
rely upon prestige suggestion. He is a well-known and much
respected and, no doubt, widely travelled man; he claims to have
'some little knowledge of human nature' whilst not professing
to 'professional knowledge'. This is an obvious trick. Secondly,
he indulges in a remarkably obvious diversion to an irrelevant
conclusion. The point was not at all whether those who trade in
armaments were 'better or worse' than 'ordinary business men',
nor whether these are 'better or worse' than 'many politicians'.
Lord Halifax's statements on both these points may be true; they
are certainly totally irrelevant. The point at issue was that armament trading is not an 'ordinary business', so that peculiar safe-
guards might be necessary. That Lord Halifax was aware of the
point, but failed to meet it, is shown in his comparison of those
'who trade in armaments' with 'ordinary business men'.

The same failure to see, or at least to reply, to the point was
evident in a speech made by Sir John Simon, in the House of
Commons, on November 22nd, 1934. He said:

> It would be very unjust to armament firms and to those re-
> sponsible people connected with them, to imply that there is

something in their business which essentially makes undesirable methods their practice.

This again is a flagrant example of failing to keep to the point and of deliberately ignoring the point in dispute. Both Lord Halifax and Sir John Simon are content to make vague statements suggesting that unjust accusations have been made, whereas the contention was that these accusations are true. Neither of them met the contention that there are certain trades (such as the opium traffic, or the white slave traffic) which are not ordinary trades and out of which it is undesirable that private persons should be allowed to make profits.

The device of 'abusing the plaintiff's attorney' when no case can be put up by the defence is recognized as a dishonest trick. Perhaps it sometimes works. A prosecuting counsel might influence a jury by speaking of the accused man as a scoundrel because the crime of which he is accused (but not yet found guilty) is an atrocious crime. Stated thus baldly, the device would be, I hope, too obvious to mislead any jurors. It can, however, be made to work if the suggestion that the accused man is a scoundrel be conveyed by subtle implications. Lord Halifax and Sir John Simon seem to me to have used this device, but on the side of the defendant, and not with any considerable degree of subtlety.

An example of another device for taking advantage of our stupidity is also provided by the Armaments Inquiry. The following account is given in the *Press Reports*:

When Sir Charles Craven[5] was being questioned by Sir Philip Gibbs yesterday, he said Messrs Vickers' trade was not particularly dangerous.

Sir Philip: You do not think that your wares are any more dangerous or obnoxious than boxes of chocolates or sugar candy? – No, or novels.

Sir Philip: You don't think it is more dangerous to export these fancy goods to foreign countries than, say, children's crackers?

Sir Charles: Well, I nearly lost an eye with a Christmas cracker, but never with a gun.

It is difficult to believe that these replies were intended to be serious. There is an obvious diversion from the point under the guise of a contemptuous joke. At least, I think it must have been meant for a joke, although it is certainly a poor one. There is a further crooked argument. The hearer might willingly assent to the suggestion that someone might 'nearly lose an eye with a Christmas cracker' although he has never been in danger from a gun. Crackers, however, are not made for this purpose, whereas armaments are made solely for the purpose of killing and wounding people and destroying buildings. But it is *armaments* that are being discussed. I hardly think this crooked argument could deceive anyone.

I shall conclude this chapter by setting out an argument that contains a considerable number of fallacious modes of reasoning and twisted thinking. I have constructed this argument for the purpose of illustrating these defects. The argument has been 'made up' by me much in the way in which a patchwork quilt is made by connecting together various pieces brought together from different sources. I do not think that any one speaker would combine in so comparatively short a speech so many dishonest devices or exhibit so many forms of twisted thinking. On the other hand, every argument that appears in this 'speech' has been used by someone or other in the course of the prolonged controversy concerning Women's Suffrage. My imaginary speaker will quote some passages from the speech made by Sir F. E. Smith (afterwards Lord Birkenhead) in moving the rejection of the Conciliation Bill, introduced to the House of Commons by Mr Shackleton in 1910.[6] In the context in which these passages are now forced (by me) to appear, they have undoubtedly a twist that is more obvious, and, perhaps more vicious, than in the original. In my opinion Sir F. E. Smith's speech was a masterpiece, regarded from the point of winning over the undecided to agreement with him.

For the purpose of examining this imaginary speech, I shall adopt the device (used in Chapter 8) of affixing small letters to those statements upon which I shall subsequently comment.

It has been truly said by Mrs Humphry Ward that 'the political ignorance of women is irreparable and is imposed by Nature.'(a) Women are incapable of forming a sound judgment on important political affairs. But it is not only the right, it is, I submit, also the duty of every voter to judge soundly and wisely of those matters that are put before him. It has been said that women have a right to exercise the parliamentary vote. But, as Sir F. E. Smith has wisely said: 'No one has an abstract right of that kind. The theory that there is such a right is as dead as Rousseau. The vote is given on approved public grounds to such citizens as in the opinion of the State are likely to exercise it for the benefit of the whole community.(b) If women have a right to vote, they have the right everywhere, including priest-ridden Italy and our great Eastern dependencies.(c) Supposing that our Indian fellow-subjects ever are enfranchised, the operation must include, not the men only, but the unillumined zenanas.' How frightful would it be even to contemplate the enfranchisement of 'the unillumined zenanas'.(*d*) Yet, if we give the vote to women in this country we cannot stop short of enfranchising the most ignorant women in our Empire. The women in this country have no need for a vote. Sir Frederick Smith challenged the House of Commons to cite one case 'where the advocates of a woman's grievance have come to the House and said, "I have established this grievance, and I ask the House to remedy it",' and have failed to get it remedied.(*e*)

If women are given the Parliamentary vote, it might happen that women combined with a minority of men should attempt to impose their views upon an actual majority of men. This would be intolerable. Women will vote together and there will be a regiment of women indeed. But the power behind the vote is force; it is by force that the law is made effective. What part can women play in the exercise of this most necessary sanction of law? No part at all. Make no mistake. Those who are working for the enfranchisement of women will not stop with the parliamentary vote. They will press for complete equality between the sexes; they will not stop short of demanding that women should sit in the House of Commons. Indeed, as Mr Gladstone so clearly saw, 'The capacity to sit in the House of Commons logically and practically draws in its train the capacity to fill every office in the State.'(*f*) That a woman should be a Cabinet Minister is too horrible to contemplate. Women have the feminine graces. Let us reserve for men the masculine part.(*g*)

To quote once more from the powerful speech of Sir Frederick Smith: 'We are told that it is no answer to say that women voters might be ignorant – that men voters are ignorant too. That is the most crude application of the doctrine of political homoeopathy to which I have ever listened. I do not assent to the gloomy view held as to the capacity of the male voter.'(*h*) Here Sir Frederick

Smith put his finger on the true answer. Women have not the capacity of men. (g) Women are women and men are men whatever be their class or rank or country. (g) It is a shameful thing that women should attempt to usurp the powers and perform the duties entrusted by Nature to men and to men alone. (i) Let them content themselves with the noble work some of them are performing so well of influencing their men to judge concerning the gravest political questions of the day. A woman's sphere is her home. There she can represent her political views to her husband and his friends; there she can play her part by exercising sweet feminine influence without sullying herself by entering into the strife and turmoil of practical politics. To be the power behind the throne is better than to be seated uneasily upon the throne itself. (j) Let me once again repeat the words of Sir Frederick Smith. 'I do not', he said, 'wish to decry the claim of women to intellectual distinction. I have never ... founded myself on some assumed intellectual inferiority of women. I do not believe it; but I venture to say that the sum total of human happiness, knowledge, and achievement would be almost unaffected if – I take the most distinguished names – Sappho had never sung, if Joan of Arc had never fought, if Siddons had never played, and if George Eliot had never written, and that at the same time, if the true functions of womanhood had not been faithfully discharged throughout the ages, the very existence of the race and the tenderest and most sacred influences which animate mankind would have disappeared.' These are weighty words. You are asked to support a movement that will prevent the true functions of womanhood, and threaten the very existence of the human race. (k) When I reflect upon the consequences that would ensue upon the enfranchisement of women I am filled with dismay. I detest this proposal. (l) Every right-thinking person, be it man or woman, agrees with me.(*m*) The alternatives are clear: Either you give the vote to women and destroy the sanctity of the home, or you reject this most iniquitous proposal and preserve that which every Englishman holds dear.(*n*)

It is not difficult to detect the absurdities in this speech, nor to discern the contradictions in it. I have indeed put them together for this purpose.

(*a*) This statement is a good example of potted thinking; it has the effect of a slogan, and conceals, I fancy, much begging of the question. The statement immediately following it is a repetition with variation in the wording. This is by no means a dishonest device. As we have already seen, it may be necessary for a speaker to repeat his points, lest his hearers be slow to take them in. It is, however, wise not to slip into the habit of supposing that every new statement advances the argument.

(*b*) The claim that women have a right to the franchise is not equivalent to the claim that they have an 'abstract right'. On the contrary, the claim was based upon the need for women, in their own interests, to be enfranchised, and it was justified on the ground that women were not more politically incompetent than men. Accordingly, the assertion that 'the vote is given on approved public grounds to such citizens as in the opinion of the State are likely to exercise it for the benefit of the whole community' involves a deliberate disregard of the point at issue. It asserts what had not been denied.

(*c*) This involves an extension of the opponent's contention, which may have been a legitimate extension, but it derives its force here from the irrelevant denial of 'an abstract right'.

(d) An appeal to emotion that is not, in itself, unjustifiable in a speech. But the appeal depends upon representing the zenanas as 'unillumined', whereas the original contention was that *all* women were politically incompetent.

(e) Simple denial of the point at issue, combined with another irrelevant conclusion. In point of fact, advocates of a woman's grievance were proposing that the grievance should be removed. Sir F. E. Smith, failing to see that their lack of a parliamentary vote was a grievance, replied, in effect, to the women that *other* grievances of theirs had always been remedied.

(f) This is indeed a logical conclusion. This point was made by Sir F. E. Smith as well. It is an effective argument against the proposal to enfranchise women, provided it be admitted that women are not fitted to be Members of Parliament.

(g) A diversion from the point at issue, which was no doubt all the more effective for being a mere tautology. The same diversion is made twice more in rapid succession. In all three cases the hearers are intended to get the impression that the speaker's opponents are contesting the indisputable fact that women are not men. The point at issue is whether the differences between women and men are relevant to the 'exercise of the vote'.

(h) This is a straightforward expression of personal opinion. If the hearers accept it as in any way supporting the speaker's contention, they should do so only in so far as they recognize that he is in a position to have expert knowledge of the matter in dispute.

(i) This is a flagrant begging of the question, reinforced by an appeal to what is in accordance with Nature.

(j) The inconsistency of the last two statements with the contention that 'women are politically incompetent' is so obvious that I should not have included it in this 'speech', were it not for the fact that exactly this inconsistency was repeated again and again both by men and by women anti-suffragists.

(k) An extreme extension of the opponent's contention, combined with the false suggestion that it has already been agreed what are the 'true functions of womanhood' and what exactly is incompatible with the exercise of them.

(l) Again a perfectly legitimate expression of personal feeling.

(m) But this legitimate expression of personal feeling is at once regarded as evidence that everyone else will have the same feeling unless he (or she) is not 'right thinking'.

(n) A dishonest conjunction of the two exclusive alternatives – either give, or not give, the vote – with two other alternatives that are not necessarily conjoined with the first pair. To assume that they are thus conjoined is to beg the question.

To protect ourselves from these tricks we must be constantly on the alert; the cost of thinking effectively is a difficult vigilance.

NOTES

1 Here, and elsewhere in this chapter, 'he' covers 'she' in accordance with convention.
2 *Formal Logic*, p. 260.
3 *The Times*, April 27th, 1938.
4 This quotation, and the two following quotations, are taken from *Inquest on Peace*, pp. 73, 74.
5 Sir Charles Craven is a director of Vickers-Armstrong, Ltd.
6 These quotations are taken from the report of Sir P. E. Smith's speech, given in *The Times*, July 13th, 1910.

14

TESTING OUR BELIEFS

A large volume might be written on the topic: *How are beliefs to be tested?* A specialist in any branch of knowledge holds many beliefs of which a layman in that subject has never heard. Such a belief either has been tested or stands in need of being tested. If the test has been passed, then the specialist may be said to have *knowledge*. Thus, for instance, a physicist knows that energy is radiated only in definite quanta. A chemist knows that carbon dioxide is formed by the direct combustion of carbon and oxygen. A botanist knows that the nourishment of a green plant is entirely derived from inorganic materials. The list might be continued, but to do so is unnecessary. A special science is a more or less systematic body of knowledge, which has been gradually acquired by the labours of scientists, i.e. of people who have

DOI: 10.4324/b22927-14

investigated carefully a certain region of phenomena, have learnt from the labours of their predecessors, and have made discoveries. The various special sciences have been developed out of the primitive beliefs about the behaviour of things (including themselves) that were entertained by those who lived before the dawn of scientific thinking. When a scientist claims to have made a discovery he is proclaiming that he has entertained certain beliefs, that these beliefs have been tested and have successfully withstood the test. To examine the nature of these tests and to evaluate the claim to success would involve an examination of the technique adopted by the scientist in question. Such an examination could be carried out only by other specialists in that science. The title of this chapter places a limitation upon the discussion, of the testing of beliefs, by introducing the word 'our'. Who are the people to whom reference is thus implicitly made, and which among the various beliefs, or sorts of beliefs, that they may entertain are to be considered? The beliefs that are to be considered in this chapter are the beliefs of ordinary people about ordinary topics.

This statement presupposes a distinction between ordinary people and those who are not ordinary. In making this distinction I am not thinking of a *Who's Who* classification, thereby assuming that there are some people who are not *who*. The distinction is between the non-expert and the expert. An expert is a person who has experience in some branch of knowledge; he has a special skill; he can speak with authority about the topics that lie within his specialized knowledge. There are, no doubt, a few great men who are experts in more than one branch of knowledge. Even these men, however, are 'ordinary people' in regard to some topics on which knowledge is possible. An expert in, for instance, physics is not necessarily an expert in theology or in political affairs. It may be assumed that each one of us entertains many beliefs about topics with regard to which we have no special expertness. These beliefs will be our ordinary beliefs.

We saw in Chapter 2 that we often hold a belief more strongly than the evidence warrants, and we hold some beliefs without having considered whether they stand in need of any evidence, and, if so, whether we are aware of any evidence in support of these beliefs. No one would think of questioning a belief until he had some reason for supposing that the belief in question was not known to be certainly true. Unfortunately we too often do not even wish to find out whether our beliefs are true. We are content to accept without testing any belief that fits in with our prejudices and whose truth is necessary for the satisfaction of our desires. It is for this reason that we fall an easy prey to skilful propaganda. We are apt to be cocksure where we should be hesitant, definite where we should be content to be more or less indefinite, vague although we might have attained precision provided that we had cared to examine the evidence.

Certainly it would be foolish to believe nothing. I think it would be psychologically impossible. A person who is always questioning what 'common sense accepts' is a nuisance to other people and a trouble to himself. There are occasions, however, when he is a much-needed nuisance. To this point I shall refer again in the next chapter. Here we are concerned to ask what are the sources of our knowledge and in what ways we may acquire fresh knowledge from those sources.

At first sight it might seem that there are four distinct sources of knowledge: (1) our direct observation of what is happening; (2) our memories of what we have thus observed; (3) testimony, that is, reports provided by other people with regard to what they have directly observed or remembered; (4) self-evident truths. On examination we find that these four sources are not independent. With regard to the fourth source little needs to be said here. If a belief were in fact self-evidently true, then it would have consequences but no grounds. Such a belief could not be justified, since to justify a belief is to adduce grounds for accepting it. We test a belief in order to find out whether there are such grounds. Self-evident beliefs have been called 'intuitions'. All ordinary people maintain that it is intuitively evident that the whole is greater than its parts. Most people would say that it is no less evident that pain is an evil to be inflicted only for the sake of attaining something worth while. I said 'most'; I did not say 'all'. Intuitions may conflict. Since an intuition of mine may conflict with an intuition of yours it is sometimes reasonable to ask ourselves whether what we intuitively believe could be reasonably doubted, and if it could not, then why not. Testimony, the third source of our knowledge, is not different in kind from the first two sources, since it consists in other people's reports with regard to what they have directly observed or have remembered, and further, in hearing this testimony we are relying upon what we now observe. The testing of beliefs accepted on testimony involves, however, considerations that are lacking in the case of beliefs based upon sense-observation and personal memories. Consequently, we shall discuss (1) and (2) together, and shall then consider (3) at greater length.

By using our senses we are provided with information primarily with regard to our immediate environment. I see in front of me some green blotting-paper. It is true that I may sometimes believe that 'that is green blotting-paper', but it turns out not to be blotting-paper at all. Usually we take 'the evidence of our senses' to be reliable. Most often it is; occasionally it is not. It does not make sense to say 'I see this, but I don't see it.' Such a statement is self-contradictory. The difficulty is that what I unhesitatingly claim to see may not be there to be seen. Perceiving involves more than being sensibly aware of something presented to the senses; it involves the activity of perceiving. This is the activity of a person, and in perceiving, the whole person is involved, not merely one or other of his sense organs.[1] I shall, however, take it for granted that, with due care, we may accept beliefs provided by our senses, testing these beliefs only when the further evidence of our senses leads us to doubt. The phrase 'with due care', in the preceding statement, comes perilously near to begging the question. Nevertheless, I shall take it for granted that we can rely upon our senses to provide us with knowledge. This is a reasonable procedure since we can test the evidence of our senses only by relying upon other evidence similarly provided. The knowledge provided by our memories is not fundamentally different from the knowledge obtained through our senses, although it is easier to have false beliefs based upon what we mistakenly believe ourselves to remember than to have false beliefs based upon what we mistakenly suppose ourselves to perceive. In remembering there is more scope for the distorting effects of prejudice.

We extend the knowledge provided by our senses and our memories by inference. We generalize from what is observed, and thence infer to what is not observed. We note an analogy between M and N, and thence infer that what is true of M is also true of N. In the foregoing chapters we have had occasion to notice that both these kinds of inference may be mistaken. Nevertheless, our ability to extend the slender stock of knowledge provided by our own sense-observations and our own memories is dependent upon our ability to make such inferences correctly.

Accepting a generalization to the effect that *All A is B* as true and noticing that *This is an A*, we infer that *This is a B*. This, it will be remembered, is a deductive inference. The truth of the conclusion is not established unless the premisses are true. The truth of the premiss *All A is B* is established either by generalization or by a previous process of deductive inference. In the latter case those premisses will need to have been established. Eventually we come to a premiss (or premisses) accepted on the basis of generalizations or regarded as intuitively evident.

Let us take as an example two statements made by Lord Baldwin; we have already made use of both these statements, but we are now concerned with them from a different point of view.

(a)   *A political audience is only imperfectly prepared to follow a close argument.*
(b)   *The speaker (at a political meeting) wishes to make a favourable impression, to secure support for a policy.*

I believe that both these statements are true. We must ask what are the grounds for holding them to be true. Naturally I do not know what answer Baldwin would give to this question, but I conjecture that any politician might reasonably give some such answer as the following:

I have had a good deal of experience of political audiences; I know that such audiences are usually made up of people of various types. Some are comparatively well-informed, but most are almost completely ignorant of the issues that are to be put before them. They vary considerably in intelligence. For the most part they have not been trained to follow a close argument; they do not know clearly what are the conditions of a sound argument. They want, or at least most of them do, to be assured that the policy of the country will be directed in the main for their own welfare. Many of them realize that they are incompetent to judge the merits of the various alternatives that may be placed before them; they are impatient to have things done. Accordingly, they easily get bored by a speaker who attempts to give his reasons at length. But this is what a close argument requires. So I conclude that a political audience is only imperfectly prepared to follow a close argument.

This reply provides the first step towards testing the belief given in statement (a). The belief is based upon first-hand experience of 'political audiences', and involves a generalization from this experience. The generalization is not at all simple. Let us contrast it with a much simpler kind of generalization.

(i)   *This buttercup is yellow, and so is that.* Indeed, *I remember that all the buttercups I have seen are yellow.*
(ii) Therefore, I conclude that *All buttercups are yellow, both those that I have seen and those that I have not seen.*

In this example (i) constitutes the premiss, (ii) the conclusion of the inference. The inference is of the kind known to logicians as 'inductive inference by simple enumeration where contradictory instances are not found.' The name is not perhaps very enlightening. The crucial word is 'instances'. It belongs to the pre-reflective stage of acquiring knowledge to recognize certain objects as resembling each other in some respects. These objects can be classed together *because* they resemble each other in those respects. Hence arise class-names. If someone says: 'That is a buttercup', he is asserting that *that* (which is sensibly present to him) is an *instance* of the class *buttercups*. Suppose that, as you are walking along the pavement, you see a motor-car approaching, and you say: 'Hullo, that's a Hillman-Wizard'. You are expressing your recognition of *that car* as belonging to the class of cars called 'Hillman-Wizards'. We are constantly making judgments of this sort: 'That is a sheep'; 'That man is Chinese'; 'That ship is a brig'; 'Those roses are Alan-Richardsons'; 'That was a very good speech.' Each of these judgments is a judgment with regard to something that it is an *instance* of a certain class. They differ in complexity, and thus, in ease of recognition. Sometimes such judgments are mistaken; in that case there is a failure in identification. With that source of error we are not now concerned. We have to consider the passage of thought from noticing that *every observed instance of a certain class has a certain property* to the conclusion that *all members of that class have that property*. Clearly, in thus inferring we run the risk of error. Nevertheless, we are bound to rely upon inferences of this kind. The conclusion goes beyond the evidence; it is based upon observed instances, but involves an assertion about what is not observed. Unless we could reasonably make assertions that go beyond the evidence, our knowledge would be confined to what we each observe and remember. Without generalization human knowledge would not have advanced, for we could not have benefited by the labours of our predecessors.

Generalizations of the sort we have been discussing are empirical generalizations, i.e. generalizations based upon experience. If our experience is meagre, we are foolish to generalize. A single contradictory instance will upset the generalization. The example of a generalization, discussed in Chapter 10, to the effect that *red-haired people are poor at history* is upset by the discovery of a single brilliant historian who has red hair. When we were discussing that example we saw that whilst an unrestricted generalization of the form *All A is B* may be false, yet a more moderate statement of the form *A tends to be B* may be true. It is reasonable to accept the unrestricted generalization provided that the observed instances upon which it is based are not relatively few in number, and that we have some grounds for supposing that, if there were contradictory instances, we should have heard of them.

The statement about *political audiences*, given on p. 220, is an unrestricted generalization. If you look back to the grounds that were (supposedly) given for the belief that *a political audience is only imperfectly prepared to follow a close argument*, you will see that the speaker began by affirming that he had 'had a good deal of experience of political audiences.' This is a hopeful beginning for a defence of the belief. He had observed instances of the sort about which his belief was a generalization. Certainly it is much more difficult to 'observe' an audience than it is to observe a buttercup. But an experienced speaker comes to sense the reactions of his audience. Notice that I say 'an *experienced* speaker', and 'comes to *sense* the reactions of his audience'. These phrases are significant. 'An experienced speaker' is a person who has had previous experience of speaking to an audience; he knows *from his own experience* what it is like to speak to an audience. Through his experience he acquires knowledge. Again, someone who has such experience may gain an apprehension of the reaction of his audience that is not unlike sense-experience. He is immediately aware of the reaction; i.e. he is not *inferring* the reaction, but, as we also say, *feeling* it. In spite, then, of the differences between seeing a buttercup and having experience of the reaction of an audience, there is an important similarity in the form of the generalization about buttercups and the generalization about political audiences. The further grounds given (on p. 221) were also hopeful for the defence of the belief. A rough attempt was made to analyse the make-up of a political audience. This analysis was expressed in a set of judgments, each of which was likewise based upon previous experiences. Finally, these judgments were regarded as justifying the deductive inference that, since audiences were composed of people like this, they would be bored by a close argument. From which the conclusion follows that such an audience is only imperfectly prepared to follow a close argument.

This reasoned defence has a logical form. It combines generalization from observed instances with deductions from other generalizations derived in the same manner. I venture to assert dogmatically that every reasoned argument has a definite logical form although not all reasoned arguments are deductive. It would not be difficult to set out this form in detail, but for my present purpose it is not necessary. It is enough to call attention to the fact that some premisses required for the defence of the belief were not stated by the speaker; it was assumed that they could be tacitly taken for granted. You will easily be able to supply these premisses.

I have said that the generalization which we have been considering was an unrestricted generalization. This is true in form and in fact. Nevertheless, we have to take note of the context in which assertions are made. When Baldwin was talking about certain characteristics of a political audience he was speaking about conditions now prevailing. He did not commit himself to the assertion that at *any time* and in *every country* a political audience is only imperfectly prepared to follow a close argument. We may easily misunderstand the import of an assertion and may do an injustice to the speaker, if we forget to take note of the context within which the assertion is made. It is not inconsistent to believe that Every S is P and yet to believe that the characteristics which belong to the objects called 'an S' may be altered in such a way that it is not true that Every S is P. Certainly a proposition of the form Every S is P contradicts a proposition of the form Not every S is P. This is so because the symbol, 'S', signifies by convention the same subject in both propositions. When, in a statement using significant words (as distinct from conventional symbols), we replace the symbol 'S' by 'political audience', then the subject is very complex. The properties that define the class political audiences are independent of some of the properties possessed by sets of people who, at any given time, make up this, or that, political audience. A political audience is a set of people gathered together in order that they should be addressed by some public speaker on a political topic. It is not unreasonable to suppose that variation in the properties which are not presupposed in what is meant by 'political audience' is not irrelevant to the truth of the statement that every political audience has some definite property symbolized by 'P'. This possibility was recognized in the defence of the belief we have been discussing for the sake of giving an example. I assume that further elaboration of this point is not necessary.

This tedious examination of a definite example was required in order to indicate how we may test one sort of belief. If a belief is derived from a generalization based upon particular instances, we must take into account the scope of the investigation. We must try to find out whether the instances are representative or are selected, whether there are likely to be contradictory instances that have not been looked for, and whether the belief in question conflicts with other beliefs for which we have equally good grounds. When there is such a conflict there are not sufficient grounds for regarding either belief as true. We must search for further evidence in the hope of establishing one belief and rejecting another. Unless it is possible to put the conflicting beliefs to this further test we ought to suspend judgment.

If you look back once more to the statements labelled (a) and (b) on p. 220, you will see that (b) is also an empirical generalization. It requires the same kind of testing as (a). We may now notice that if we accept both (a) and (b), we shall be tempted to conclude that *a speaker addressing a political audience will not offer a close argument*. I have yielded to this temptation. I confess that I long ago entertained this belief. The fact that Baldwin, who is an expert in these matters, also holds it did but confirm my belief. It would be possible to derive the belief that *a political speaker will not put forward a close argument* from observation of the behaviour of political speakers and generalizing from these observations. Here again we should need to be careful not to confine our observations to one type of political speakers or to one type of political audiences. If we omit these precautions we may fall into the mistake of inferring from selected instances. This precaution is always necessary; it is relevant to every one of the statements made in the defence, since, ultimately, the premisses used in the argument must be based upon observation of instances.

I wish now briefly to consider how someone might come to be convinced – that political speakers will not put forward a reasoned argument when they are addressing a political audience – not by generalizing from his own experiences, but by accepting the premisses of an argument that entails this conclusion. This conclusion does not follow directly from statements (a) and (b); it requires some additional premisses. I will set out the arguments in full, enclosing in brackets those premisses which have not been stated, but the assumption of which is logically necessary to establish the conclusion:

(1) *A political audience is only imperfectly prepared to follow a close argument;*

(2) *[A speaker who uses an argument which the audience is not prepared to follow will not make a favourable impression;]*

(3) *[A speaker who presents a close argument is using an argument which a political audience is not prepared to follow;]*

(4) *Every speaker (to a political audience) wishes to make a favourable impression, to secure support for a policy;*

Therefore, *No speaker (to a political audience) will put forward a close argument.*

It is irrational to accept these four premisses and deny the conclusion. Someone who had not previously believed what is stated in the conclusion but was now convinced of the truth of the premisses ought to accept the conclusion. If he did so, then he would have acquired fresh knowledge, and this knowledge would have been gained through a deductive inference. This statement is true subject to the condition that the premisses are true. If one, or more, of the premisses were false, he would not have good grounds for his belief, even if the conclusion were in fact true. This point has already been considered, and I shall not pursue it farther. I wish only to stress the fact that our knowledge about the world is derived partly from empirical generalizations, partly from deductive inferences from these generalizations.

Some of these generalizations each of us makes for himself; the majority of those we accept are accepted upon the testimony of other persons. The greater part of our knowledge about any topic is due to our acceptance of the labours of other people. I confess that I should be very much surprised if anyone were to doubt this statement. I shall not attempt to justify it, but will content myself with reminding you that, if you claim to know anything that goes beyond the direct evidence of your senses and is not supplied by what you remember, then you are relying upon testimony. Ask yourself why you believe that George V is dead (supposing that you do believe it). Ask yourself why you believe that sugar is a carbohydrate, or why you believe that Belgium is more densely populated than Brazil, or why you believe that an election was held in Russia on December 12th, 1937, or why you believe that Mr Anthony Eden resigned from the Cabinet in February of this year (1938) because he differed from the foreign policy of the Prime Minister – supposing that you do entertain any of these beliefs. You will find that at least part of the evidence for any one of these beliefs is based upon testimony – upon what you have been told by other people, or have read in books or in newspapers or some other appropriate journals.

From the point of view from which this book is written the fact that we must rely upon testimony is of great importance. For most of the purposes of our everyday life we need to think effectively. We want to draw true conclusions from true premisses. If we are sick, we want to find a doctor upon whose statements we can rely. If we want to go by train from Euston to Glasgow, we want to know what trains are available for that purpose. If we want to learn how to sail a yacht, we want advice from those who are expert in the craft of sailing. Constantly we are forced to rely upon the advice of other people; we have to rely upon others to supply us with information which we have not the time, or the opportunity, or the skill, to discover for ourselves. In short, the acceptance of testimony is indispensable for the fulfilment of our desires. Since we must act, knowledge of the conditions relevant to our action is essential.

We have already noticed that, from the point of view of the origins of our knowledge, testimony is not a logically independent source of knowledge, since in accepting testimony we are using our senses or relying upon our memories. Testimony is, however, a means of acquiring knowledge about topics of which we have not, and do not expect to have, first-hand experience. Testimony provides us with indirect knowledge. The beliefs we accept upon testimony need to be scrutinized carefully. In addition to the mistakes to which we are all liable in our own observing and our own interpretation of what we have observed, we have to make allowance for prejudices that we may not share and for deliberate dishonesty that we may not suspect. It would, indeed, be relevant here to consider the crooked arguments that other people may try to foist upon us. These we have already discussed. Consequently, we need now only note that in relying upon testimony we must beware of crooked arguments, provided that there are any grounds for suspicion that they may be used, and that we must satisfy ourselves of the credentials of the experts whose advice we seek.

To take an extreme example. A headmistress of a school was appointing a new housekeeper. One candidate stood out from the rest by reason of the excellence of the testimonials she presented. The headmistress knew the writer of one of these testimonials and had reliance upon her judgment. This candidate was appointed. She turned out to be lacking in just those qualities that were essential for this particular post, although these qualities were attributed to her in the testimonials. Being much puzzled by this discrepancy, the headmistress investigated the matter. She discovered that the 'testimonials' were forgeries. You will have noticed that I spoke of 'the writer of one of these testimonials' and asserted that the headmistress had confidence in 'the writer'. I then said that the testimonials were forgeries. They had been written by the candidate herself. In presenting the case, however, I was presenting it in the way in which it had been accepted by the headmistress. The person whose name was printed at the foot of the testimonial was assumed by the headmistress to be the writer. This assumption is generally made and is usually correct. I believe that few applicants for posts in schools or colleges present forged testimonials, although to do so would not be usually attended by much risk in those cases where the originals of the printed, or typed, copies do not have to be produced. In the case we have been considering, the headmistress believed that she was being provided with the testimony of a person whom she knew to have expert knowledge about the sort of characteristics required in a school housekeeper. Her belief that the *assumed* writer was an expert upon whose judgment and accuracy she could rely was not mistaken. The mistake lay in taking it for granted that the assumed writer had in fact written the testimonial.

In our attempts to discover what is going on in our own country and in foreign countries we are forced to rely upon newspapers and other writings. In Chapter 7 I pointed out some of the difficulties we encounter owing to the fact that our Press is relatively a controlled Press, or, as Mr Chamberlain put it, 'a combination of a factory, commercial business and a profession'. In this chapter I am anxious to call attention to another obstacle than propaganda. This obstacle is due to our habit of assuming that what is not reported in our favourite newspaper (or newspapers, if we like more than one) could not have been worth reporting, and that what is reported is so reported as to bring out its full significance. We tend to assume that all the information we require about the political situation will be provided by our daily paper, whichever that may be. This is a mistake. Partly for the reasons mentioned in Chapter 7 there must be selection with regard to what is reported. To save much needed space a précis has often to be substituted for report in direct speech and important letters from public men have at times to be summarized. We cannot complain of this procedure since we are content to have newspapers that are the product of the combination of a factory, a commercial business and a profession – the elements of the combination being in order of precedence correctly stated by Mr Chamberlain. This being so, it is desirable to consult newspapers of different political complexions if we wish to be well informed of what is taking place at home and abroad. Otherwise, we may miss items of importance. The phrase 'items of importance' is significant. To repeat a point that I have stressed throughout this book – *importance* depends upon the point of view. Accordingly, those who control our newspapers stress what is important from their point of view, and slur over, or omit entirely, whatever may conflict with it.

Two examples of significant omission may make this point clear.

The question of the formation of some sort of 'Popular Front' in this country is considered by many people to be of considerable importance. Some non-Conservatives are ardently in favour, others are as ardently opposed to any such formation. The Labour Party are, in the main, opposed, whilst those who are of the political persuasion represented by the *New Statesman and Nation* are, in the main, in favour. At the Aylesbury by-election in May of this year (1938), the Labour Party candidate was urged to withdraw in favour of a 'Popular Front' candidate. His withdrawal was strongly opposed by the local Labour Party; and he was not withdrawn. Meanwhile, various conferences were voting for or against proposals for a 'Popular Front'. The National Conference of Labour Women rejected 'by an overwhelming majority proposals for a Popular Front'. This quotation is taken from a letter, published in *Forward* (Saturday, May 28th, 1938), and signed 'Mary Sutherland, Chief Woman Officer, Labour Party, Transport House.' The following extracts from this letter deal with this question of newspaper omissions:

> I think it may be of interest to your readers to know how this important news item was treated in the Popular Front Press.
>
> The *News Chronicle* on May 11th carried no report of the discussion nor the vote. On the following day – one day late – it had a few lines tacked on to a report of a speech by Mr Attlee at the Public Demonstration held in connexion with the Conference.
>
> The *Daily Worker* made no mention of the matter at all. The *Tribune* and *Reynolds* at the week-end were also silent and the *New Statesman and Nation* contained a contemptuous reference to it.
>
> The following week's *Tribune* (May 20th, 1938), in the course of a somewhat peevish description of the Conference, referred to the 'unhealthy submissiveness to authority of the majority of the delegates.'

The reference in the *New Statesman and Nation* (May 14th) occurs in a paragraph headed: 'By-elections and Transport House', and is as follows:

> Transport House, however, despite some local Labour pressure to withdraw in Mid-Bucks, remains quite unmoved by the demands for any sort of 'Popular Front' based on local electoral arrangements with the Liberals; and this week, on a resolution proposing collaboration with both Liberals and Communists,

the Labour Women's Conference voted as Transport House wished by a very large majority.

No doubt the writer of the letter to *Forward* regarded this reference as 'contemptuous', since the Women's Labour Conference is reported as having 'voted as Transport House wished.' Certainly the implications of the statement are that 'working-class women' have not minds of their own.

In a later letter to *Forward* (Saturday, June 4th) Mary Sutherland stated that, since writing her first letter, she had 'seen a copy of *Reynolds* of May 15th, which carries a report of the National Conference of Labour Women, including a few lines about the conference decision on the Popular Front.' She adds:

> This copy was sent to a reader, who protested to *Reynolds* about their failure to mention the conference.
>
> I regret, therefore, that I said that *Reynolds* was silent, as it appears that certain editions did mention the matter, but when readers as far apart as Glasgow, Essex, Portsmouth and London had had copies containing nothing about the conference, my conclusion was not unjustified: and rank-and-file Labour women, who are loyal supporters of *Reynolds*, can be forgiven for believing that a conference which represents over a million and a half organized working women, is worthy of notice in *every* edition.

This incident is, I believe, fairly representative. Papers that support the Popular Front are only too ready to minimize the importance of any agitation against its formation. And conversely, a reader who, for example, had followed the accounts of the Aylesbury by-election only in the *Daily Worker* would have a totally different impression of what was happening from that of a reader who had followed accounts only in *Forward*. Those who read only what are called 'the more reputable papers' would have, I think, some difficulty in discovering at all that a considerable number of people are being agitated by the possibility of the formation of a Popular Front.

The second example of significant omission concerns the letter recently written by Lord Cecil to Lord Lucan, in which he requested that the Government Whip should not be sent to him, since he could not be treated 'any longer as even nominally a supporter of the Government'. This step was taken by Lord Cecil as a result of Mr Chamberlain's attitude to the bombing of British ships by the insurgents in Spain.

Whatever may be our attitude on this question, we may surely regard Lord Cecil's refusal of the Government Whip as a matter of political importance, that is, of sufficient importance to warrant a full report of his letter in all the 'reputable newspapers'. The way in which this incident was reported provides a striking example of the significance of omissions in the Press. I propose, for the sake of example, to consider in some detail the reports given of this incident in various newspapers. Lord Cecil's letter was sent to Lord Lucan on Friday, June 24th, and was presumably received by him on June 25th. I propose to begin by quoting in full the report given in *The Times* (Monday, June 27th). This report appears in the 'Home News' page, under the title 'LORD CECIL AND THE PRIME MINISTER,' with the sub-heading 'GOVERNMENT WHIP DECLINED.' The report is as follows:

Our Parliamentary Correspondent writes:
    Lord Cecil has requested that the Government Whip be no longer sent to him, since he cannot, in view of the Prime

Minister's speech on the bombing of British ships by Spanish insurgents, allow himself to be treated as even nominally a supporter of the Government.

Lord Cecil explains, in a letter to Lord Lucan, that his feeling that Mr Chamberlain's attitude is indefensible does not arise from a wish to take either side in the Spanish War. The ships bombed were acting lawfully in pursuit of their trade, and the attacks were not accidental but deliberate. The Prime Minister admitted that the attacks were illegal, but he declined to take any action, military or economic, to protect British lives and property; all that he would do was to send Notes, which had been quite ineffective.

Lord Cecil adds that he does not recall any incident in British history at all comparable, and it seems to him to be inconsistent with British honour and international morality.

This report, you will observe, is in indirect speech. Not only did The Times not consider it worth while to print the letter in full; further, it gives not a single quotation from it. The effect of this form of report is to depersonalize what Lord Cecil had written. To bring out this point I shall quote in full the first two and the last two paragraphs of Lord Cecil's letter:

My dear Lucan, – In spite of the fact that for some time I have felt unable to vote for most Ministerial measures you have been good enough to send me the Government Whip.

I am much obliged to you, but after the Prime Minister's speech about the bombing of British ships by the insurgents in Spain, I feel bound to ask you to stop doing so in future.

. . .

I do not recall any incident in British history at all comparable. I do not believe that any other British Prime Minister has ever made a speech like that of Mr Chamberlain. It seems to me inconsistent with British honour and international morality.

Holding that opinion, I feel that I cannot honestly allow you to treat me any longer as even nominally a supporter of the Government. With much regret. Yours very sincerely,

CECIL

I have quoted these paragraphs from the *Manchester Guardian*, which reports the letter in full, without interspersed headlines. The middle paragraph I have omitted; the gist of it is given in the second paragraph of *The Times'* report. I have omitted it, partly for reasons of space, partly because I am not here concerned to take sides with regard to Mr Chamberlain's policy; my sole concern is to bring out, by means of a detailed example, the dangers to which we ordinary people are exposed in our reliance upon the information we obtain from the newspapers. I shall now compare the reports, or lack of reports, of Lord Cecil's letter in various newspapers upon which some of us are wont to rely to supply us with information. I shall make a list giving the amount of space devoted to the report, in the case of each newspaper mentioned, adding brief comments as required. The figures in parentheses give, where stated, the circulation to the nearest thousand.[2]

Evening Standard (June 25th, p. 3). Letter reported in full, and interspersed with headlines. 10½ inches. (405,000.)

Manchester Guardian (June 27th, p. 9). Letter reported in full (8 inches), with short introductory comment. Total report, 10½ inches. The Leader (p. 8), entitled 'A Policy's Results,' quotes in full the last paragraph but one of the letter.

Daily Telegraph (June 27th, p. 6). Letter reported in part only, but the condemnatory paragraphs (reported in indirect speech in *The Times*) are given in full. 4 inches. (Over 700,000.)

A comment is made (p. 12) on 'Lord Cecil, Cross-Bencher', pointing out that the 'only surprise about his move is that he did not make it some time ago,' since for some time he has spoken from the cross benches. The comment concludes: 'Lord Cecil's geographical move, whatever his political associates may have thought of it, was welcomed by the reporters, who for the first time found his speeches approaching audibility.' (Comment upon this comment would be superfluous.)

The Scotsman (June 27th, p. 11). Letter reported in full, interspersed with headlines, preceded by brief comment. 9 inches.

News Chronicle (June 27th, p. 13). Letter reported in full, interspersed with headlines. 10 inches. Editorial comment. (1,334,000.)

The Star (June 25th, p. 6). Letter reported in full. 13½ inches. (493,000.)

Daily Herald (June 27th, p. 8). Letter reported in part, the whole sense being given; condemnatory paragraphs quoted in full, interspersed with large headlines. 10 inches. (Over 2,000,000.)

Observer (June 26th). No report. (214,000.)

Daily Express (June 27th). No report. (2,507,000).

Sunday Express (June 26th, p. 17). Brief statement. 1 inch. (In excess of 1,400,000.)

Daily Mail (June 27th, p. 12). Brief statement as follows:

Viscount Cecil has decided that he can no longer be treated as 'even nominally a supporter of the Government', and has asked that the Government Whip should not be sent to him.

He has taken this step, he says, as a result of the Prime Minister's attitude toward the bombing of British ships in Spain. (1,531,000.)

This is all that the *Daily Mail* reports. The brief statement is headed 'Lord Cecil and Spain,' not – as might have been expected – 'Lord Cecil and the Government.'

The statement in the *Sunday Express* is very similar to that in the *Daily Mail*, but it is headed 'Lord Cecil declines the Government Whip.'

Birmingham Post (June 27th, p. 7). Full report. 7 inches.

Yorkshire Post (June 27th, p. 7). Letter reported in full. 7 inches.

Daily Independent, Sheffield. No report.

The Sunday Times (June 26th, p. 24). Letter reported in full, interspersed with headlines, preceded by brief comment. 9 inches. (Over 300,000.)

It will be noticed that, so far as the London Press is concerned, the only newspapers (of those mentioned above, which include all I have been able to examine) which reported the letter in full were the *Evening Standard*, the *Star*, the *Daily Herald*, the *News Chronicle*; the widely read *Scotsman* and *Manchester Guardian* also reported in full. *The Times*, *Daily Mail*, and *Daily Telegraph* gave reports that were misleading both in brevity and in form.

I do not wish to suggest that, had some other incident been selected, there would not have been a considerable variation in the papers that respectively published full reports, brief statements, or no reports at all. On the contrary. My chief reason for selecting this incident was that it occurred at the time when I was looking for an example of significant omission. The points that I wish to stress are that omissions are significant and are, by the nature of the case, difficult to detect. They can be detected only if we form the habit of consulting newspapers representing different political views. That this should be necessary is deplorable. We are considering not *views*, but *news*. No one, I imagine, wishes all newspapers to be written from the same point of view. In my opinion, at least, it is a gain to a nation that there should be newspapers representing many different shades of opinion. Indeed, as I pointed out in Chapter 7, there is in this country a considerable degree of uniformity in the newspapers with the largest circulation. Just as the Government, in a democratic country, is healthier when there is a strong Opposition, so is the Press in a more satisfactory condition when there are newspapers of rival views, but with, approximately, the same circulation. We do, however, need correct and adequate *news*, in order that we may have the necessary information upon which to base our judgments and form our views about political affairs.

Many ordinary people are puzzled to know just how much truth there is in, say, atrocity stories from Spain, or in accounts of 'the Red Menace', or 'the spy racket in Russia'. We are easily tempted to attach equal weight to all the statements we read, or to believe more firmly those statements that are made most impressively or that happen to chime in with our prejudices. If we desire to test our beliefs, we shall do well to seek for information in newspapers of rival views. For example, if we were to find any admission in The Times of atrocities committed by General Franco's forces, we should reasonably accept the statement; whereas, if we find admissions by those of 'Left' sympathies that the Spanish Government have been guilty of atrocities we should likewise be reasonable in accepting these admissions as providing good evidence. As a further example, we may consider the question of religious toleration in Spain. Sir Arnold Wilson, in a letter to The Times (November 25th, 1937), said:

Neither the Duke of Alba nor General Franco can 'guarantee' anything at this stage except 'complete toleration'. The phrase means one thing to us in India and the Colonies and something else at home. It is neither fair nor reasonable to expect it to be defined more exactly. But we know that it is not and will not be extended to Christians by the Government of Barcelona.

This letter was replied to by the Rev. A. Capo (Methodist Minister in Barcelona), an extract from whose letter was published in *The Times*, on December 6th, 1937. I quote part of the extract:

I wish to state that while we here have no information as to the religious tolerance on the side of the Franco Government, we do know that in Barcelona all the Protestant churches are open for services and attended by good congregations and that this is with the consent and approval of the authorities of Barcelona. The services are celebrated with the accustomed ritual, without interference or opposition of any sort.

The publication of this extract in *The Times* may, I think, be regarded as evidence of its authenticity. The original letter from Sir Arnold Wilson was printed in full in the large print given to 'Letters to the Editor'; the Methodist Minister's reply was given in extract under 'Points from Letters.' But it was given. It is reasonable to attach more weight to this evidence than would be the case had this letter appeared in a newspaper favourable to Barcelona.

It is not, I think, necessary to multiply examples in order to show that we need to adopt to the news we find in our newspapers the attitude we recognize to be reasonable in assessing the weight to be attached to the testimonials produced by candidates to a post. If we happened to know that the writer of such a testimonial was extremely hostile to the candidate in question, we should recognize that any good point assigned to the candidate was honestly attributed to him by the writer. The judgment would be disinterested. Anyone who has had much experience in reading testimonials is likely to admit the difficulty of eliciting the relevant facts from a set of testimonials. One learns to note carefully what is not said, as well as what is said. I am optimistic enough to believe that most writers of testimonials on behalf of candidates for posts say what they believe to be true. It does not follow that their beliefs are in fact true, but with that consideration we are not now concerned. The point is that there is some likeness between eliciting the facts about a candidate from the evidence presented by his testimonials and eliciting the facts about a controversial topic from the evidence presented in the reports of different newspapers. The latter task is much more difficult owing both to the nature of the inquiry and the degree of reliableness of the witnesses. In our attempts to form a reasoned judgment upon, say, the state of unemployment, the likelihood (or otherwise) of a slump, or the foreign policy of the Government of the day, we are not, I believe, given as much help as might reasonably be expected. Our greatest obstacles are to be found rather in omission of vital evidence or in distortion of evidence than in deliberate mis-statement or in direct lies, whether we are considering parliamentary debates or information provided in the Press. With regard to the latter source of information there is the further difficulty of disentangling the *news* – i.e. reports of what has happened – from the *views* – i.e. judgments, made by the newspaper writer, concerning the significance of what has happened.

Those of us who wish 'to know the facts' are indeed somewhat in the position of jurors who have to 'judge' from the evidence submitted to them whether or not the prisoner in the dock is guilty. The prisoner knows whether he is guilty or innocent; the defending counsel may also know the truth; some of the witnesses may know, some may not. Let us suppose that the prisoner is guilty, that his counsel and some of the witnesses know that he is, but that some of the witnesses mistakenly believe him to be innocent. In such a case those who know the prisoner to be guilty are concerned to conceal the truth; they may find it necessary to tell deliberate lies; they will seek to distort the evidence, to avert as far as possible any chance that one of the deluded witnesses will blurt out an inconvenient fact. The defending counsel will seize every opportunity to make a point in favour of the prisoner. The prosecuting counsel, on the other hand, will seek to produce only that evidence that tells against the prisoner; he will attempt to discredit as much as possible the evidence that appears to make for the prisoner's innocence, he will do what he can to build up a case against the prisoner both by the cross-examination of witnesses and by a skilful marshalling of the circumstantial evidence. The jurors, listening to both sides, have to come to a decision; they must make up their minds whether the prisoner is guilty, and, if so, what is the degree of his guilt; or they must regard the conclusion as 'not proven'.[3]

I have been assuming that the jurors have to make up their minds and form their judgment upon the basis of circumstantial evidence. Evidence is said to be 'circumstantial' when a set of facts taken together point to a definite conclusion even though a single fact, taken in isolation, would not suffice to indicate that conclusion. Circumstantial evidence is cumulative. Each distinct item in the evidence points in the same direction. 'Under certain circumstances,' as we say, 'the only reasonable conclusion is so and so.' To say that the conclusion is one that it is reasonable to assert is not to say that it must be true. We are most of us familiar with heroes of detective stories who are 'entangled in a web of circumstantial evidence' through a series of coincidences that belong, it must be confessed, rather to fiction than to fact. It is enough here to point out that circumstantial evidence is capable of leading us to form a reasonable judgment. What is more relevant to my purpose is to emphasize the consideration that, so far as our opinions about public affairs are concerned, we are seldom in so favourable a position as are jurors listening to the evidence in a court of law. The jurors know which part of the evidence is provided by the prosecuting counsel and the witnesses for the prosecution, and which part is provided by the other side. They are thus in a position to know, and thus to make allowance for, the respective points of view.

It might be objected that it is the business of the witnesses to provide evidence, not of the counsel. This objection would not hold. In the sense in which we are concerned with the estimation of evidence, anything is 'evidence' that is provided for the sake of enabling us to form a judgment. The speeches of counsel are designed with a view to leading the jurors to make a certain judgment, namely the judgment favourable to the counsel's side. The selection and arrangement of the items of information elicited from the witnesses give to these items just that significance that makes them 'evidence of such and such'.

How, then, does the position of ordinary people who are trying to come to reasonable conclusions with regard to public affairs differ from the position of jurors whose duty it is to assess the evidence given in a court of law? The resemblance has already been stressed. Governments, whether British, Russian, French, German, Italian, or Japanese, are at times anxious to conceal 'the facts' both from their own people and from those of other countries. To secure this end a Government may be guilty of evasion, of skilful misrepresentation, even of deliberate lying. We ordinary people have to elicit the truth from such evidence as we can discover. We cannot assume that there is anyone anxious to help us in eliciting the truth. We have to take note of the trend of events by comparing what is said by one person at one time with what he says at some other time, or by different persons on different occasions. We have to evaluate the credentials of the authors of conflicting reports. In doing so we must be prepared to make allowance for the point of view. Herein we are faced with a difficulty from which the jurors are free; we may not be able to guess the point of view. It is true, as Baldwin has said, that a politician resembles an advocate in that he has to defend a policy. This limitation upon his candour can be allowed for, if we know what his policy is and bear that important point in mind. But our difficulties do not end here. There is no impartial judge to give us a summing up – reminding us of the evidence we heard some days ago, at the beginning of the trial, pointing out the significance of this or that item of evidence, showing us precisely what are the doubts to be resolved. All this we must do for ourselves, unless we are content to rely upon our journalists to make up our minds for us. The leading articles in the newspapers perform, in some fashion, the business of 'summing up', but without the impartiality which we expect from a judge. Moreover, we are seldom in a position to know when 'the evidence' has been completed.

To remember the evidence is difficult. Our memories are short. It is at times difficult to acquit politicians of taking advantage of the ease with which we forget. What is said one day may be flatly contradicted a little later without our noticing the contradiction because we have forgotten all about the former statement.

Compare, for instance, these statements:

All my information goes to show that trade prospects, in general, are good and that the country can feel with confidence that progress made in 1937 will be maintained in the coming year.

This statement was made by Mr Oliver Stanley, reported in the *Sunday Times* on December 26th, 1937.

In the first four months of this year not only had there been a slackening in the increase of production that had been going on before, but in some trades an actual decline.

This statement was also made by Mr Oliver Stanley, but on May 25th, 1938.

These two statements are not, it will be observed, in flat contradiction. It is not logically impossible that all the information Mr Oliver Stanley had up to December 26th, 1937, should show that trade prospects were good and that in the four months immediately following there should be a slackening in increase and even an actual decline. If the former statement is true, then we can only conclude that the President of the Board of Trade was not well served by those who supplied him with 'information'. Perhaps we should be less ready to accept this view if we noticed that Mr Chamberlain was reported – in the same number of the *Sunday Times*, namely, December 26th, 1937 – as having said:

The talk of an on-coming slump is not only exaggerated, but dangerous.

Perhaps it would also be helpful to remember that there had been some discussion in *The Times*, during that month, of the need for 'increasing business confidence'. A letter was published on December 18th, in which Mr J. M. Keynes vigorously supported the view that 'the fear of a slump may be itself a contributory cause for creating one'. I myself believe Mr Keynes's statement to be true. Possibly Mr Stanley also believes it. Possibly this belief led him to make the reassuring statement which I have already quoted.

I have selected this example because it is comparatively innocuous. Some of us may remember other occasions and other issues of even greater importance to the nation when our statesmen have put forward comforting statements, which they later denied quietly. It may be remembered that Baldwin informed the British public, not long after the 1935 election, that a statesman's lips may be 'sealed' even at the very moment (say at a General Election) when he is deliberately professing to tell us the truth and nothing but the truth. It would not, in my opinion, be reasonable to ask Cabinet Ministers to tell us 'the whole truth', for 'us' covers not only the people in their own country but also anyone anywhere who has access to the same channels of communication. But if we do not know the whole truth, if some of the evidence most vital for our purposes in deciding about a policy be concealed from us, then we cannot be in a satisfactory position for estimating the significance of what we do know. We should then be unable adequately to test any belief that we may have come to entertain. There is no short and easy way of overcoming this obstacle.

As a final example we might consider the recurrent treason trials in Russia. Certain reports appearing in our newspapers may be accepted as data, i.e. as true reports of what happens. For example, it would not be reasonable to doubt that Zinoviev and Kamenev were accused, tried and declared to be guilty of conspiracy against the Soviet Union; further, that they were subsequently executed. But it is not so easy to determine whether they were in fact guilty, and if so, of what precisely they were guilty. Suppose that we accept further the reports of their 'confessions'. How are we to decide whether these confessions were genuine or not? Those who are friendly to the Soviet Union must have found it difficult to credit them; those who were hostile were in no less difficulty, although for opposite reasons. It is not my concern to take sides in this matter. I cite these 'Treason trials' merely as a good example of the sort of difficulties against which we have to contend if we desire to know what is happening either in foreign countries or in our own country. Those who know do not always tell; those who tell do not always know.

NOTES

1   See A. W. P. Wolters: *The Evidence of Our Senses*, p. 5. The reader who is interested in pursuing this topic further would find this book very useful. It is brief, clear and excellently written.
2   These figures are based upon information kindly supplied to me by the newspapers in question.
3   It is true that, according to English law, the *verdict* 'not proven' cannot be given, but the jurors may make up their minds that the guilt of the prisoner is not proved; in that case, they must return a verdict of 'not guilty'. This is a point in which the comparison I am making does not hold in detail.

15

EPILOGUE

DEMOCRACY AND FREEDOM
OF MIND

The *Times* for December 11th, 1937, had for its first leader an article entitled 'Democracy on Paper'. It begins as follows:

> All Russia goes to the polls to-morrow, and it is pertinent, though perhaps unkind, to recall the passage in which Marx pointed out that the essence of bourgeois democracy was that 'the oppressed were permitted once every few years to decide which particular members of the oppressing class should mis-represent them in Parliament.' This formula, it is true, does not

DOI: 10.4324/b22927-15

> altogether apply to Sunday's gigantic dumbshow. The Russian
> voters are not permitted to decide anything at all. They cannot
> indeed claim to be taking part in an election, for to elect – in the
> Russian language even more unequivocally than in the English –
> means to choose.

The *Observer*, on the following day, made comments of a similar kind upon the Russian polling day. So far as my information goes – which is not very far – I believe these caustic comments to have considerable justification. I believe also that similar strictures could be truly made with regard to polls held recently in Germany and in Austria. Elections in this country are not in this sense unfree. We are proud to consider ourselves a democracy; we claim to have freedom of election, freedom of speech (including freedom of the Press) limited only by the laws of libel, sedition and blasphemy, and freedom in religion. No doubt there are certain qualifications to be made; it is probable that most people would admit that without economic freedom there cannot be political freedom, and that lacking economic security no man can be regarded as economically free. But, even if these admissions be granted, it will be contended that, by and large, we in this country do have institutions that may properly be described as democratic. It is not to my purpose to dispute these contentions. Nor shall I attempt to determine what characteristics are essential to democracy. It is enough if it be granted that it lies in our national temper to dislike obvious governmental restrictions. We like to feel ourselves to be free. In short, we value civil liberties.

I cannot pretend to make this *we* precise. I do not believe that it could be truthfully maintained that all British citizens have the power to impose their wills upon those who govern, limited only by the clash of interests between one citizen and another. I deliberately omit, however, any discussion of such political obstacles to freedom as we may encounter. I am not concerned with politics. My topic is freedom of mind. Unless I can think freely I cannot think effectively. Here 'I' stands for any person. If I want to make up my mind upon any problem of political action, I must be able to deliberate freely. If it were in fact true that we were all politically and economically free, still it would not follow that we were possessed of the freedom of mind without which, in my opinion, no democratic institutions can be satisfactorily maintained.

In this book I have tried to point out some of the obstacles that impede us in our attempts to think to some purpose: the difficulty of freeing our minds from blinkers, the difficulty of resisting propaganda and of being content to be persuaded where we should have striven to be convinced, the difficulties of an audience dominated by an unscrupulous speaker and the difficulties of a speaker who has to address an audience that is lazy and uncritical – in short, the difficulties created by our stupidity and by those who take advantage of that stupidity. Finally, there is the difficulty of obtaining information – the difficulty of knowing how to discover reliable testimony. It is this last difficulty that I wish to emphasize now.

I will take an example from my own experience, for here only am I sufficiently well informed. When the General Strike of May 1926 occurred, I was completely ignorant of the events that had led up to it. My sympathies, i.e. the implications of my general point of view, were somewhat waveringly in favour of the miners. I realized, however, that such judgments as I felt able to make were not well informed. Accordingly, I sought to discover 'the facts of the matter' – to use the glib phrase wherewith an uninstructed person is wont to approach matters of great moment. I found great difficulties in ascertaining 'the facts'. The stopping of the newspapers by the strikers increased my difficulty. Subsequently I read various accounts in different newspapers. I was struck by the way in which one newspaper asserted 'the plain facts' are so and so, whilst another asserted 'the simple fact' is – the opposite. How, then, could I decide between the miners and strikers on the one hand and the mine-owners on the other? Unless I did know what exactly were the points at issue, what each side sought to gain, what were the facts in the mining industry itself, I could not form an instructed judgment with regard to the problem. My ignorance made me unfree. To feel thus unfree is not pleasant. Out of this feeling may arise the temptation to give up thinking about the problem or to delude oneself into the belief that it is settled as soon as we can talk about the problem in terms of vague and unidentified abstractions. I select three examples to make this point clear.[1]

Lord Oxford and Asquith, during the General Strike, asserted:

We should have lost all sense of self-respect if we were to allow any section of the community at its own will, and for whatever motives, to bring to a standstill the industrial and social life of the whole nation. It would be to acquiesce in the substitution for Free Government of a Dictatorship. This the British people will never do.

Mr Baldwin asserted:

Constitutional Government is being attacked ... Stand behind the Government, who are doing their part, confident in the measures they have undertaken to preserve the liberties and privileges of the people of these islands. The laws of England are the people's birthright. The laws are in your keeping. You have made Parliament their guardian. The General Strike is a challenge to Parliament, and is the road to anarchy and ruin.

Rudyard Kipling published in Mr Churchill's British *Gazette*, 'A Song of the English', which runs:

> Keep ye the Law – be swift in all obedience –
> Clear the land of evil, drive the road and bridge the ford.
>> Make ye sure to each his own
>> That he reap where he hath sown,
> By the peace among Our Peoples let men know we serve the Lord.

It is a profitable exercise in the attempt to think clearly to try to identify 'the community', 'the people' (whose birthright is said to be the Laws of England), 'Our Peoples', and 'we', as these words are used in the above quotations from distinguished men. What is the cash value of these large abstractions? The task of identifying the reference of these words I leave to you.[2] I do not lack the experience of having allowed myself to be befooled with words. It is very easy to believe oneself to be thinking when one is only stringing together words that have a warm familiarity and an emotive significance. We are not thinking unless we know *what* it is we are 'thinking about'. It is probably true that 'the British people' will not acquiesce in 'the substitution for Free Government of a Dictatorship'. It is probably true that 'the peoples of these islands' will 'stand behind the Government' as soon as these people are persuaded that the Government 'have undertaken to preserve the liberties and privileges' that are their 'birthright'. Lord Oxford and Mr Baldwin showed themselves to be great parliamentarians in making these pronouncements. Rudyard Kipling showed himself to be an effective advocate of the policy he favoured, when he admonished 'the English':

> Make ye sure to each his own
> That he reap where he hath sown;

but we cannot follow his advice until we know who has sown and whether he who has sown is able to reap that which he sowed.

We (i.e. you or I, any you and any I) cannot each of us make our own investigations with regard to the vast majority of the problems upon which we are called to make decisions. I (Susan Stebbing) must rely upon the expert knowledge of the physician when I am sick; I must rely upon Bradshaw when I want to know what trains are available to take me from King's Cross to St Andrews; and so on. Frequently I am forced to say: 'This person's testimony is reliable'; 'that newspaper's report is to be trusted'. I am forced to say this; if my belief in the reliability of the testimony is false, then I am not free to decide. If such information as I have is not to be trusted, then I lack freedom of decision. For this reason, those who control the Press have power to control our minds with regard to our thinking about 'all public transactions'. A controlled Press is an obstacle to democracy, an obstacle that is the more dangerous in proportion as we are unaware of our lack of freedom.

At the outset of this book I raised the question whether the English are peculiarly illogical. At the conclusion I wish to state my opinion that we English are not politically minded. We do not take a passionate interest in political affairs; we do not want the trouble of political responsibilities. I am aware that many people would dissent from this judgment. We are accustomed to hear that 'the English' have 'political genius', and that parliamentary institutions and the British Commonwealth are in no small part due to this political genius. But what does 'the English' stand for here? In my opinion the answer is that it stands for the ruling class, educated for political purposes, trained from birth to undertake the responsibilities of ruling. The vast majority of English people want to be governed peaceably, and want to be free to pursue their own unpolitical interests. If democratic government means government by the consent of the governed, then we have a democratic government. If democratic government means that the voice of the people prevails, then we can hardly be said to have a democratic government. This is not because 'the voice of the people' is heard but not heeded; it is because there is no 'voice of the people to be heard'. This statement certainly needs qualification. There have been occasions when the majority (or at least a strong and effective minority) of the English people have felt so strongly about some political matter that they have found a voice and compelled the politicians to listen. These occasions are rare. The voice will be a mere *flatus vocis* unless it speaks out of the clearness and fullness of the head.

I, for my part, am not politically minded. I am thoroughly English; I do not want to accept political responsibilities. Unfortunately I cannot avoid them. Neither can you. We are confronted, I believe, with only two alternatives: either we must freely decide to support (or to oppose) this or that political measure, or we must acquiesce in the decisions made by those who control us. My contention is that for deciding freely it is essential to know whatever is relevant to that decision. I believe that 'to decide freely' and 'to decide' are synonyms. I have used the pleonasm 'decide freely' only in order to emphasize the point that there is no middle way between *deciding* and *acquiescing* in that which *others* have decided for me. Ignorance of the relevant facts is incompatible with freedom to reason with regard to them. I am not free to reach a reasoned conclusion with regard to the questions at issue in the General Strike of 1926 unless I know what had happened and what was happening. This example could be replaced by others. I cannot reach a reasoned conclusion with regard to the authorship of the *Epistle to the Hebrews* unless I am conversant with the historical circumstances and am aware of the criteria relevant to the decision. I cannot reasonably pursue a line of conduct unless I know what are the alternative actions open to me, what will most probably be the effects of these actions, which of these effects I desire to see realized. To decide presupposes deliberation. We do not deliberate in the void.

Some people have supposed that to be reasonable is incompatible with being enthusiastic. Personally I do not think so. 'Enthusiasm' is, however, a word with a strong emotional meaning; further, it is both vague and apt to be ambiguous in usage. If 'enthusiasm' be taken to mean 'unreasoning passionate eagerness', then, no doubt, enthusiasm is incompatible with reasonableness. If, however, 'enthusiasm' mean 'intense eagerness', I see no incompatibility. We can be enthusiastically for a cause *about* which we have reasoned dispassionately, i.e. impartially with due regard for the relevant evidence. I do not dispute, nor, taking note of the etymology of the word 'enthusiasm', could it reasonably be disputed, that the enthusiastic pursuit of a cause has often led to an intolerant interfering with the freedom of other persons. I would go farther and would maintain that it is desirable that we should develop in ourselves a habit of sceptical inquiry. Our enthusiasms stand in need of being from time to time revised; like our other mental habits, they are all the better for being occasionally overhauled. A mind in blinkers is a mind that is unfree. For this reason it is well that we should sometimes suffer the nuisance of having our uncritically held beliefs questioned, that we should be driven to find reasonable grounds in support of that which we passionately hold to be true. Should we be able to find such grounds, then our belief will be reasonable and yet not less passionately held. Concerning considerations such as these I have, I hope, already said enough in this book. My point of view with regard to this topic can be summed up in the statement: He alone is capable of being tolerant whose conclusions have been thought out and are recognized to be inconsistent with the beliefs of other persons. To be tolerant is not to be indifferent, and is incompatible with ignorance. My conclusions have been reasonably attained in so far as I have been able to discount my prejudices, to allow for the distorting effects of your prejudices, to collect the relevant evidence and to weigh that evidence in accordance with logical principles. The extent to which I can achieve these aims is the measure of my freedom of mind. To be thus free is as difficult as it is rare.

NOTES

1   I take these quotations from Leonard Woolf's *After the Deluge*, Chapter III.
2   I have pointed out elsewhere the ambiguous and thus misleading use of such words. *Set Logic in Practice*, pp. 71–4.

INDEX

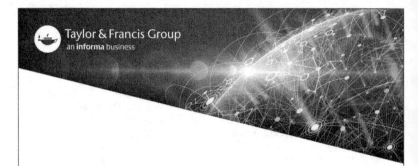

Printed in the United States
by Baker & Taylor Publisher Services